Soldiers, Sutlers, and Settlers

NUMBER TWO

The Clayton Wheat Williams

TEXAS ★ LIFE ★ SERIES

Major funding for this series was provided by
CLAYTON W. WILLIAMS, JR.
Director, Texas Mercantile Corporation

Soldiers, Sutlers, and Settlers

GARRISON LIFE ON THE TEXAS FRONTIER

By Robert Wooster

Illustrated by
Jack Jackson

TEXAS A&M UNIVERSITY PRESS
College Station

LIBRARY OF CONGRESS CATALOGING-IN-PUBLICATION DATA

Wooster, Robert, 1956–
  Soldiers, sutlers, and settlers.
  (The Clayton Wheat Williams Texas life series ; no. 2)
  Bibliography: p.
  Includes index.
  1. Texas–History–1846–1950. 2. Frontier and
pioneer life–Texas. 3. Fortification–Texas–History–
19th century. 4. United States. Army–Military life–
History–19th century. I. Title. II. Series.
F391.W92 1987   976.4'05   87-1948
  ISBN 0-89096-356-8

To Pat

Contents

Illustrations

Preface

The Clayton Wheat Williams Texas Life Series provides an excellent opportunity to examine various aspects of everyday life in Texas. The experiences of soldiers, settlers, and traders at military posts along the Texas frontiers are an important part of this remarkable heritage. At these often remote outposts, men, women, and children of different racial and cultural backgrounds strove to create an environment suitable for military purposes as well as civilian life.

The close of the Mexican War allowed the U.S. Army to establish numerous forts both along the Rio Grande and ahead of western settlement, a process that continued for the next half-century. Throughout this period, new forts were built and old positions abandoned as patterns of civilian expansion and Indian resistance changed. By about 1890, however, the growth of the railroads combined with increased civilian and military pressure to decimate the Indians of Texas. The present volume thus covers the years from 1848 to 1890, during which the U.S. Army maintained its strongest and most significant frontier presence in the Lone Star State.

Several problems complicate any detailed discussion of the daily life of those living in the forts. Fundamental to understanding the military frontiers is the recognition that the army occupied a constantly changing array of forts, subposts, and temporary camps rather than a single line of static defensive positions. To further complicate our understanding of the period, the military failed to elaborate a clear, consistent Indian policy, as I have attempted to show in another work (Yale University Press, forthcoming). Guided by a constantly changing cast of characters with little interest in finding equitable or effective solutions to the nation's Indian "problem," the army's actions and reactions against Indians were inconsistently conceived and inconsistently applied. As such, the military occupied and abandoned a series of haphazardly placed posts which varied according to location and to theories in vogue at the time they were built.

In attempting to deal with these problems, my purpose has been to present an accurate description of life at these complex military forts in a manner which appeals to the general reading public as well as the interested scholar. In so doing, I have emphasized the interrelationships between blacks and whites, soldiers and civilians, and men and women at the army's Texas posts. Seeking to explain and understand rather than to lionize or castigate, I have attempted to point out the failures along with the triumphs of those who occupied the military frontiers.

Several words of explanation and introduction are necessary. Quotations have been reproduced in their original form in order to retain the delightful flavor of my subjects, except in rare cases when errors in grammar or spelling detract from the meaning. Because of limitations of space and the general requirements of the Texas Life Series, footnotes are limited to citations of (1) direct quotations, (2) sources of special information not generally available, or (3) particularly noteworthy primary or secondary sources. The essay on sources is intended to serve as an annotated bibliography as well as a detailed guide to further reading. Again, the goal has been to present the material in a fashion useful to the educated and interested non-specialist as well as the traditional scholar.

Numerous groups and individuals made significant contributions to the production of this book, and deserve more than the brief acknowledgments that I can offer. Obvious thanks are extended to Clayton W. Williams, Jr., for recognizing the vital role that academic achievement, the arts, and literature will have in the future of Texas. Jack Jackson merits recognition for his interest in the text and his striking illustrations in this volume. Thanks to a grant from the Jean and Price Daniel, Jr. Foundation, I worked for the Texas State Historical Association as scholar in residence at the Sam Houston Regional Library at Liberty, Texas, from 1985 to 1986, during which time I completed most of the manuscript. Finishing touches were added after I was hired as assistant professor by Corpus Christi State University. To these employers I offer my sincere gratitude.

Several individuals deserve additional accolades. I owe a special debt to the staffs of the Barker Texas History Center and the Fort Concho Research Library, especially Ralph Elder and William Richter. Dr. Lewis L. Gould, former chairman of the Department of History at the University of Texas at Austin, was instrumental in bringing attention to a struggling graduate student. James A. Michener, for whom I had the distinct good fortune to work from 1982 to 1985, performed a similar service on my behalf. John Kings and Lisa Kaufman were among my coworkers and friends during this very special time of my life. I thank Jim, John, and Lisa for all that they taught me. Fellow graduate students Jim Boyden and Sally Graham provided constant friendship and support of just the right kind as well.

At some point in my life, I hope to be able to express my thanks to my family in terms that reflect the true depths of my feelings. At this juncture, the best I can offer is my gratitude to my mother and father, Edna and Ralph Wooster, who did the right things at the right times. Most important was their constant love. My wife, Pat Thomas, carefully edited the manuscript. I wish that I could give more than the traditional but well-deserved thanks for her work. In partial repayment for the time, effort, and thought I devoted to it rather than to her, I offer this book.

Soldiers,
Sutlers, and Settlers

CHAPTER ONE

Moving to Texas

How much they will suffer is sad to contemplate.

−Lt. Clinton W. Lear

On a blustery October day in 1851, a young American officer scanned the newly selected site for Fort Phantom Hill, Texas. Lt. Clinton W. Lear grudgingly acknowledged that a certain degree of wind-swept beauty characterized the region north of present-day Abilene. Yet, as he later confided to his wife: "We are like the dove after the deluge, not one green sprig can we find to indicate that this was ever intended for man to inhabit. Indeed, I cannot imagine that God ever intended white man to occupy such a barren waste. The ladies will have to live in tents all winter; how much they will suffer is sad to contemplate."[1]

Lear's description of Fort Phantom Hill proved accurate. Established above the junction of the Elm and Clear forks of the Brazos River to protect westbound emigrants from Indian attack, the site lacked adequate supplies of both timber and water. The army abandoned the post after less than three years of occupation, and either Indians or soldiers burned the abandoned buildings shortly thereafter. While troops occasionally occupied the grounds after the Civil War, the post's charred remains lent a ghostly quality to the landscape of the Phantom Hill area.

Other forts had a more lasting tenure upon the Texas countryside. Forty years after Lear saw Phantom Hill, Surgeon James P. Kimball and his new bride returned from their European honeymoon to the Texas frontier. Mrs. Kimball described their approach to Fort Clark, near Brackettville:

> At the top of a rocky ledge, gates opened before us and we entered the fort. The bugle was just sounding Retreat, and the tempered sunset light lent a rosy charm to the rather severe and rectangular stone quarters. The vine-

1. Lear to Mary, Nov. 19, 1851, in George H. Shirk, "Mail Call at Fort Washita," *Chronicles of Oklahoma* 33 (Spring, 1955): 28.

covered verandas, tiny lawns, and trim rows of China trees (Pride of India) bespoke careful home-making; for these trees were planted in trenches blasted out of the solid rock and filled with soil; the grass was a layer of sod placed over the out-cropping limestone.[2]

The army's occupation of Fort Clark sharply contrasted with its futile efforts at Phantom Hill. In the summer of 1852 soldiers began work on the post, which commanded both the San Antonio–El Paso road and a traditional Indian trail from the southern plains to Coahuila. The rich soil and abundant timber and grazing lands enabled the military to occupy the position until after World War II. The quarters and buildings of the old post have since been restored to form a private residential community.

From 1846 to 1890 the U.S. Army built or occupied thirty-five forts and numerous additional temporary camps within the state of Texas. Some posts, such as

2. Maria Brace Kimball, *A Soldier-Doctor of Our Army: James P. Kimball, Late Colonel and Assistant Surgeon-General, U.S. Army* (Boston: Houghton Mifflin Co., 1917), p. 121.

Forts Concho, Stockton, and Worth, served as forerunners of permanent civilian settlements. At other posts, Forts Lancaster, Quitman, and Terrett, for example, civilian communities did not survive after the soldiers' departure. But whatever the eventual outcome, the experiences of those whose lives touched these military posts form a vital chapter in Texas' nineteenth-century development.

Before 1845 several governments had attempted to protect new settlers in the American Southwest from Indian attacks. As the Spaniards moved north into the present-day states of Texas, New Mexico, Arizona, and California, they relied increasingly on the presidial system, with colonists rather than professional soldiers supplying most of the manpower. Disastrous uprisings among Indian tribes and increased threats from England, France, and Russia in the New World

forced Spanish authorities to revise their defenses. Although frontier conditions never allowed complete uniformity, the presidial soldiers as a whole became more proficient during the eighteenth century. In Tejas, towns such as Goliad and San Antonio began to develop in the shadows of these military complexes.

The Spaniards never had sufficient funds or personnel to subdue the wandering tribes north of the Rio Grande. Following her revolution against Spain, Mexico maintained several of the former Spanish military bases in that troubled northern province. While the troops provided some defense against Indian raids, the Mexican army became increasingly embroiled in disputes with local settlers

over proper government authority, conflicts that culminated in the Texas Revolution. Having gained their independence, the Texians in turn established camps and forts along their frontiers to blunt Indian attacks. Republic troops inflicted several costly defeats on hostile tribes, but they, like their Spanish and Mexican predecessors, proved unable to quell every Indian threat.[3]

In the late 1840s observers calculated that some thirty thousand Indians re-

3. Philip Wayne Powell, "Genesis of the Frontier Presidio in North America," *Western Historical Quarterly* 13 (Apr., 1982): 125–42; Max L. Moorhead, *The Presidio: Bastion of the Spanish Borderlands* (Norman: University of Oklahoma Press, 1974), pp. 3–114.

mained in Texas. Texian and Mexican soldiers and contagious diseases had all but exterminated the coastal Karankawas. In addition, the Republic of Texas had driven out most of the Cherokees, along with the remnants of the Caddo confederacies that had once inhabited East Texas. A plan devised in 1854 to set up reservations on the Brazos and Clear Fork rivers was inadequate and unpopular, and by 1859 Indians still living on those lands had been pushed north of the Red River. However, the more warlike Comanches, Kiowas, and Kiowa Apaches in the north and west, as well as the various Apache tribes in the south, still challenged the Anglo presence.

Formally occupying Texas after the ratification of the Treaty of Guadalupe Hidalgo in 1848, the U.S. Army was assigned the unenviable task of trying to stop the warfare that had become virtually a way of life among Apache and Comanche tribes, who had violently opposed the intrusions of Spaniards, Mexicans, and Americans. The continued hostility of Mexicans who had been uprooted from their homes in Tejas by unfriendly governments in Austin and Washington, D.C., posed additional problems for the regulars in blue. The army hoped that a series of forts constructed in advance of white settlement might counter these threats. Bearing little resemblance to European castles, Spanish presidios, or the wooden stockades often seen in western movies, the army's Texas posts were instead collections of buildings grouped in a rough square without protective walls. From these bases the military conducted raids and launched large-scale offensives as it had done across the Midwest. As supply bases and defensive outposts the forts remained a key to frontier protection.[4]

Existing posts were clearly inadequate to cope with the demands of defending the vast territory. Brig. Gen. George Mercer Brooke, commanding the Department of Texas (then called Military Department No. 8), thus began an extensive construction program in 1849. Along the lower Rio Grande, Fort Duncan, Fort McIntosh, and Ringgold Barracks reinforced Forts Brown and Polk, which had been built during the Mexican War. To the north Brooke added Forts Inge, Lincoln, Martin Scott, Croghan, Gates, Graham, and Worth.

Even the new defensive lines failed to stem Indian attacks. Texans demanded better protection, one newsman arguing that the infantrymen who currently occupied the posts were "as much out of place as a sawmill upon the ocean." Upon Brooke's death the newly appointed commander of the Department of Texas, Bvt. (Brevet) Maj. Gen. Persifor Smith, established Forts Belknap, Phantom Hill, Chadbourne, McKavett, Terrett, and Clark in a huge arc across the plains. Forts Mason, Merrill, and Ewell had also been added to guard particularly troublesome areas. The western defensive system now consisted of two cordons of forts. Ideally, in-

---

4. See Robert M. Utley, *Frontiersmen in Blue: The United States Army and the Indian, 1848–1865* (1967; reprint, Lincoln: University of Nebraska Press, 1981), pp. 70–72; Francis Paul Prucha, *The Sword of the Republic: The United States Army on the Frontier, 1783–1846* (1969; reprint, Bloomington: Indiana University Press), p. 356; Roy Eugene Graham, "Federal Fort Architecture in Texas during the Nineteenth Century," *Southwestern Historical Quarterly* 74 (Oct., 1970): 165–88.

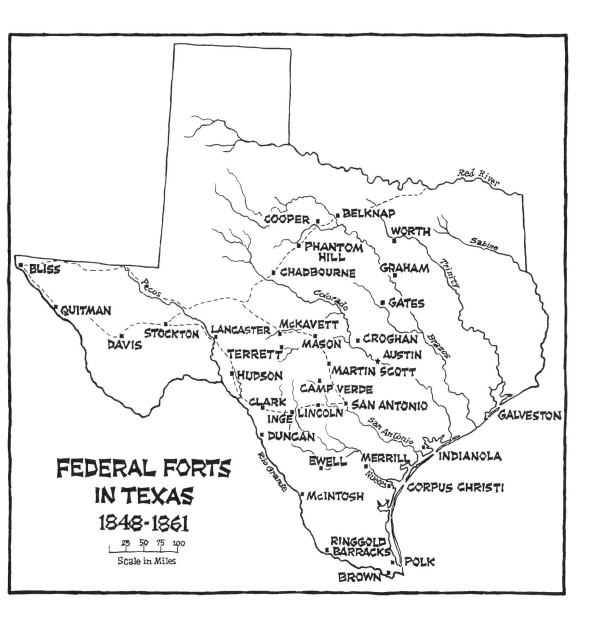

FEDERAL FORTS
IN TEXAS
1848-1861

25 50 75 100
Scale in Miles

fantry stationed at the outer posts would alert the mounted troops based at the inner positions to the incursions of Indian raiders.[5]

To the double line in the west and the string of posts along the Rio Grande Smith added a series of forts on the San Antonio–El Paso road. First established in 1849, Fort Bliss was reactivated in 1854. Fort Davis was established in the midst

5. *Texas State Gazette* (Austin), Jan. 12, 1850, p. 161.

of the Davis Mountains the same year, and Fort Lancaster was built in present-day Crockett County in 1855. Camp Cooper, an important bastion in northern Texas, was opened in 1856. Forts Hudson, Quitman, and Stockton reinforced the line in 1857, 1858, and 1859, respectively.

In the wake of the Federals' evacuation of Texas in 1861, Confederate and state units guarded the frontiers during the Civil War. Despite their presence the withdrawal of the stronger regular troops occasioned an increase in Indian raids. Although the beleaguered pioneers tried to defend themselves by "forting up" in specially constructed blockhouses and walled settlements, the more extended settlers grudgingly retreated to the east. Only after the war did the western push resume. Bluecoats returning to the frontier reoccupied Forts Belknap, Bliss, Brown, Chadbourne, Clark, Davis, Duncan, Hudson, Inge, McIntosh, McKavett, Mason, Quitman, Ringgold, and Stockton. The army also built new outposts ahead of the westward push of migrants. Five large forts met the changing frontier conditions after 1866—Richardson, Griffin, Concho, Elliott, and Hancock. Several additional bases, such as Camps Del Rio and Peña Colorado, were set up in response to threats in West Texas.[6]

Authorities used a variety of methods to select the exact locations of the Texas forts. In 1851, Secretary of War Charles Conrad instructed General Smith to find sites that could be easily supplied, protect citizens, and fulfill the nation's treaty obligations with Mexico. More specific guidelines were rare. Usually the army simply issued orders for the establishment of a post in a general area. A commission of officers then chose the position, although the exact procedures of selecting the commission and determining the location varied. In scouting for a site for Camp Cooper, for instance, Lt. Col. Robert E. Lee, son of Gen. Henry "Light-Horse Harry" Lee and future Civil War combatant, brought along a junior officer to help him examine the country before making a firm decision.

Under ideal circumstances the position under consideration offered water, grazing, timber or stone for building, and arable soil for gardening. In practice it often proved impossible to meet each of these conditions, the location of a reliable water supply being a special obstacle. Over the years the army abandoned several Texas positions, including Forts Belknap and Chadbourne, because of the lack of sufficient water. In stark contrast to the dusty plains, flooding could pose a hazard to frontier garrisons near major rivers. Following an 1886 deluge, for example, the Rio Grande broke the temporary dike protecting Fort Hancock. The stench arising from the saturated soil left the areas occupied by married troops uninhabitable. Likewise, the floodwaters raging from the Concho River in 1882 destroyed a great deal of the town of Ben Ficklin and threatened to engulf Fort Concho itself.

Yet special circumstances sometimes demanded the establishment of a fort in an area despite physical limitations. Following the recommendations of a rov-

6. Marilynne Howsley, "Forting Up on the Texas Frontier during the Civil War," *West Texas Historical Association Year Book* 17 (Oct., 1941): 71–76.

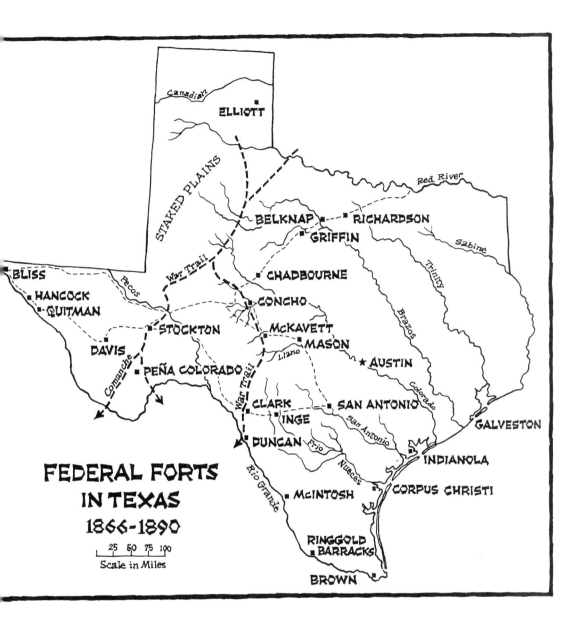

FEDERAL FORTS IN TEXAS 1866-1890

25 50 75 100
Scale in Miles

ing inspector, the army constructed Fort Lancaster on the San Antonio–El Paso road. The limestone hills ringing the fort magnified the summer sun's inexorable glare, and the lack of rain usually ruined the post's gardens. But a subsequent report again testified to the fort's strategic value. Situated in a region inhabited by Indians, the post served as a necessary shelter and resting point for weary travelers and migrants and was credited with saving many lives.

In other instances military observers disagreed about the suitability of a particular site. Department Commander Persifor Smith, having engaged some

Apaches in a brisk skirmish during his tour of West Texas in 1854, was well aware of the danger of travel in the trans-Pecos region. To protect emigrants, Smith chose to establish Fort Davis some 210 miles east of El Paso in a beautiful valley surrounded on three sides by steep cliffs. Fearful that Indians might fire down from the cliffs into the fort, junior officers disagreed with Smith's decision and sought to move the post farther out on the prairie. Smith remained adamant, and the fort was originally built in the canyon; however, soldiers rebuilt Fort Davis on the safer site after the Civil War.

Texas' ownership of her public lands, assured by the joint resolution of annexation, posed additional problems. In other states and territories the army simply occupied areas owned by the federal government and thus paid no rent or lease. In Texas, however, speculators could purchase land from the state and then lease the site to the army at exorbitant rates. A San Antonio banker, for example, held the land title at Fort Duncan. Terms agreed to in 1856 called for annual payments of $1,560 plus $10,000 for back claims. By the 1870s the lease had risen to $2,400 a year. Subsequent War Department plans to purchase outright the lands at many forts were eventually scuttled as army officers pointed out that the positions would be useless once the Indians had been crushed. As a result, the problem was never fully resolved.[7]

Individual commanders might also alter the sites selected for a prospective post, with pecuniary interests among both officers and civilians often becoming a factor. In the summer of 1867, Gen. Philip H. Sheridan ordered a four-man board of officers to find a good position for a new post. The board members duly selected a site in what later became Tom Green County. Capt. George G. Huntt and four troops of the Fourth Cavalry moved in to begin construction. But Huntt deemed the commission's site unsuitable and moved the post twelve miles, to the junction of the North and South forks of the Concho River. Huntt claimed that the new position, dubbed Fort Concho, would protect the two sawmills and its workers along the river. Whatever the actual reasoning may have been, Huntt's change certainly pleased the San Antonio transportation company of Adams and Wickes. Already working on several government contracts, the firm's owners apparently learned of the proposed fort in the Concho River area through their army connections. The San Antonio company bought the land just before the military acted, thus reaping the benefits of both their new government lease and the correspondingly inflated values of the nearby real estate. Although his connection with Adams and Wickes was never proved, the army later dismissed Huntt for his action.[8]

A military garrison was an important boon to local entrepreneurs, who realized the economic benefits of the army's presence. They often mounted major

7. Herbert Hart, *Pioneer Forts of the West* (Seattle, Wash.: Superior Publishing Co., 1967), pp. 49–51; various reports in H. Exec. Doc. 282, 1874, ser. 1615, pp. 1–46; Fort Elliott Papers, Barker Texas History Center, Austin, Tex. (hereafter cited as BTHC).

8. Post Medical Returns (hereafter PMR), Fort Concho, p. 1; Huntt to Davis, Sept. 5, 28, 1867, Fort Concho Post Returns 1867–68 (microfilm, Fort Concho Research Library, San Angelo,

campaigns aimed at securing new posts near their businesses. Noting the projected transfer of three additional companies to Fort Richardson, the editors of the Jacksboro *Frontier Echo* remarked, "Send them along, the more the merrier." As the *Echo* noted, the arrival of an army paymaster "increases the supply of 'medium'" on the cash-starved Texas frontier. In analyzing the suggested relocation of Fort Davis to Presidio del Norte in 1876, General Sheridan noted that "the recommendation is probably in the interests of the town of Presidio del Norte, which wants to get a market for the sale of grain and other articles of commerce of which the traffic in whiskey largely exists."[9]

The army's dependence on Congress for appropriations also made it essential to include legislators in the location process. The Texas delegation's generally promilitary stance after Reconstruction, especially that of Senator Samuel B. Maxey, often guaranteed special treatment for the Lone Star State. The culmination of Texas' efforts can be seen in 1878. Considering a new post between either Forts Concho and Elliott or Forts Sill and Griffin, Sheridan bluntly asked the Texas delegation "to fix the most suitable point."[10]

Yet the relationship between the army and the state was not always friendly. Texans sharply criticized the regular army's inability to prevent Indian depredations, and the Federal occupation of Texas during Reconstruction further angered many of the state's inhabitants. In return, military men charged that Texans deliberately exaggerated the magnitude of Indian attacks, so that troops enforcing Reconstruction laws would instead be transferred to the frontiers. War Department threats to withdraw troops from Texas altogether only heated the controversy, and the uneasy tenancy continued to trouble army officials for years to come.

The consequences of these problems were not lost on contemporary observers. Frederick Law Olmsted, a noted antebellum traveler who later designed New York's Central Park, believed Fort Duncan to be "badly placed, in a military point of view, being commanded from the hills in the rear." Having witnessed the federal government's failure to protect the Rio Grande frontier during the 1850s, another citizen concluded that "there is no systematic plan of defence—none whatever." Such charges proved well founded; political and economic considerations often outweighed military convenience or necessity.[11]

MF 67); Herschel Boggs, "A History of Fort Concho" (Master's thesis, University of Texas, 1940), pp. 8–9; Greg Melton, "Trials by Nature: The Harsh Environment of Fort Concho, Texas" (Master's thesis, Abilene Christian University, 1981), p. 13.

9. *Frontier Echo* (Jacksboro), Aug. 11, Sept. 25, 1875; Sheridan quoted in Belknap to Secretary of Interior, Jan. 23, 1876, Letters Sent by the Secretary of War Relating to Military Affairs, 1800–89, National Archives, Washington, D.C., Record Group 107 (hereafter cited as NA, RG), (microcopy 6, vol. 79, reel 72).

10. Maxey to wife, June 17, 1876, Samuel B. Maxey Papers, Texas State Archives, Austin; Sheridan to Sherman, Mar. 19, 1878, box 19, Philip Sheridan Papers, Library of Congress, Washington, D.C.

11. Frederick Law Olmsted, *A Journey through Texas: A Saddle-Trip on the Southwestern Fron-*

With the effects of such difficulties still lingering, the complex process of staffing a remote outpost began shortly after the location had been determined. Recent West Point graduates often viewed the move to the frontier as an adventure. Accused by fellow classmates of theft at the academy, Orsemus Boyd eagerly went west to escape his reputation. Boyd's young wife, having seen no other military establishments, naively expected their new post to be similar to the Point. More experienced families realized that their transfer to Texas would be only one of a seemingly innumerable series of moves. One army wife lived at nineteen different stations in the West, including four different forts in Texas. An officer estimated that he had traveled or campaigned over ten thousand miles in a single four-year period.

Some dreaded the constant changes. Ellen M. Biddle, stationed with her husband in post–Civil War Jackson, Mississippi, particularly feared the move to the frontier. Texas seemed an especially wild outpost, far from the cultural graces she had known in the East or in the South. Upon her husband's transfer, she recalled, "I thought my heart would break to give up my dear little home, my garden and flowers, in which I had taken such interest, and the dear friends whom I had learned to love so dearly; besides I had such a horror of Texas, and I was not very well. But it had to be done."[12]

Soldiers came to Texas by a variety of routes. For at least part of the trip some of the more adventurous officers boarded steam locomotives. In early 1860, Lt. Col. Robert E. Lee rode the train from Washington, D.C., to New Orleans, a journey lasting three and a half days. Ten years later another officer and his wife made the ride from Boston to New Orleans in six days. From New Orleans most travelers caught a ship to Texas; the railroad from that city to Houston was not completed until 1881. Other delays proved common. In 1873, for example, a young wife and daughter took the railroad cars from Philadelphia to Texas, only to be delayed almost a month by a cholera quarantine at Denison. Individual officers who opted to travel by stagecoach found the vehicles uncomfortably overcrowded and subject to attacks by bandits. To make matters worse, poor roads frequently forced the riders to get out and walk to rest the horses.

Oceangoing vessels carried other officers the entire journey to Texas. Rough weather and seasickness claimed many a land-loving soldier or dependent. Although the officers and their families generally got along well with the ship's captains, unforeseen problems with the crews often prevented everyone from getting much rest. A fire and a near mutiny highlighted one particularly notable journey. The soldiers, refusing to sleep below the deck because of the heat, kept the sailors awake instead. Fistfights broke out and forced the officers to station a raw lieu-

tier, ed. James Howard (1857; reprint, Austin: Von Boeckman-Jones Press, 1962), p. 174; Mrs. William L. Cazneau (Cora Montgomery), *Eagle Pass or Life on the Border* (1852; reprint, Austin, Tex.: Pemberton Press, 1966), p. 153.

12. Ellen McGowan Biddle, *Reminiscences of a Soldier's Wife* (Philadelphia: J. B. Lippincott Co., 1907), p. 60.

tenant on deck to prevent further outbreaks. "I had no trouble whatever," he re-called, "although some of the men had threatened to throw me overboard."[13]

The experiences of leading fresh recruits to their outfits in Texas could test even the stoutest of spirits. The men who had joined up in the larger eastern cities found themselves routed to a "center of instruction"—foot soldiers to David's Island or Governor's Island, New York; cavalrymen to Carlisle Barracks, Pennsylvania, or Jefferson Barracks, Missouri; and artillerymen and a few infantrymen to Newport Barracks, Kentucky. Enlisted men were supposed to learn the rudiments of their new professions at these centers. Yet demands for reinforcements from the western posts forced officials to rush fresh recruits ahead to their frontier stations in groups ranging from a dozen to two hundred. It was assumed that they would receive their basic training from their companies in the West.

The volunteers, tired of the cramped barracks and poor food at the depots, were an undisciplined lot, prone to desertion. Space was always at a premium aboard the transport vessels; finding no space below on their old side-wheelers, some enlisted men slept on deck. A recent West Point graduate, Lt. Zenas R. Bliss, recalled with horror his first command on board a troopship. With no noncommissioned officers available and senior officers refusing to help, he tried to issue rations: "The men formed in single rank and as soon as the barrel of pork was opened, someone gave a push and they all piled on top of the pork and in a minute it was gone. I finally got it issued, but I am not quite sure that it was a very equitable division."[14]

Upon their arrival in Texas—usually at Galveston, Indianola, or Corpus Christi—everyone eagerly debarked from the cramped transports. The next few days deteriorated into a confused melee as units regrouped and readied for the march inland. Many seized the opportunity to go on alcoholic binges; others, having used their enlistments to gain free passage to Texas, promptly deserted. The transfer from ship to shore took a particular toll on wives and dependents. The shortage of proper tents forced even junior officers and their families to double up in unfloored hospital tents. In the confusion possessions were often left unguarded and exposed to the elements on the beaches and wharves.

The overland journey could prove equally trying. In the fall of 1855 the newly organized Second Cavalry Regiment began its march to Texas from Jefferson Barracks, Missouri. While the regiment's equipment, property, and surplus baggage were forwarded by sea to Indianola, the elite new outfit went by land. Sixteen of its officers became generals for the blue or the gray during the Civil War; nonetheless, the Second Cavalry's march to Texas was a far from auspicious debut. Torrential rains in early November slowed progress to a crawl. Sixty-mile-an-hour north winds hit the column the following month. Shivering troopers

13. Zenas R. Bliss Reminiscences, BTHC, 1:3–5, 12.

14. H. H. McConnell, *Five Years a Cavalryman: Or, Sketches of Regular Army Life on the Texas Frontier, Twenty Odd Years Ago* (Jacksboro, Tex.: J. N. Rogers and Co., 1889), p. 20; Bliss Reminiscences, 1:2–3.

tried to warm their tents by filling holes dug under the canvas with hot coals. Meager Christmas celebrations on the trail included issues of whiskey for the soldiers and eggnog for the officers. They struggled in to Fort Belknap two days later, only to be faced with insufficient quarters and fuel. An accidental forest fire that erupted near the post several days later seemed an appropriate conclusion to the regiment's journey.

Despite such difficulties, the pleasures of easily paced travel often outweighed the inconveniences of camp life. While the troops walked or rode horses and mules, wagons carried supplies and dependents. A two-wheeled light spring carriage called an "ambulance," drawn by two or four mules, became a favorite among officers' wives. Typical of heavier wagons was the one built by Studebaker, a four-

wheeled vehicle about ten feet long and three and a half feet wide. The typical 1875 model sported blue body paint and a white canvas top inscribed with the regimental number and company letter.

With wagons crammed full of children, dogs and cats, personal possessions, and company equipment, the bustling entourage seemed to be in perpetual motion. One officer's wife rode on a rocking chair anchored to the floor of her ambulance. Various supplies, including a tin washbowl and pitcher, books, lunch

basket, bags, shawls, and cups, were strewn around her in the carriage. Canteens of milk and water, field glasses, sewing basket, lantern, liquor case, water casket, shotgun, revolver, her husband's saber and pistol, and two dogs with their assorted puppies rounded out the wagon's contents.

Along the road soldiers and dependents found ingenious ways to make their long sojourns more comfortable. Lacking a proper perambulator, Mrs. Orsemus Boyd carried her baby in a champagne basket, which gently rocked the child as the carriage rolled ahead. Others accumulated great supplies of portable camp furniture and cookware. While families of limited resources subsisted on regular rations, the luckier travelers added ham, soft bread, rice, eggs, tomatoes, chocolate, molasses, and cakes to their fare (although Lieutenant Colonel Lee joked that "cake cannot travel with cavalry long"). Those of all ranks hunted game to supplement their diets along the way. As the columns passed civilian homes and small settlements, the troops issued what Elizabeth Custer recalled as "a fusillade of the wittiest comments, such as only soldiers can make" at the bewildered Texans. To avoid marching during the heat of the day, some commanders sounded reveille as early as 2:00 A.M. They frequently halted in the early afternoon to allow the animals to graze before sundown. Sunday marches were often suspended as well.[15]

However, the easy camaraderie of the road could only partly alleviate the hardships of camp life and travel in the nineteenth century. While Indians rarely attacked large military parties, members of the caravan had to keep a vigilant watch. To make matters worse, army columns making the overland crossing frequently lacked the slightest notion of the best route to follow. Sometimes inadequate planning brought on severe water shortages. On other occasions the troops lost their way, retracing their steps to known landmarks or wandering blindly across unfamiliar terrain. Flash floods transformed tranquil streams into raging torrents within a matter of minutes. Unwary travelers who failed to take precautionary measures while fording the high waters, or who made camp too close to a riverbank, could pay for their miscalculations with their lives.

In spite of the dangers, most had fond recollections of life on the trail, later admitting that they had deliberately maintained a slow pace. As Zenas R. Bliss later noted, "Travelling on the road in Texas was very delightful to those who liked it, and nearly everybody did, who was not scared to death about Indians." Most would have agreed with Elizabeth Custer's assessment of her family's quarters in Austin. "I went into the building with regret," recalled Mrs. Custer, who always enjoyed the pleasures of camp and field. She described her room in the old Blind Asylum as having three windows that she and her husband kept open at night. Yet, "Notwithstanding the air that circulated, the feeling, after having been so long out of doors, was suffocating. The ceiling seemed descending to smother us."[16]

A staggering variety of animal and plant life awaited the new Texans, most of whom saw the wildlife as at least partial recompense for the crude quarters.

15. Mrs. Orsemus Bronson Boyd, *Cavalry Life in Tent and Field* (1894; reprint, Lincoln: University of Nebraska Press, 1982), pp. 94, 245–46; Lee to Annie Lee, Mar. 25, 1860, in Francis Raymond Adams, Jr., "An Annotated Edition of the Personal Letters of Robert E. Lee, April, 1855–April, 1861" (Ph.D. diss., University of Maryland, 1955), pp. 592–93; Elizabeth B. Custer, *Tenting on the Plains, or General Custer in Kansas and Texas*, 3 vols. (1897; reprint, Norman: University of Oklahoma Press, 1971), 1:140–41.

16. Bliss Reminiscences, 5:230–31; Custer, *Tenting on the Plains*, 1:216–17.

The post surgeon at Fort McKavett, in western Menard County, observed predators including gray wolves, coyotes, brown bears, wildcats, and cougars. Turkeys, gophers, antelopes, deer, buffalo, jackrabbits, and wild horses also roamed the area. In the air buzzards, eagles, crows, ducks, geese, quail, owls, doves, swans, and plovers circled the fort. Nearby rivers teemed with perch, bass, trout, gar, and eel. Observers also spotted rattlesnakes, king snakes, black snakes, cottonmouths, bull snakes, horned frogs, tarantulas, and centipedes in the region.

The state's tremendous range of plant life was equally impressive. The surgeon at Fort Davis identified 56 genera and 237 species of plants near the site. Cottonwoods and willow trees grew along the creeks, with small oak, pine, and cedar trees gracing the hills. Cacti and Spanish daggers thrived on the prairies. A profuse array of wild flowers exploded in a brilliant rainbow of colors during the region's short rainy season. Texas wild flowers impressed even such a critical observer as Ellen Biddle, who, upon seeing the fields near Brenham, admitted that "I must say for Texas that I have never seen in any State or Territory such quantities of wild flowers of all colours and wonderfully beautiful; great fields of them as far as the eye could reach."[17]

Many newcomers to Texas reserved their most vehement complaints for the state's unpredictable climate. The garrison at Fort Worth, situated on an unprotected high plain above the Trinity River, baked in the hot sun in summer and froze during northerly winds in winter. Fort Duncan, protected from northers by hills on the north and east sides, suffered from drenching rains and excessive heat for much of the year. Winters also proved temperate at Fort McIntosh, but recorded summer temperatures of 107 degrees in the shade quickly made the soldiers forget their January good fortune. Those lucky enough to serve at beautiful Fort Davis praised its moderate summer climate. On the other hand, residents of Ringgold Barracks firmly believed it to be the hottest place on earth.

The landscapes surrounding the forts varied markedly across the state. Fort McIntosh lay along one bank of the Rio Grande about fifty feet above the river's low-water point. The loose, sandy soil, intense heat, and southeasterly winds allowed for little nearby vegetation save mesquite and prickly pear. Fort Lancaster was about twenty-five feet above the bed of Live Oak Creek in a hot basin surrounded by six-hundred-foot limestone hills. Overland travelers to Lancaster found the last leg of their journey a terrifying stagecoach descent down the cliffs. One soldier wrote that the first sight of Fort Stockton, in the midst of the Pecos desert, "caused many sad hearts" because it "looked in the distance like a camp of Mexican carts."[18]

The harsh environment at Fort Concho, established at present-day San

---

17. PMR, Fort Davis, pp. 37–46; Biddle, *Soldier's Wife*, p. 68.

18. Report of Perrin, 1852, 34th Cong., 2d sess., S. Exec. Doc. 827, pp. 360–61; "Statistical Report on the Sickness and Mortality in the Army of the United States," 36th Cong., 1st sess.,

Angelo, plagued the occupants throughout the fort's twenty-two-year occupation. Poor soil, insufficient timber reserves, and sporadic rainfall were only a few of the fort's problems. High spring winds and the generally dry climate made fires extremely dangerous. The post's physical isolation compounded the difficulties,

S. Exec. Doc. 52, ser. 1035, p. 192; Report of Anderson, 1852, 34th Cong., 1st sess., S. Exec. Doc. 96, ser. 827, pp. 393, 396; Bliss Reminiscences, 5:188.

as did the extreme weather conditions, which included droughts, dust storms, freezes, hail, and tornadoes. Scorpions, snakes, fleas, bats, and centipedes added to the misery of those occupying the Concho River fort.

Although Concho's residents might have disagreed, most sites received higher marks from contemporary observers. A series of hills and oak groves sheltered Fort Croghan from northers. One officer, while admitting that Fort Martin Scott was "pleasantly situated," enthusiastically concluded that "no place on the line is more remarkable for its beauty and fitness in every respect" than Fort Graham. A cottonwood grove shaded quiet Fort Bliss. Camp Verde, occupied by Texas Rangers after its evacuation by Federal troops, also won acclaim from occupants for its natural beauty.[19]

Reflecting an oft-voiced cultural theme, comparisons with Europe and the Mediterranean abounded. Capt. William G. Muller likened life along the Mexican border to that "of Old Spain, with the Alcalde, the Padre, the guitar and the fandango." Teresa Vielé compared her first impressions of the Rio Grande with those she imagined of the Nile: "It only wanted a few swarthy, turbaned men, and a sphinx or two, to complete the illusion." Sgt. H. H. McConnell believed that the glorious Texas sunrise must rival that of the Alps. While some travelers "may grow rapturous over the sunny skies of Italy, or descant in glowing terms on the climate of la belle France," he doubted the existence of a "sunnier, fairer or more favored clime than Texas."[20]

In occupying a series of fixed defensive positions against Indian attacks, the U.S. Army was continuing traditional policies implemented earlier by Spain, Mexico, and the Republic of Texas. In theory, a clear strategic plan, based on regional defense rather than on local demands, would guide the overall selection process. A well-watered area with adequate timber and pastureland, slightly ahead of white settlement, provided the army's ideal position. Throughout the West, however, planners found that economic and political considerations outweighed purely strategic concerns. In addition, some locations that had initially appeared suitable revealed unanticipated problems once they were occupied by several hundred enlisted men and their families.[21]

Officers and enlisted men generally looked on their trips to Texas as part of a marvelous adventure. The prospect of life in the Lone Star State itself was not met with universal enthusiasm. Yet in conquering the Indians and the wild lands of Texas, most saw themselves as helping their country achieve its manifest destiny. Engaged in a cooperative effort, these travelers, like their nonmilitary counterparts, firmly believed that they were staking a rightful claim to the entire continent.

Most army wives shared the views of their male comrades. Approaching the West with a mixture of apprehension and cautious optimism, they saw the hardships of frontier military life as a challenge. Lydia Lane and her army officer husband, to whom she had been married less than a year, landed at Corpus Christi

19. Whiting to Deas, Jan. 21, 1850, 31st Cong., 1st sess., S. Exec. Doc. 64, ser. 562, pp. 239–43.

20. William G. Muller, *The Twenty Fourth Infantry Past and Present* (1923; reprint, Fort Collins, Colo.: Old Army Press, 1972); Teresa Griffin Vielé, *Following the Drum: A Glimpse of Frontier Life* (1858; reprint, Lincoln: University of Nebraska Press, 1984), p. 99; McConnell, *Five Years a Cavalryman*, p. 180.

21. Robert Wooster, "The Military and United States Indian Policy, 1865–1903" (Ph.D. diss., University of Texas, 1985), pp. 135–40.

to find yellow fever ravaging the city. She later expressed with eloquence her personal determination: "It was dreadful news to us, as there was no escape, no running away from it, nothing to do but land, take the risk, and trust in Providence. However, I had 'gone for a soldier,' and a soldier I determined to be."[22]

22. Lydia Spencer Lane, *I Married a Soldier; or, Old Days in the Old Army* (1893; reprint, Albuquerque, N. Mex.: Horn and Wallace, 1964), p. 22. For scholarly examinations of these attitudes toward the West, see Sandra L. Myres, *Westering Women and the Frontier Experience, 1800–1915* (Albuquerque: University of New Mexico Press, 1982), p. 36, and William H. Goetzmann, *Army Exploration in the American West, 1803–1863* (1959; reprint, Lincoln: University of Nebraska Press, 1979), pp. 17–18. For a contrasting view, see John Mack Faragher, *Women and Men on the Overland Trail* (New Haven, Conn.: Yale University Press, 1979), pp. 86–87, 109, 143.

CHAPTER TWO

Building a Frontier Fort

They are adapted neither to health nor to comfort.

—Acting Assistant Surgeon W. E. Taylor

In 1854, Lt. Zenas R. Bliss arrived at Fort Duncan exhausted by the trials of his long journey from the eastern seaboard to southwestern Texas. As his column approached Duncan, several of the garrison's officers rode out to meet them, extending a generous welcome in the process. Yet the lack of vacant quarters on the post at Eagle Pass soon disappointed the young West Post graduate. Undaunted, Bliss opted for temporary housing:

> My tent was pitched on the parade ground and the Quarter-Master gave me some grain sacks for a carpet. I pegged them down on the ground, moved in my trunk and without chair, table or bedstead, commenced life at a frontier Post.
>
> Life in tha[t] tent was anything but pleasant. Every few days, a Norther would spring up and the dust would fly in such clouds, that one could not see and my bed and clothing would be covered with it. . . . Besides the elements, I had other things to contend with. It was a fine joke for the young officers on their way back home, to loosen my tent cords so that if the wind came up during the night, my tent would cave in.[1]

While Bliss eventually obtained more suitable quarters, his experiences were not unusual. Time after time the War Department, beset by rapid changes along America's frontiers, proved unable to coordinate an individual post's needs with its limited construction budget. The army might, for instance, establish a fort in a region that seemingly would require defense for years to come. Yet the money invested at that position often proved wasted when changing settlement patterns or failures in the site's water supply led to evacuation of the garrison. Increasing military requirements created additional problems. A base that comfortably

1. Zenas R. Bliss Reminiscences, BTHC, 1:35.

housed four companies of regulars commonly found its facilities overburdened by the arrival of additional companies sent to strengthen regional defenses. Such failures inevitably affected daily life at the frontier garrisons.

Aware of the problems, the army drafted a series of model building plans for its military posts. Unfortunately, these generally applied only to structures defined as permanent. As such, the forts on both the Atlantic and the Pacific coasts benefited from careful, though by no means perfect, engineering and architectural design. By contrast, experience had taught the army that expanding white settlement often rendered frontier military positions obsolete. Such was obviously the case in Texas. Not surprisingly, the army classified few of the nineteenth-century Texas forts as permanent and was reluctant to pour large amounts of money into positions that might soon be obsolete. This reasoning, however sound financially, afforded little comfort to the soldier who lived in an overcrowded shanty with a leaky roof.

Whatever judgments might be made about such decisions, interests of health and humanity demanded that the troops secure temporary shelter as quickly as possible. Various canvas structures, including the Sibley tent; the more common A, or wall, tent; and the famous shelter-half, or pup, tent, served this purpose. Eager for added protection from the elements, troops often placed wooden pickets around the sides of the tents. Also popular was the prefabricated Turnley cottage, which included locks, keys, sashes, and blinds. Three men could set up this structure in four hours.[2]

Until the completion of permanent housing at Fort Terrett, Lt. Richard W. Johnson was one of those forced to live in a tent. Taking a practical outlook on his predicament, Johnson divided his tent into two rooms. Swarms of fleas caused him more concern than did the region's deadly rattlesnakes. As was common frontier practice, he placed the foot of each bedpost in a pan of water before going to bed, to prevent the pests from ruining a good night's sleep.

Picket cottages provided a somewhat more solid solution to the housing problem. Workers first dug a rectangular ditch one to two feet deep along the proposed perimeter of the building. Next they placed large posts at the four corners of the ditch. Then they set smaller wooden posts into the trench, perpendicular to the ground rather than in the parallel fashion of the traditional log cabin, forming rude walls. With good lumber at a premium, the soldiers shaped window and door frames out of wood salvaged from packing crates. The men filled in the chinks with wood chips, mud, and lime. Across the tops of the rough pickets they laid a few wooden frames, to which they anchored makeshift roofs of canvas and straw.

Opinions on the serviceability of these crude structures differed widely. Ener-

2. Willard B. Robinson, *American Forts: Architectural Form and Function* (Urbana: University of Illinois Press, published for Amon Carter Museum of Western Art, 1977), pp. 85–184; Roy Eugene Graham, "Federal Fort Architecture in Texas during the Nineteenth Century," *Southwestern Historical Quarterly* 74 (Oct., 1970): 180–88; "Report of Surgeon General Conley," Col. M. L. Crimmins Papers, BTHC.

getic roommates quickly outdistanced their less enterprising comrades. Such men made a number of improvements, boarding the floor, forming a carpet out of condemned blankets, and lining the walls with canvas. Windows and a fireplace might complete the interior. Yet even the best picket buildings aged quickly and required constant maintenance. As the shanties aged, rain and snow poured through cracks and crevices. Although they were intended to provide only short-term shelter, the exigencies of the service often meant that at many posts they continued to be used as housing for many years.

If permanent buildings replaced such temporary quarters, the shortage of timber forced builders to substitute locally available materials for wood. Adopting the Spanish style of architecture, the army hired Mexicans to teach its troops how to build flat roofs and to make adobe bricks. By August, 1870, the garrison at Fort Concho was producing one thousand bricks a day, though the terrific heat from the oven and sun made it necessary for a commissioned officer to oversee the troops to keep them working. Heavy rains and poor local materials eventually halted the brickmaking. This effort having failed, the builders at Concho

turned to stone for construction, as did their compatriots at several other posts. At Fort Duncan the men of Company C, First Artillery, contributed eighty dollars from their personal funds to the construction of stone barracks. Workers at Camp Hudson used a mixture of gravel and lime for walls. Although the building process was slow, such structures proved cool in summer and warm in winter.

Whatever materials were used, congressional limits on military spending forced the army to employ enlisted personnel for much of the construction work. Post quartermasters thus hired soldiers from the ranks to serve as carpenters, wheelwrights, blacksmiths, stonemasons, saddlers, clerks, teamsters, and woodcutters. Army officials recognized the adverse consequences of using troops as common laborers. Too many garrisons gathered wood or erected housing instead of practicing their military skills. Despite continued congressional parsimony, the army hired significantly more civilian employees after the Civil War. In the fall of 1868, for instance, more than 150 carpenters and masons worked at Fort Richardson, and between 100 and 200 civilians worked at Fort Davis during a period of heavy construction. In March, 1868, while only 5 soldiers were employed on extra duty

at Ringgold Barracks, no less than 372 men were hired to build a national cemetery and assist in general construction.[3]

Considering the unskilled workmen, the patchwork materials, and the irregular plans, it is not surprising that sharp contrasts marked the various forts of Texas. The ultimate in enlisted men's barracks was found at Ringgold. Each of the four two-story buildings was designed to house one company. The first story included rooms for reading, washing, dining, drilling, and storing of miscellaneous supplies, as well as additional cubicles for the first sergeants. The second story was a large dormitory with ample space and bedding for each man. Some believed that these were the finest barracks in the country.

3. H. H. McConnell, *Five Years a Cavalryman; Or, Sketches of Regular Army Life on the Texas Frontier, Twenty Odd Years Ago* (Jacksboro, Tex.: J. N. Rogers and Co., 1889), p. 159; PMR, Fort Davis, Jan.–Apr., 1869, pp. 105–17; "Report of Persons and Articles Employed and Hired at Brownsville, Texas, during the month of March, 1868," William A. Wainwright Papers, BTHC.

Few other posts possessed housing rivaling the grandeur of Ringgold, though some barracks were indeed impressive. Plans for barracks at Fort Duncan compiled in 1860 proposed a series of 20-by-120-foot buildings, each designed to house one company. Every structure was to have a 10-foot porch, eleven windows, seven doors, and two fireplaces. Including shingle roof, stone walls, and labor, the cost of each building was estimated at $827.45. Postbellum Fort Davis included several roomy company-size barracks. The best such structures were 27 by 186 feet, each having two squad rooms separated by a 12-foot passageway. A 27-by-86-foot wing, divided into a kitchen, a mess room, and a storeroom, stood at the end of the passageway. The 12-foot-high squad rooms also had space for sergeants' quarters and offices. A fireplace, windows, and a ceiling ventilator provided heat and air

for the adobe complex. Two hundred feet behind the barracks, an 8-by-24-foot sink served as the company's latrine.[4]

By contrast, the serviceability of company billets at other forts was often

4. PMR, Fort Davis, 1872, pp. 9, 12; packet 12, Fort Duncan Records, BTHC.

found wanting. Fort Griffin's garrison lived in forty small frame huts designed
to house four men apiece. Each hut, measuring a cramped 8½ by 13 feet, had
a door, two windows, a fireplace, and a shingle roof. Made of green timber, the
tiny shacks leaked badly after the wood shrank and were ovens in the dry summer heat. At Fort Concho efforts to concrete the floor of the enlisted men's quar-

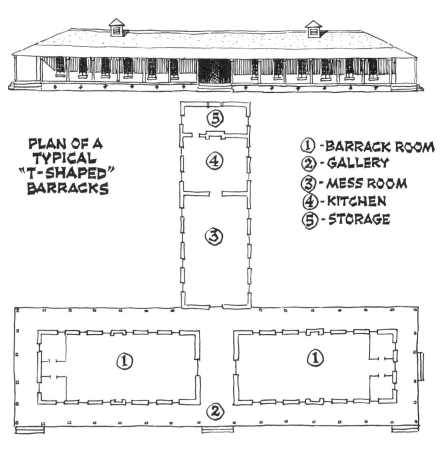

PLAN OF A
TYPICAL
"T-SHAPED"
BARRACKS

① - BARRACK ROOM
② - GALLERY
③ - MESS ROOM
④ - KITCHEN
⑤ - STORAGE

ters failed miserably. As of December, 1868, no provision had been made for warming the barracks at Fort Brown, although the post had been occupied for almost twenty years. The exasperated surgeon at Fort Bliss concluded that, "as the occupancy of their present quarters by the troops is, perhaps, deemed a military necessity for all the time being, I shall allude to them no further than to say that they are adapted neither to health nor to comfort."[5]

Military officials measured the housing at army posts in terms of air space per man—and all too often found the structures woefully inadequate. The 1863 regulations specified a minimum of 426 cubic feet of air space per man south of the 38th parallel. Such regulations were often ignored; at Fort Concho, for example, the air space was only 296 cubic feet per man. Medical officers also charged that the official standard itself was inadequate. The doctor at Fort Elliott complained that levels of 500 to 700 cubic feet were insufficient; a level of 403 cubic feet was called too low by the surgeon at Camp Peña Colorado. The opposite situation could be found at spacious Ringgold Barracks, where quarters allowed 1,000 cubic feet of air space per man.

The quality of officers' housing proved similarly varied. Ringgold Barracks, with its permanent garrison along the Rio Grande, again set high standards. By the 1870s a series of 54-by-40-foot buildings housed commissioned personnel. With one and a half stories and eight rooms, each building held three officers. A captain occupied half of the house, thus appropriating the four rooms to which official regulations entitled him. Two lieutenants split the remaining four rooms of the house, their allotments also meeting army specifications. By 1872 the nineteen officers' houses at Fort Davis seemed satisfactory; the single-storied structures, which housed one family each, had front and rear porches. That had not been the case during the 1850s, when, to avoid the scramble over quarters, junior officer Richard Johnson bought a hospital tent, put it over a rough frame, built a crude fireplace, and, as mentioned earlier, divided this "miserable hovel" into two rooms.[6]

Conditions similar to those at pre–Civil War Fort Davis were common. At Fort Clark, Lydia Lane described her jacal picket cottage as "a funny little house." A chimney in the middle of the flimsy wooden structure divided the bedroom from the sitting room. The Lanes also had a separate kitchen, as was common at the frontier posts. Their house was slightly removed from the other quarters, and Mrs. Lane recalled that the "Indians could have crept in upon us, taken our scalps, and ridden away without being molested." It was, as she noted, "a wretched place to live in."[7]

5. PMR, Fort Griffin, p. 9; Herschel Boggs, "A History of Fort Concho" (Master's thesis, University of Texas, 1940), p. 13; PMR, Fort Concho, Dec. 31, 1874, p. 164; PMR, Fort Brown, Dec., 1868; PMR, Fort Bliss, July, 1878.

6. PMR, Ringgold Barracks, p. 6; PMR, Fort Davis, 1872, p. 9; Richard W. Johnson, *A Soldier's Reminiscences in Peace and War* (Philadelphia, J. B. Lippincott and Co., 1886), p. 86.

7. Lydia Spencer Lane, *I Married a Soldier; or, Old Days in the Old Army* (1893; reprint, Albuquerque, N.Mex.: Horn and Wallace, 1964), pp. 37–38.

Pests of all sorts infested virtually every building. The green logs used in construction shrank as time passed, and "the rats and mice came and went without ceremony" in the Lanes' house at Fort Clark. Although Lt. J. J. Brereton occupied "one of the best" rooms at Fort Duncan, he still kept an umbrella handy in rainy weather and maintained a wary eye for falling adobe. Roaches "covered the kitchen floor until it was black." At Fort Bliss, the indomitable Mrs. Lane reported that "the quarters were tolerably good." Unfortunately, cracks in the thatched roof meant that "there was nothing to prevent a snake dropping in on us whenever he felt inclined."[8] In 1860 the besieged Robert E. Lee described his morning regimen to his wife:

> I get in a tub of water every mng [morning], scrutinize closely with my spectacles on every garment that I put on, & before I am dressed I am attacked. I have my articles of camp furniture taken out & washed, no use. I mentioned to someone the other day, that I had had to get up two or three times in the night, disrobe & examine myself & bed, & still be afflicted. They said they had found that was the worst plan. It was better to keep quiet, you only aroused them by lighting your candle, & after a little while you did not mind them. I see no relief for me, for I am so awkward in catching them, but retreat.[9]

The prerogatives of rank further complicated the search for decent housing at Texas forts, for senior officers had their choice of domiciles, occupied or not. Upon the arrival of a new unit a captain might spot a neat little house occupied by a first lieutenant. The latter, having been evicted, might then push a lowly second lieutenant out of his former home in a process known as "falling bricks." Sometimes this meant doubling up officers in the existing buildings. Other officers pitched tents to avoid the scramble. One resourceful officer attached two small tents to a hospital tent, framing and flooring the entire lot. A servant slept in another tent at the rear; cooking was done in yet a fifth canvas structure.

While a few bachelors gallantly gave up their quarters to junior officers with families, the housing shortages more often led to endless bickering. In early 1870, in an effort to clear up problems at overcrowded Fort Concho, Lt. Col. William R. Shafter ordered that captains and lieutenants could occupy only one room plus a kitchen, more generous army regulations notwithstanding. "Decided discord" resulted. After a flurry of charges and countercharges, two officers who had complained too vehemently were placed under arrest, and several others were threatened with similar action. Social relations at the post reached a new low.[10]

---

8. Ibid., pp. 37–39, 72; J. J. Brereton, Jan. 4, 1878, in R. C. Crane, ed., "Letters from Texas," *West Texas Historical Association Year Book* 25 (Oct., 1949): 112.

9. Lee to Mrs. Lee, May 2, 1860, in Francis Raymond Adams, Jr., ed., "An Annotated Edition of the Personal Letters of Robert E. Lee April, 1855–April, 1861" (Ph.D. diss., University of Maryland, 1955), p. 626.

10. PMR, Fort Concho, Jan., 1870, p. 153, Feb., 1870, p. 157, May, 1870, p. 169; Dinmick to AAG, Aug. 31, 1869, and Notson to Gamble, Aug. 31, 1869, Appointment, Commission and Per-

Lt. Col. Robert E. Lee was caught in a similar shuffle at Fort Brown resulting from an exchange of garrisons in 1856. On temporary duty as a member of a court-martial, he saw three wives and their families forced out of their homes. Two officers gave up their rooms to allow two of the women to stay indoors; the third couple had to be satisfied with a tent. Lee himself was reduced to sharing his room with two other officers. Writing his wife in Virginia, he reluctantly concluded that "the more I see of Army life in Texas, the less probability do I see your ever being able to join me here."[11]

With space at a premium the more resourceful officers and wives found a number of ways to spruce up their tiny abodes. The officers at Fort Belknap, where only two stone structures had been completed in 1854, were credited by one observer with having used "taste and ingenuity" in making the best of a bad situation. In 1857, Fort Mason offered "habitable, though homely quarters," with married officers occupying two rooms plus a kitchen and their single counterparts one room each. The vine-covered cottages at Fort Brown presented an attractive officers' row. Flower beds surrounded many such residences at Fort Concho. Mrs. Lane's house at Fort Bliss was fairly comfortable. It had a carpet-covered canvas floor, adobe walls, and a thatched roof, and she remembered seeing only one snake and very few insects indoors.[12]

Although housing was often inadequate, military officials took more stringent efforts to ensure that post hospitals met at least minimal standards, especially after 1865. Good and bad soldiers alike saw the need for a comfortable hospital. Here the conscientious could find a few comforts to help their recovery; the malingerers might enjoy the hospital's special diet and a few days' rest. Patchwork floors, filthy bedding, incomplete medical journals, and disordered medicine cabinets marked a few infirmaries, but most such structures were the post showpieces. The hospital at Fort Concho, for example, was plastered throughout. Fire buckets and axes with printed directions were stored in the halls of the twenty-four-bed structure in case of fire. Stoves and fireplaces heated the building, which one contemporary observer estimated had cost $56,000.[13]

Eventually lamps were installed at the front entrances of many hospitals to aid the sick arriving after dark. Separate kitchens often provided special diets. Several infirmaries were rebuilt in accordance with the widely held belief that hospital poisons would saturate any structure after ten years. At Fort McKavett the original infirmary's leaky roof exposed patients, furnishings, and medical supplies to rainfall. However, a new structure later resolved the problem. By 1871,

---

sonal Branch, Letters Received 3046-1876, NA, RG 94 (microfilm, Fort Concho Research Library, MF 13).

11. Lee to Mrs. Lee, Nov. 19, 1856, in Adams, "Lee Letters," pp. 211–12.

12. James Parker, *The Old Army: Memories, 1872–1918* (Philadelphia: Dorrance and Co., 1929), p. 215; Lee to Mrs. Lee, Apr. 12, 1857, Adams, "Lee Letters," p. 328; Lane, *I Married a Soldier*, p. 72.

13. McConnell, *Five Years a Cavalryman*, pp. 164–65; PMR, Fort Richardson, June, 1872, pp. 269–70; Boggs, "History of Fort Concho," p. 12.

Fort Brown boasted a forty-eight-bed brick hospital. Painstakingly contructed according to the General Plan for Hospitals issued in 1867, the fine new building was completely surrounded by a twelve-foot-wide porch.

The post's other structures rarely matched the hospital in quality. Particularly squalid were the post guardhouses. Although Fort Brown possessed an excellent infirmary, the sunken floor of its guardhouse forced prisoners to sleep in the mud during wet weather. Tobacco juice, smoke, human filth, and the lack of even the most basic cleaning could make a guardhouse a virtual deathtrap. In August, 1870, forty-eight men were crowded into the jail at Fort Richardson. One was in solitary confinement in a cell 8 by 8 feet, nine were crowded in three other cells of the same size, and the remaining thirty-eight prisoners were packed in a 24-by-12-foot room. Conditions had improved but little four years later, when the post surgeon described the guardroom as "hot and suffocating in summer, damp and dark in winter and foul and uncomfortable always." By then most prisoners were confined in a 21-by-10-by-8-foot room with an earthen floor. Two

22-square-inch openings provided minimal ventilation. The older cramped structures were still standing.[14]

The typical frontier fort also contained a collection of auxiliary buildings. Most secure were the stone magazines that held the garrison's store of powder and ammunition. Other structures varied in size and quality. Fort Davis eventually had an adobe bakery, a smithy, a carpenters' shed, a commissary, and two stables, all of fairly good construction. The stable at Ringgold Barracks was, however, "a mere sham," for the enormous expenditures for the post's quarters had exhausted the building funds. Troops attempting to reoccupy Fort Quitman after the Civil War found virtually every building in shambles. "During heavy rain yesterday, the guardhouse fell in and guard and prisoners narrowly escaped injury," reported one officer. He added that the "houses are not fit to stable cattle in. . . . the offices are all dripping and filled with mud. . . . Quarters have a wagon load of silt on rugs, furniture, etc. . . . The post is a disgrace to the government and a gross injustice to troops to station them there."[15]

Sanitary facilities on the frontiers were primitive. Most troops bathed in nearby rivers until the 1880s, when several post doctors mounted strong campaigns to establish bathhouses. They achieved only mixed results. Some posts received new zinc-lined bathtubs, pipes, and hot-water tanks. Assistant Surgeon R. C. Newton achieved less success at Fort Elliott. In January, 1885, he called for a structure large enough to allow each soldier to take two baths a week. Reducing sickness and the spread of diseases through better sanitation "might elevate the moral tone of this command," Newton argued. Despite continued recommendations, in the fall of 1886, War Department authorities disapproved his request for a four-to-six-tub bathhouse.[16]

Toilet facilities proved especially troublesome on the older and larger posts. Communal latrines were usually behind the company barracks. Officers used separate outhouses behind their own quarters. The two privies generally consisted of underground zinc-lined vaults, which needed periodic cleaning and replacement. Both officers and men took great pains to avoid latrine duty, a problem compounded by a chronic shortage of lime and disinfectant. The results were clearly evident. As time passed, the amount of human excrement tested even the strongest of sensibilities. Some medical officers hoped to separate the urinals from the privies and to convert the vaults into dry-earth operations that could be "used by numbers of people and still remain odorless." Properly fitting

---

14. PMR, Fort Brown, July, 1868; PMR, Fort Richardson, Aug., 1870, p. 181, Dec., 1874, pp. 110–11.

15. PMR, Fort Davis, pp. 9–11; Walter C. Conway, ed., "Colonel Edmund Schriver's Inspector-General's Report on Military Posts in Texas, November 1872–January 1873," *Southwestern Historical Quarterly* 67 (Apr., 1964): 573–74; George Ruhlen, "Quitman: The Worst Post at Which I Ever Served," *Password* 11 (Fall, 1966): 116.

16. PMR, Camp Peña Colorado, Jan. 31, 1888, p. 145; PMR, Fort Elliott, Jan. 4, 1885, p. 185, Nov. 1, 1885, p. 28, Oct. 3, 1886, p. 72.

toilet seats and the regular use of dry soil to cover the vaults also reduced discomfort.[17]

The condition of the officers' privies drew similar fire. Overuse and shabby construction often rendered the privies unusable. Green lumber inevitably shrank and created large gaps in the flooring, which, according to one doctor, permitted "offensive and unhealthy gases to escape, and these unhealthy gases must necessarily be inhaled by the occupant of the privy." To make matters worse, the distance from houses to outhouses forced the officers' wives "to run the gauntlet of the whole back part of the officers' quarters whenever they wished to go there."[18]

The houses of the married enlisted personnel and the laundresses received similar criticism from sanitary inspectors. Separated from the company barracks, these quarters comprised a motley collection of buildings dubbed "suds row." Those at Fort Richardson in 1870 consisted of several 9-by-21-foot picket structures covered with canvas. The post doctor, noting that many laundresses lived and worked in areas unprotected from the sun, suggested that each be given two rooms with a veranda to shade her workplace. An inspector suggested that the married men and the laundresses should have homes that were "an ornament rather than an offence to the eye." He believed that such structures should have exterior latticework similar to that used in the officers' quarters and be arranged in neat blocks rather than irregular clusters.[19]

Despite such recommendations, housing supplied to married men and laundresses remained substandard. Insufficient appropriations as well as the low priority given to such projects by many post commanders contributed to the lack of effective action. The animosity between the medical department, responsible for judging the health of a post's structures, and the quartermaster's department, responsible for construction, further hampered remodeling efforts. At least one soldier, Sgt. Thomas Drury, gave up waiting for government action. With a family to consider, Drury spent about a hundred dollars to build his own house at Fort Duncan. No record can be found of any response to his request for reimbursement by the government.[20]

Construction was an ongoing affair at the Texas posts. Noting the haphazard houses of stone, adobe, log, mud, and canvas at Fort Duncan during the 1850s, one observer remarked that "had [the buildings] been deposited on the ground as a result of a cyclone there would have been no less regard for regularity or uniformity." Subsequent reoccupation of Duncan after the Civil War brought great improvements, including almost entirely new quarters.

17. PMR, Fort Elliott, Jan. 11, 1885, p. 186.
18. PMR, Fort Davis, Nov. 30, 1881, p. 324.
19. PMR, Fort Richardson, Dec., 1870, p. 198; PMR, Ringgold Barracks, July 13, 1876, p. 279; PMR, Fort Brown, Dec., 1871.
20. Miller J. Stewart, "Army Laundresses: Ladies of the 'Soap Suds Row,'" *Nebraska History* 61 (Winter, 1980): 423; M. L. Crimmins, ed., "Colonel J. K. F. Mansfield's Report of the Inspection of the Department of Texas in 1856," *Southwestern Historical Quarterly* 42 (Jan., 1939): 244.

The situation at Fort Brown in July, 1868, appears to have been typical of the oft-changing architecture of Texas forts. Its garrison included 241 infantry-men living in two newly completed barracks with a third in progress, 82 infan-trymen in temporary wooden structures designed to hold 4 men each, 65 cavalry troopers quartered in a temporary barracks, and 11 officers residing in houses.[21]

Construction work did not always lead to improved conditions. Surgeon William N. Notson complained in February, 1871, that twelve different men had been in command of Fort Concho since his arrival three years earlier. Their differ-ing views on construction had added to costs and slowed progress as each undid the labors of his predecessor. Erratic funding also created shortages in construc-tion materials, which meant that expensive civilian laborers were sometimes paid for doing nothing. Buildings remained half-finished when money was cut off. J. B. Girard's cryptic comments of late 1880 capture this frustration. On October 27 he optimistically reported that "work on new laundry began." On December 20 he wrote, "Work on laundry discontinued leaving building unfinished."[22]

Texas civilians also built their own forts, but in a very different form. The withdrawal of U.S. regulars from Texas early in 1861 left settlers vulnerable to In-dian attacks. While state troops ranged the frontiers, their numbers were never adequate to provide effective defense. Consequently, western settlers left to their own devices often grouped together for communal defense. Fifteen miles below Camp Cooper on the Clear Fork of the Brazos, about 120 people built "Fort Davis," a 300-by-325-foot stockade. Beginning work in October, 1864, the citizens even-tually erected rude walls with bastions at each corner to protect the twenty solid picket houses in their homemade fort. One occupant described her home as hav-ing three rooms, plank floors, doors with locks, and two fireplaces. It was, she concluded proudly, "the best house in the place."[23]

Although similar fortifications were built elsewhere, the regular army's sprawl-ing bases were typical of the Texas military frontiers. Adequate congressional funding was essential to provide satisfactory quarters. If such monies were forth-coming, the availability of local materials further affected construction. And al-though post–Civil War regulations required post surgeons to file periodic sanita-tion reports, the attitude taken by the post's commander was crucial. His interest, or lack of it, often determined whether sanitary recommendations were put into practice or ignored. An energetic officer who carefully surveyed the construction and sincerely cared for the welfare of his men might, through the force of his will, secure much better facilities than conditions otherwise warranted. Yet with-out firm enforcement by the fort's highest authority the dirtier jobs of cleaning privies and butcher pens were not carried out.

---

21. Johnson, *A Soldier's Reminiscences*, p. 64; PMR, Fort Brown, July, 1868, p. 1.

22. PMR, Fort Concho, Feb., 1871, p. 201, Feb., 1872, p. 253; PMR, Fort Davis, Oct. 27, 1880, p. 282, Dec. 20, 1880, p. 284.

23. Samuel P. Newcomb Diary, Jan. 1, Feb. 1, 1865, BTHC; Susan E. Newcomb Diary, p. 33, BTHC.

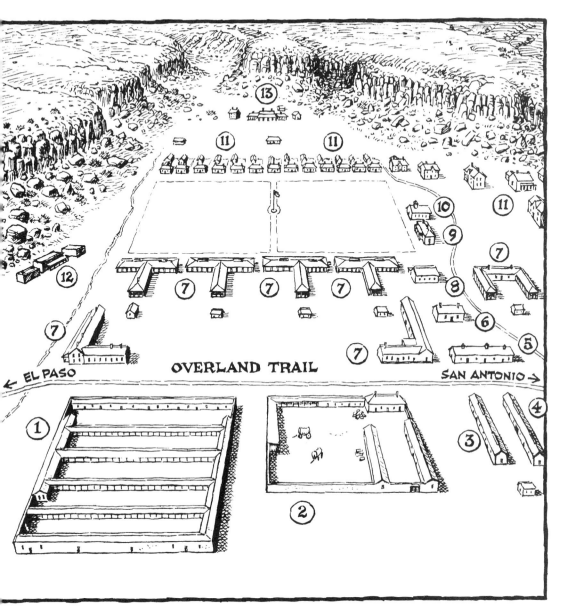

AT FORT DAVIS, TYPICAL OF ALL TEXAS FORTS, ENLISTED MEN'S BARRACKS ⑦ FACED "OFFICERS' ROW" ⑪ ACROSS THE PARADE GROUND. HEADQUARTERS ⑨ AND A CHAPEL-SCHOOLHOUSE ⑩ DOMINATED THE NORTH END OF THE QUADRANGLE, WITH THE POST SUTLER'S ⑫ TO THE SOUTH. BEHIND THE BARRACKS STOOD THE CAVALRY STABLES ①, QUARTERMASTER'S STABLES ② AND STORE-HOUSE ③, GRANARY ④, COMMISSARY ⑤, BAKERY ⑥, AND GUARDHOUSE ⑧. THE MAGAZINE WAS USUALLY A DISTANCE AWAY — AT DAVIS, BEHIND THE HOSPITAL ⑬ — AS WERE THE LAUNDRESSES' QUARTERS. FORTS WERE RARELY ENCLOSED BY WALLS.

The typical nineteenth-century military post was composed of a group of buildings erected at different times by different persons for different purposes. The structures formed a rough square, with company barracks on one side and the officers' quarters on the opposite side. The hospital, storehouses, and auxiliary structures formed the other two sides of the fort. The central area was used as a parade ground, with a flagpole invariably placed in the center. As one soldier recalled, "There is nothing to prevent Indians or anyone else, from riding through the posts in any direction. They are built simply for quarters, and their localities for defence, is seldom thought of. They are placed so as to have a level place for a parade, convenient to water &c., without any expectation that they will ever have to stand a siege."[24]

As national agents defending settlers from Indian attack and committed to aiding western expansion, those who resided at the ramshackle frontier stations believed that their suffering advanced an important and necessary cause. Although they lived in a hospital tent during the 1850s, Richard Johnson later commented that he and his wife were "happy and contented." Lydia Lane called Fort Lancaster "the worst of all the posts in Texas" but admitted that "the ladies I have met at the post seemed cheerful and contented." O. M. Knapp's laconic description of the time the Rio Grande flooded at Fort Bliss in 1867 further exemplifies this attitude. "Yesterday a store house went in and the blacksmith shop will be gone tomorrow," he informed his mother. "So it is with life."[25]

24. Bliss Reminiscences, 1:119–20.
25. Johnson, *A Soldier's Reminiscences*, p. 86; Lane, *I Married a Soldier*, pp. 44, 76; Knapp to Mother, May 19, 1867, Obadiah M. Knapp Papers, BTHC.

CHAPTER THREE

The Soldiers

. . . an epitome of the world.

—Sgt. H. H. McConnell

One prominent historian has called the U.S. Army "a child of the frontier." Indeed, the army's connection with frontier defense can scarcely be overestimated. Although the Continental army had performed well in the Revolutionary War, many Americans opposed a large standing army, fearing that such a force threatened their hard-earned liberties. Defense, they maintained, should be left to the state militias. However, Indian raids and the continued presence of British troops in the Northwest Territory led Congress in 1784 to organize the First American Regiment, which became the nucleus of the regular army.[1]

By 1812, when frontier problems attracted closer scrutiny by national leaders, the regular force had grown to more than six thousand men. Yet inadequate training, inept leadership, and organizational quagmires marked military efforts during the second war with England and led John C. Calhoun, secretary of war from 1817 to 1825, to advocate a series of reforms. Calhoun's interest in West Point helped spur that institution to begin producing graduates who gradually professionalized the American officer corps. He also proposed the establishment of a skeletal regular force, with an overabundance of officers and units, which could be augmented with volunteers in times of emergency. Although Calhoun's plan was not implemented, his enthusiasm and hard work injected a needed stimulant for the formation of America's armed forces.

During the era dominated by Andrew Jackson and his policies, the army established a new series of forts ahead of white settlement. In theory the military was to protect both whites and Indians. Yet continued western migration made

---

1. Francis Paul Prucha, *The Sword of the Republic: The United States Army on the Frontier, 1783–1846* (1969; reprint, Bloomington: Indiana University Press, 1977), p. 394; Russell F. Weigley, *History of the United States Army* (enl. ed., Bloomington: Indiana University Press, 1984), pp. 80–82.

the army's job increasingly difficult. Sparking debates that continued for the remainder of the century, a few officers attributed the frontier violence to impatient whites who demanded ever-increasing amounts of land from Indians. Such objections, however, rarely deterred restless frontiersmen and failed to fundamentally alter national policy. Emigrants continued to push west, and the army moved with them. By the eve of the Mexican War the regular army, which occupied posts in western Arkansas, Missouri, and the upper Mississippi River valley, had grown to almost nine thousand men.

After temporarily expanding the army to forty thousand men during the war with Mexico, Congress reduced its strength to under fourteen thousand soon after the war ended. Frontier problems did not disappear as easily. By 1853 the territorial gains of the mid- to late 1840s—Texas, Oregon, and the Mexican Cession (California and the Utah and New Mexico territories)—had stretched the tiny army over fifty-four stations. Responding to calls for a larger force to guard the new lands, Congress added two cavalry and two infantry regiments to the existing establishment of four artillery, eight infantry, and three mounted regiments. Artillery regiments comprised twelve companies; infantry and cavalry, ten each. A company serving on the frontier had seventy-four men at full strength. A colonel commanded each regiment, assisted by a lieutenant colonel and two majors. A captain led each company, with the aid of a first and a second lieutenant.

The Civil War brought a tremendous expansion of American armed forces. By 1865 more than 2 million men had worn the Union blue; about 900,000 had fought under the Confederate Stars and Bars. But postwar reductions were swift: a force of 54,000 men was the maximum authorized in 1866. In 1869 an upper limit of 37,313 was set. The following year Congress reduced the maximum to 30,000 enlisted men and in 1874 set an effective limit of about 27,000. The post–Civil War army contained forty regiments; four of these, the Ninth and Tenth Cavalry and the Twenty-fourth and Twenty-fifth Infantry, were composed of black enlisted men. The officer corps remained lily white until 1877, when Henry O. Flipper was appointed to the Tenth Cavalry.[2]

Although lines of authority were complex, the army divided the country into divisions, departments, and districts. The Lone Star State, largely encompassed in Department 8 in 1848, was renamed the Department of Texas in 1853. Except for the Civil War era, it remained a separate department or district for the rest of the century.

Texas was partitioned into districts and subdistricts which were often reorganized over time. In 1869, for example, Texas (then known as the Fifth Military District) included the subdistricts: Rio Grande (including Forts Brown, Ringgold, and McIntosh), Pecos (Forts Duncan, Clark, McKavett, and Concho), Brazos (Fort Griffin and Richardson), and Presidio (Forts Stockton, Davis, Quitman, and Bliss). The commander of each post was usually selected by the department head, with occasional interference from War Department bureaucrats. Post commanders corresponded with subdistrict, district, and department headquarters.

The army's duties were not solely military. In addition to guarding the western frontiers and both the Atlantic and Pacific coasts, the army was used to oversee reconstruction of the southern states after the Civil War, establish national parks, escort scientific teams, and put down labor unrest. The army's varied duties, plus the huge geographic area for which it was responsible, meant that the frontier forts were thinly garrisoned. In 1849, for example, each of the army's six Texas posts had an average of 116 men. Although more than one-fifth of the entire U.S. Army was stationed within the state's borders by 1856, Texans called for still more military support. To their dismay problems in Kansas, Utah, California, and Oregon forced the transfer of some of these men. By 1860 only 1,238 troops were serving in the fourteen military posts in Texas, an average of slightly less than 90 regulars per fort.[3]

---

2. Robert M. Utley, *Frontier Regulars: The United States Army and the Indian, 1866–1891* (New York: Macmillan Co., 1973), pp. 12, 16.

3. Robert Wooster, "The Military and United States Indian Policy, 1865–1903" (Ph.D. diss.,

After Texas seceded in early 1861, the withdrawal of federal forces was a devastating blow to frontier settlers. State officials quickly raised volunteer units to fill the breach, but with a large portion of Texas' fighting men and resources going to the Confederacy, these outfits never amassed sufficient numbers or adequate supplies. Against these weakened forces Indians stepped up their raids, forcing the retreat of white settlement as much as a hundred miles during the Civil War. Only the subsequent return of the regulars to Texas after the war encouraged western migration to begin anew. By 1868 more than 4,500 troops occupied the Lone Star State. As late as 1890 more than 2,200 soldiers were still patrolling Texas.[4]

Although between 10 and 30 percent of the entire regular army was stationed in Texas at various times, the numbers of troops available for duty remained pitifully small. In March, 1853, for example, Fort Chadbourne had five companies of the Eighth Infantry. If these outfits had been filled to their maximum allowable strength, they would have composed a formidable force of more than 400 officers and men. There were, however, only 15 officers and 225 enlisted men on company rolls. Of that total 12 officers and 77 enlisted men were absent from Fort Chadbourne on detached service or on leave. Nineteen others were under arrest, and sickness claimed 7 more. Forty-three were on extra duty. Thus the five infantry companies stationed at Fort Chadbourne could list a total of 3 officers and 79 men as ready for action.

Post–Civil War figures present a similarly unimpressive picture of army strength. As the War Department funneled recruits into the cavalry, infantry units became mere skeleton forces. In May, 1870, the Twenty-fourth Infantry Regiment listed only 17 officers and 136 men as present for duty. Fifteen commissioned officers and 100 troops were on detached service, in confinement, in hospitals, or absent with or without leave. Seventy-one recruits had just arrived and were awaiting assignment. Three companies had no officers. Company G had only 7 men in its ranks. At peak efficiency was Company A, with 2 officers and 27 men present for duty and another 16 of all ranks on the rolls.[5]

The disparity in strength between cavalry and infantry regiments widened after the annihilation of Lt. Col. George A. Custer and much of the Seventh Cavalry at the Little Bighorn in 1876. Responding to calls for more mounted

University of Texas, 1985), pp. 17–20; Report of Jones, Nov. 28, Secretary of War, Annual Report (hereafter cited as SW, AR), 1849, p. 182; Davis to Latham and others, Sept. 24, 1856, Letters Sent by the Secretary of War Relating to Military Affairs, 1800–1889, NA, RG 107 (microcopy 6, Lamar University, Beaumont, Texas, 38:272); Report of Cooper, Nov. 28, SW, AR, 1860, pp. 218–23.

4. For numbers, see Reports of Townsend, Oct. 20, SW, AR, 1868, pp. 764–77, Oct. 11, SW, AR, 1875, pp. 146–47; Report of Drum, Oct. 11, SW, AR, 1880, pp. 11–14; Report of McKeever, Oct. 7, SW, AR, 1890, pp. 78–79.

5. Fort Chadbourne, Mar., 1853, Reports from U.S. Military Posts, 1800–1916, NA (microcopy 617, Fort Concho Research Library, MF 39); Returns from Regular Army Infantry Regiments June 1821–December 1916: Twenty-fourth Infantry December 1866–December 1872, NA (microfilm, Fort Concho Research Library, MF 27).

troopers, Congress authorized the army to raise another 2,500 cavalrymen to meet the emergency on the northern plains. After the crisis ended, Congress maintained the upper limit of 25,000 by taking troops away from infantry companies to compensate for the cavalry increases. While allowing 100 men per mounted troop, this practice set a 37-man limit on infantry companies. In effect, then, the new measures reduced the average infantry company to fewer than 25 men.

In increasing the percentage of mounted men, Congress adopted a policy long advocated by civilians and military personnel. Editors of the *Texas State Gazette* reasoned that the foot soldiers were "almost as useless as so many lobsters" against mounted Indians. Having first experimented with mounted volunteers, in 1833 Congress created two dragoon regiments, adding a second regiment during the 1830s. A regiment of mounted riflemen was organized in 1846. Secretary of War Charles Conrad received permission to mount infantry stationed in Texas in 1850, but the experiment was a failure. In 1855, responding to the growing need for reliable horse soldiers, Congress authorized two new cavalry regiments. No less than ten mounted regiments constituted the post–Civil War mounted forces.[6]

Cavalry units received their share of criticism, with opponents pointing out that cavalry regiments cost twice as much as foot soldiers. And while mounted troops did well on short expeditions, on longer marches, especially in winter or over terrain devoid of forage, the infantrymen often outstripped their cavalry counterparts. In the end man often proved stronger than horse. Seeking to overcome this obstacle some soldiers rode mules rather than horses. The heavier rifle carried by the foot soldier also gave him more range than that of the mounted man. The need to detail one man in four to guard the horses during combat further reduced the cavalry's firepower.[7]

Civilians—and Texans in particular—were harshly critical of the apparent inability of regular cavalry and infantry to cope with the guerrilla tactics of the Indians. It was ludicrous, they argued, for troops drilled in European-style formations to try to catch the mobile warriors. "How can they protect us against Indians," argued Sen. Sam Houston, "when the cavalry have not horses which can trot faster than active oxen, and the infantry dare not go out in any hostile manner for fear of being shot and scalped!"[8]

The volunteer frontiersmen also received criticism from both their army rivals and the citizens they were supposed to protect. In 1857 the War Department estimated that the country could have saved $30 million over the preceding twenty years by replacing expensive volunteers with regulars. Sgt. H. H. McConnell admitted that the Texas Rangers were "tolerable Indian fighters" but maintained that "most of their time was occupied in terrorizing the citizens and 'taking in the town.'"

---

6. *Texas State Gazette* (Austin), July 12, 1851; Report of Conrad, Nov. 30, SW, AR, 1850, pp. 4–5; Report of Scott, Nov. 30, SW, AR, 1850, p. 114.

7. Report of Ewell, Feb. 10, SW, AR, 1855, pp. 59–61.

8. *Congressional Globe*, 33d Cong., 2d sess., 1855, p. 440; ibid., 31st Cong., 2d sess., 1851, p. 722.

After serving with a mixed command of regulars and volunteers along the Rio Grande, Bvt. Lt. Col. William J. Hardee concluded that "the volunteers . . . evinced much energy and intelligence, and obeyed my orders; but in irregular cavalry, where the horses are owned by the volunteers, it must be expected that they will consider the preservation of their animals as paramount to other considerations." Commenting on Indian troubles near Eagle Pass in 1866, J. W. Light reported: "I see that there has been a Proposition . . . to rase Rangers again. I am of the opinion the remidy is as bad as the disease. These Ruyed assed Rangers aint worth a Huraw in Hell."[9]

Despite such criticism circumstances sometimes forced army commanders to use the volunteer troops to supplement their meager forces. State governors called out the irregulars on many other occasions. In Texas these men, as well as the more established Texas Ranger organization, came to be known collectively as Rangers. Paid by the state, they operated against outlaws and Mexicans as well as Indians, free of the red tape that often paralyzed regulars. Yet the federal government refused to fund such troops on a regular basis; unwilling to spend large amounts of state monies, the Texas legislature left the job of guarding the frontiers largely to the U.S. Army.

As a result the regular army assumed most of the duties associated with frontier defense even in Texas. The officers, a mixture of professionals and amateurs, veterans and greenhorns, diligent guardians of the nation's borders and incompetent fops, were the backbone of the regular forces. Considering their small numbers and the miserly level of congressional appropriations, these officers performed their lonely tasks well.

The typical officer serving in Texas between 1850 and 1880 was about thirty-three years old; in later years the average age was a bit older. About 30 percent of these men were accompanied by their wives. For the entire period less than one officer in ten was foreign born. Before the Civil War more than half of the army officers in the Lone Star State had been born in the South. After 1865 most of the officers came from the Middle Atlantic and western states. Although the army made room for a few men commissioned from the ranks, the chances of such a promotion were extremely slight.[10]

West Point graduates filled over two-thirds of the army's commissioned positions during the 1850s. After the Civil War, Congress specified that former volunteers were to hold many of the vacant posts (one of every four second lieutenancies, for example), but subsequent army reductions later raised the ratio of

9. Report of Cooper, SW, AR, 1857, pp. 84–87; H. H. McConnell, *Five Years a Cavalryman; Or, Sketches of Regular Army Life on the Texas Frontier, Twenty Odd Years Ago* (Jacksboro, Tex.: J. N. Rogers and Co., 1889), p. 296; M. L. Crimmins, ed., "The Second Dragoon Indian Campaign in Texas," *West Texas Historical Association Year Book* 21 (Oct., 1945): 56; J. W. Light to Black, Oct. 17, 1866, Reading W. Black Papers, BTHC.

10. Based on manuscript returns from U.S. census, 1850, Bexar, Medina, Navarro counties; census, 1860, Maverick and Stockton counties; census, 1870, Maverick, Presidio, and Starr counties; census, 1880, Kinney and Wheeler counties.

West Pointers. Appointments to the academy were often politically motivated; nonetheless, the cadets who went on to serve in Texas came from varied backgrounds. Charles J. Crane, son of the president of Baylor University, tried life as a farmer and later as a cowboy before the sight of a well-dressed officer lured him into the army. Crane solicited his appointment from Congressman D. C. Giddings in June, 1872. John Bell Hood's father wanted his son to follow in his footsteps and become a doctor. But John refused his father's offer to send him to Europe to complete his medical studies and secured an appointment to the academy through a maternal uncle. During the Civil War he became one of Texas' most famous fighting men.

Not all the cadets represented America's elite. One young plebe described his classmates as a "motley, almost fantastic crowd of boys from every State and territory in the Union. There were graduates of colleges dressed in the height of fashion . . . and rough handed country boys, awkward, uncouth, jeans clad farmers' sons." At times cadet society was almost savage, and students could be ostracized for a particular misdeed, personality trait, or skin color. These young men faced a four-year program that concentrated on traditional European tactics and engineering. Few received sufficient instruction in fighting Indians, drilling men, or carrying out the routine administrative tasks they would encounter at the country's western forts.[11]

Despite the problems most graduates emerged from West Point with a strong sense of professionalism and tended to favor fellow alumni during their careers. They subjected non–West Pointers to severe criticism for lack of formal military education. Regulars bitterly pointed out that these civilian appointees owed their commissions to political connections rather than military qualifications. While some of the officers were indeed incompetent, the lack of West Point training was not a prerequisite for excellent service. Nelson A. Miles, for example, performed well during the nation's civil conflict and became one of the foremost Indian fighters of his day despite his lacking a formal military education.

Whatever their training, young officers on the Texas frontiers faced tremendous obstacles. One veteran remembered that green officers could barely handle the simplest tasks of mounting the guard, dispensing rations, riding, or drilling their men. He described the typical young subaltern as "a sort of unfinished boy who is not fit for anything particularly, except to act as recorder on a 'board of survey,' go on as 'officer of the guard,' act as 'file close' at drill, or to perform such other duties as may relieve the older officers from some of the drudgery of routine."[12]

Fortunately, bewildered newcomers eventually became experienced veterans. Even so, army life could prove trying to even the most experienced soldier.

---

11. David S. Stanley, *Personal Memoirs of Major-General D. S. Stanley, U.S.A.* (Cambridge, Mass.: Harvard University Press, 1917), p. 18; Charles J. Crane, *Experiences of a Colonel of Infantry* (New York: Knickerbocker Press, 1923), pp. 55–56.

12. McConnell, *Five Years a Cavalryman*, p. 219.

Although the forts were not completely removed from society's amenities, a well-educated officer might find the enforced isolation of the far-flung Texas posts maddening. Some, such as Capt. George Armes, succumbed to the political in-fighting that could paralyze a garrison. Armes was involved in at least four courts-martial. His career (along with his autobiography) is filled with tales of arrests, politics, and condemnations of fellow officers. In 1880 his counsel testified that Armes "is a monomaniac on the subject of people or persons connected with the army, his regiment and post, and trying, as he styles it, to rob him of his commission, to press him and to oppress him, and that a conspiracy exists to this end."[13]

Others vented their frustrations in a different fashion. One of Fort Graham's captains was tried on charges of embezzling, removing public letters from the adjutant's office, and "exposing in the most degrading manner in a public alley in the Town of Austin, Texas, the privacy of his person, by taking down his pantaloons and assuming the usual stooped posture for the performance of an office of nature." He resigned from the army in June, 1851. While serving as a traveling army paymaster, O. M. Smith reported that his companion, Maj. Isaac S. Stewart, was "drunk the entire 47 days we were absent, having several attacks of tremens and was almost unbearable at times." Stewart resigned his commission shortly afterward.[14]

Failure and depression could ruin even the most brilliant of military careers. Ranald Slidell Mackenzie, son of naval officer and author Alexander Slidell Mackenzie, graduated at the top of the West Point class of 1862. Distinguishing himself in several Civil War actions, he was promoted to brigadier general of volunteers at the tender age of twenty-four. Ulysses S. Grant pronounced him "the most promising young officer in the army." Mackenzie continued to impress his peers in the Indian Wars that followed, leading a successful raid into Mexico that culminated in the victory at Remolino in 1873. In the following year he won another decisive victory over hostile tribes at Palo Duro Canyon, in the Texas Panhandle.[15]

Junior officers idolized Mackenzie, who worked hard to secure their promotions. But the seven wounds he received in the Civil War and the Indian Wars weakened him physically, and his intense nature made him increasingly irritable and explosive. He eventually became preoccupied with his growing rivalry with

13. Testimony of George Paschal, June, 1880, Records of the Office of the Judge Advocate General, Court Martial Case Files, George A. Armes, NA (microfilm, Fort Concho Research Library, MF 20); George A. Armes, *Ups and Downs of an Army Officer* (Washington, D.C.: privately printed, 1900).

14. Sandra L. Myres, "Fort Graham: Listening Post on the Texas Frontier," *West Texas Historical Association Year Book* 69 (1983): 45; Escal F. Duke, "O. M. Smith—Frontier Pay Clerk," *West Texas Historical Association Year Book* 55 (1969): 48.

15. Ernest Wallace, *Ranald S. Mackenzie on the Texas Frontier* (Lubbock: West Texas Museum Association, 1964); Robert McHenry, ed., *Webster's American Military Biographies* (New York: Dover Publications, 1978), p. 266.

Nelson A. Miles for promotion to brigadier general. In 1883 a former subordinate found Mackenzie, now at San Antonio, "greatly changed in appearance; he had lost flesh and erectness of carriage. Even his head seemed to have lost part of its splendid shape and size." Although Mackenzie had won his coveted star a year earlier, the long campaigning, the harsh frontier life, and his personal intensity of purpose had destroyed his health. He was forced to retire in 1884; he died in 1889, apparently a victim of syphilis-induced insanity. Army life in Texas could indeed take its toll.[16]

Texas also claimed the army career of Henry Flipper, the first black graduate of West Point. Born a slave in Thomasville, Georgia, Flipper secured his appointment to the academy in 1873. One classmate remembered that Flipper "behaved himself very well indeed, and was generally liked by his classmates but no one openly associated with him, and anyone seen doing so would have been 'cut' by the Corps." Young Flipper overcame the snubs and graduated in 1877. Appointed

16. Crane, *Experiences of a Colonel of Infantry,* pp. 113, 139–40; Robert G. Carter, *The Old Sergeant's Story: Winning the West from the Indians and Bad Men in 1870 to 1876* (New York: Frederick H. Hitchcock, 1926), p. 18; Wallace, *Mackenzie,* p. 195 n. 8; Sheridan to Sherman, Dec. 28, 1883, Philip Sheridan Papers, box 43, Library of Congress.

second lieutenant in the black Tenth Cavalry Regiment, he served at Forts Concho and Davis, where he again encountered intense prejudice among fellow officers. On New Year's Day, 1881, a traditional time for visiting among officers, Flipper received only one caller, Lt. Wade Hampton (ironically, Hampton was the nephew of a former Confederate general). "The rest of the officers of the Post were hyenas," Flipper asserted. The unfortunate man was court-martialed in 1882, the victim of trumped-up charges of conduct unbecoming an officer.[17]

The vast majority of officers who served in Texas, however, met no such tragic fates and carved out respectable careers. Comrades remembered William A. Thompson, whose outstanding service enabled him to rise from the ranks to become a major, as "a jolly, rollicksome fellow" who delighted in spreading unfounded rumors about Indian massacres to nervous army brides while they were on the Texas trails. Lt. Eugene Beauharnais Beaumont, who was subsequently awarded the Congressional Medal of Honor for gallantry during the Civil War, also proved

17. Donald R. McClung, "Second Lieutenant Henry O. Flipper: A Negro Officer on the West Texas Frontier," *West Texas Historical Association Year Book* 47 (1971): 20–31; Crane, *Experiences of a Colonel of Infantry*, p. 55; Henry O. Flipper, *Negro Frontiersman: The Western Memoirs of Henry O. Flipper*, ed. Theodore D. Harris (El Paso: Texas Western College Press, 1963), p. 20.

to be a popular traveling companion. Beaumont, who had jet-black hair and moustache, wore a slouch hat, and had pistols hanging ominously from his belt, was a good singer and storyteller, making the hardships of army life more bearable for all those around him.[18]

Family affairs and personal concerns took up much of the officers' spare time and energy. Col. Benjamin Grierson, stationed in Texas in the 1880s, worried about his children and his career. A music teacher before the Civil War, Grierson volunteered and became a cavalry officer despite a deep-rooted distrust of horses stemming from a childhood accident. Grierson led several notable raids against Confederate forces in the western theater and remained in the army after the war, receiving a colonel's post in the Tenth Cavalry. Criticized by racists for commanding a black regiment and for being too sympathetic to Indians, he never won the fame of more spectacular peers like Mackenzie and Miles. Grierson's personal life was no easier than his professional career. He endured the deaths of three of his children; two others suffered from serious mental illnesses.

Lt. Col. Robert E. Lee's letters from Texas to his wife and family in Virginia express another father's concern for his loved ones. A veteran of the Mexican War, Lee came to Texas with the illustrious Second Cavalry Regiment in 1855. While trying to guide his son Robert's education from afar, he warned: "Let him never touch a novel. They paint beauty more charming than nature, & describe happiness that never exists. They will teach him to sigh after that, which has no reality, to despise the little good that is granted us in this world, & to expect more than is ever given."[19]

His advice to his nephew Fitzhugh Lee revealed a similar melancholy. Commenting that most junior officers in Texas were unhappy, he added, "My experience has taught me to recommend no young man to enter the service." Yet, while torn by concern about his wife's chronic illness and his family's Virginia plantation, he remained bound by his devotion to duty and honor. Remaining aloof from the youthful antics of his junior officers, he found joy in simple pleasures— solitary walks along the Rio Grande, good food, and the acquisition of small luxuries. Only his beloved Virginia's secession from the Union could overwhelm his commitment to the army and cause him to resign his commission.[20]

If the officers formed the professional backbone of the frontier forces in Texas, the enlisted men composed the limbs and sinew of the body. Except for the Civil War years the American army of the nineteenth century depended on volunteers.

18. Capt. R. G. Carter, *On the Border with Mackenzie; Or, Winning West Texas from the Comanches* (Washington: D.C.: Enyon Printing Co., 1935), pp. 21–27.

19. Lee to Mrs. Lee, Aug. 18, 1856, in Francis Raymond Adams, Jr., "An Annotated Edition of the Personal Letters of Robert E. Lee, April, 1855–April, 1861" (Ph.D. diss., University of Maryland, 1955), pp. 156–57.

20. Lee to Fitzhugh Lee, Nov. 1, 1856, in ibid., p. 196; Lee to Mrs. Lee, Mar. 28, Apr. 12, 1856, in ibid., pp. 106, 113–14; Lee to Williams, Jan. 22, 1861, in ibid., pp. 718–19.

Infantrymen signed up for three years; the cavalry required a five-year stint. Recruiters winked at the legal enlistment ages of twenty-one to thirty-five. Health requirements were minimal. Having no way to document their identities, deserters often enlisted under false names and lied about their previous military service. Married men were discouraged from joining, and blacks could not serve until after 1862.

In contrast to the officers, a decided majority of the regular troops were foreign-born. More than 60 percent of the enlisted men at five posts in Texas listed foreign birthplaces in the 1850 census. Ten years later the figures were even higher—71 percent foreign-born at Fort Stockton, 77 percent at Fort Duncan, and 82 percent at Fort Davis. More than 40 percent of the enlisted men at these posts came from Ireland. Of the remainder Germans and Britons dominated, but virtually every European country had at least one representative. Post–Civil War figures reveal a slightly smaller foreign-born element, although foreign-born soldiers remained in the majority among white regulars in Texas. Of the American-born soldiers serving in Texas, most came from the Middle Atlantic states, primarily New York and Pennsylvania. New England and the South were represented roughly equally, with westerners just behind. Of course, the number of western-born troops increased after 1865, reflecting the country's shifting population.

The average age of privates, corporals, and sergeants in Texas before the Civil War was twenty-six, most being between twenty-three and thirty-five years old. Some, such as fourteen-year-old French musicians Henry Van Dycke and Louis Tousel, who played in a company band, did not fit the mold. As might be expected, noncommissioned officers were slightly older than privates. According to manuscript census returns, 10 percent of the troops at Fort Lincoln in 1850 could not read or write. Seventeen of the 243 soldiers at Ringgold Barracks in 1870 were similarly handicapped.

The induction of blacks into the regular army during the 1860s altered the makeup of the forces serving in Texas. In 1870, 287 of the 289 black enlisted men at Fort Davis listed birthplaces in the United States; of these, 244 were from the South. Only 5 were natives of New England. Their average age was twenty-five; almost 10 percent were thirty years old or older. Fort Duncan statistics reveal a similar story. Less than 3 percent of the black troops at that post were foreign-born. The overwhelming majority (184 of the 222-man garrison) came from southern states, and 160 of these men either could not read or write. Their average age was between twenty-four and twenty-five, just under 6 percent having reached their thirtieth birthdays.

The situation had changed by 1880. While nationality figures were similar to those reported earlier, soldiers were on the average much older than those in earlier forces. One company of the all-black Twenty-fourth Infantry at Fort Clark averaged thirty-one years old. Almost 40 percent of the soldiers at Forts Clark and Elliott had passed their thirtieth birthdays. Trumpeter Lucienne Bassen, Com-

pany C, Eighth Cavalry, a fifty-five-year-old native of Switzerland, was the oldest enlisted man at the two posts.[21]

Typical was Company F, Sixteenth Infantry, which served in Mississippi, the Indian Territory, Texas, and Utah after 1865. The youngest recruit during the period 1866–91 was fifteen years old; fifty-six-year-old John Wansler, a thirty-year veteran, was the oldest. Seventy-nine percent joined the army when they were in their twenties. Their average height was 5 feet 6½ inches. More than one-fourth of those who enlisted in Company F gave their occupations as "laborers." Another one-fourth were farmers or former soldiers, and the rest were clerks, shoe-

21. See n. 11 above.

makers, bakers, carpenters, printers, cooks, painters, firemen, physicians, painters, and barbers. More than one-third left the army with honorable discharges,
but 23 percent deserted at one time or another during their tours of duty. Thirteen percent received disability discharges, and 2 percent died in the service.[22]

Descriptive accounts reflect this wide representation of American society.
Sgt. John Charlton, "rebellious of parental authority," ran away from home and
enlisted. Another runaway, Pvt. Henry Langford Thayer, hoped to remain in his
mother's good graces. He wrote, "I have done and said a great many things in
my past life which I would give a good deal if I could undo but it has all been

22. Robert F. Bluthardt, "The Men of Company F," *Fort Concho Report* 15 (Summer, 1983): 3–9.

done or said either through thoughtlessness or ignorance and not through wicked-ness." The guarantee of food, board, salary, uniform, and medical services per-suaded others to enlist, particularly during times of national depression (1857–59 and 1873, for example). Overeager recruiters lured gullible lads into the army with promises of exciting service in bountiful western lands. With most jobs unavail-able to them because of racial discrimination, blacks saw the army as a way to get an education and improve their status.[23]

At first glance the recruits seemed to be a motley collection of bounty jump-ers, criminals, and ne'er-do-wells. One army wife charged that a group of enlistees she saw at Burlington, Vermont, was largely composed of deserters from the Brit-ish army. Capt. Robert G. Carter described one first sergeant as a gambler who routinely managed to acquire most of his outfit's money soon after payday. An-other had served a sentence for mutiny in the navy and had done time in the guardhouse for murder after joining the army. Typical of the less than admirable enlistees was William E. Smith, a twenty-five-year-old Harrison County native who joined Company B, Tenth Cavalry, in 1881. During his colorful service Smith received a five-dollar fine and a sentence of one year at hard labor in the guard-house. He was eventually given a dishonorable discharge, but not before he was sent to Alcatraz for forgery and running up debts to the government by over-drawing both his clothing and ordnance allowances.

Yet experience led many critics to qualify their statements about soldiers in the American army. The enlistees tended to be more independent and self-reliant than their counterparts in armies of other countries, displaying the demo-cratic tendencies of the nation which they served. One civilian remembered most of the soldiers at Fort McKavett as "awful high class, educated, very fine people" with a wide range of occupations. One soldier, for example, was the son of a pro-fessor at Dublin's Trinity College who, having spent all of his money while tour-ing New York, was too ashamed to ask his father or his friends for return fare to Ireland. Instead, he joined the U.S. Cavalry.[24]

Veterans of foreign and domestic wars also enlisted in large numbers. Joe Jamison lent a distinguished presence to the Sixth Cavalry. A former English dragoon, Jamison had reportedly been one of the six hundred hussars immortal-ized by Alfred, Lord Tennyson's "Charge of the Light Brigade" at Balaklava, and he wore the Victoria Cross. Another soldier of fortune had fought with the Brit-ish, the Confederates, and Maximilian in Mexico before joining the U.S. Army.

---

23. Carter, *Old Sergeant's Story*, p. 53; Max L. Heyman, Jr., "A Letter from a Soldier in Texas," *Panhandle-Plains Historical Review* 27 (1954): 70–72; Don Rickey, Jr., *Forty Miles a Day on Beans and Hay: The Enlisted Soldier Fighting the Indian Wars* (Norman: University of Oklahoma Press, 1963) pp. 17–32; Jack D. Foner, *Blacks and the Military in American History: A New Perspective* (New York: Praeger Press, 1974), p. 55; James A. Bennett, *Forts and Forays: A Dragoon in New Mexico*, ed. Clin-ton E. Brooks and Frank D. Reeve (Albuquerque: University of New Mexico Press, 1948), p. 3.

24. George A. Forsyth, *The Story of the Soldier* (New York: D. Appleton and Co., 1900), pp. 82, 88; McConnell, *Five Years a Cavalryman*, pp. 13, 22–23; "Statement of Mr. R. H. Flutsch," Fred-erick Rathjen Papers, BTHC.

More common were veterans of the Mexican War or the Civil War. Dissatisfied with civilian life and unable to find suitable employment, these former soldiers returned to the army for stability and security.

The enlisted ranks also held a few of American society's more fortunate sons. Twice-wounded Thomas Hall Forsyth, commissary sergeant at Fort Davis, was subsequently awarded the Congressional Medal of Honor. Forsyth enjoyed his service life-style, his wealthy family background offering him alternatives not usually available to most of the volunteers. He enjoyed dancing and music and subscribed to several eastern newspapers. He played chess and whist, directed the post talent show, and joined the local Odd-Fellows and Good Templars lodges.[25]

Edward Briscoe's checkered career seems more typical of that of an enlisted man in Texas. A native of Maryland, Edward enlisted in Company B of the Tenth Cavalry at age twenty-three. Standing just over 5 feet 6 inches tall, with a scar on his left thumb and another near his left eye, Briscoe had been promoted to sergeant, demoted to private and then promoted to farrier but arrested for drunkenness and disorderly conduct, the second sentence being remitted to permit his promotion to corporal. Despite his conduct when he was off duty, he was termed "an excellent soldier" upon his reenlistment.[26]

All things considered, H. H. McConnell's summary of his fellow soldiers seems well founded:

> A Company of eighty men is an epitome of the world, and comprises representatives of every class. There was the honest, plodding fellow, ready for every duty; the "old soldier," looking with contempt on everything and everybody except the antebellum officers and men; the quiet young fellows, just from the volunteer service and full of pranks and fun, regarding their enlistment as a joke; the "smart Aleck," always ready to shirk every duty; and the "malingerer," always on hand for the hospital, and prompt at morning sick-call.[27]

25. For reference to the Good Templars, see Doug McChristian, "The Commissary Sergeant: His Life at Fort Davis," *Military History of Texas and the Southwest* 14, no. 1 (1978): 28, fn. 43.

26. Records of the U.S. Regular Army Mobile Units, 10th U.S. Cavalry, NA, RG 391 (microfilm, Fort Concho Research Library, MF 78).

27. McConnell, *Five Years a Cavalryman*, p. 88.

CHAPTER FOUR

Laundresses, Dependents, and Civilians

. . . a demoralizing influence.

—Acting Assistant Surgeon H. L. McIntyre

The frontier forts of Texas were not simply army bases occupied solely by military personnel. They were often bustling communities that attracted merchants, laborers, settlers, and dependents. The military brought along laundresses to do the soldiers' washing. Women and children accompanied their army husbands and fathers to their western stations. Civilians, including representatives of every segment of nineteenth-century American society, also congregated around the posts. Despite the criticism they often received from the army, these nonmilitary inhabitants were neither entirely trustworthy nor utterly unscrupulous. They were a fascinating collection of individuals who sought to make their way as best they could in a frequently changing environment.

Many women who lived at the army posts did so in an official military capacity. In 1802 the U.S. Army adopted the British system of detailing a group of washerwomen to a specific company. Appointed by the company captain, laundresses worked on a piece-rate basis at a scale set according to local prices by a post council. The rates varied; a soldier paid fifty cents to two dollars a month for his washing. Officers spent upwards of five dollars a month. The women collected their pay from their clients directly at the pay table. Army regulations allotted four laundresses to each company and specified that each woman was to receive one ration a day from the military.

Many laundresses were married to enlisted men and lived in quarters separate from the regular barracks. Sgt. H. H. McConnell described the scene at "Suds Row": "Situated on the outskirts of every military post may be seen a collection of huts, old tents, picket houses and 'dugouts,' an air of squalor and dirt pervading the locality, and troops of shock-haired children and slovenly looking females of various colors completing the picture. These are the quarters of the married soldiers and of the laundresses, known in army parlance as 'Suds-ville.'"[1]

A survey of the censuses at Fort Duncan from 1850 to 1870 indicates that the women averaged slightly over twenty-seven years of age. All the women working at Fort Duncan at the time of the 1850 and 1860 censuses were foreign-born. Most of them were natives of Ireland; others came from the German states, France, Switzerland, and Mexico. In 1870 two black laundresses (one born in Missouri, the other in Arkansas) served the buffalo soldiers of the Ninth Cavalry. Swarms of children inevitably accompanied these women. Few of the youngsters were foreign-born, indicating that their immigrant mothers and fathers had lived in the United States for some time.[2]

Not all the laundresses limited their activities to those specified by army regulations. Some increased their income substantially by adding prostitution to their work schedule. Aware of the situation, Assistant Surgeon Archibald B. Campbell, stationed at Ringgold Barracks, was among those who suggested that the troops do their own washing. Labeling the women at the post "a nuisance," he attributed half of his hospital cases to venereal diseases caused by their presence. In a similar argument Fort McKavett's Dr. Rufus Sharpe noted that "a few cases of *venereal* have appeared during the past month [August, 1870], originating with the laundresses."[3]

Whatever their predilections, the women must have found cleaning the heavy woolen army uniforms worn during the nineteenth century a daunting task. Nonetheless, most reports indicate that they did a satisfactory job. The laundresses did their washing on rocks or scrubboards along a river or creek near the post. The shortage of soap at many of the forts made their job even more difficult. Given the long hours such washing required, even the most diligent laundresses had difficulty keeping up their "Suds Row" houses. Of shabby construction and poor-quality materials, the quarters drew severe criticism from post medical officers.

Congress, having noted these complaints and seeking to cut government spending whenever possible, investigated the issue in 1876. Some officers supported the existing system in congressional hearings. One division commander, noting the connection between women and morality commonly made during that era, testified that the laundresses had "a harmonizing and beneficial effect upon the men." Another exclaimed, "Of course these women cost money—most women do!" He added that he thought that "they, like the personality of their sex, are worth all they cost." E. O. C. Ord, commanding the Department of Texas, took a more practical line of defense, testifying that many of the army's best noncom-

---

1. H. H. McConnell, *Five Years a Cavalryman; Or, Sketches of Regular Army Life on the Texas Frontier, Twenty Odd Years Ago* (Jacksboro, Tex.: J. N. Rogers and Co., 1889), p. 211.

2. Based on manuscript returns, U.S. census, 1850, Bexar County; 1860 and 1870, Maverick County.

3. PMR, Ringgold Barracks, Dec. 24, 1876; PMR, Fort McKavett, Aug., 1870, p. 181.

missioned officers were married to laundresses. These men could not afford to reenlist if their wives were unemployed, and for its part the army could not afford to lose this cadre of stable soldiers. Instead, Ord suggested that the number of laundresses in black regiments, which he believed needed the women's presence, should be doubled.[4]

4. Hancock to Banning, Feb. 25, 1876, 44th Cong., 1st sess., H. Rept. 354, ser. 1709, p. 25;

Others discounted the need for laundresses. "Soldiers can do their own washing," commented William Tecumseh Sherman, commanding general of the army. From Fort Brown, Texas, an officer suggested that Chinese immigrants might do the job for less. Col. George L. Andrews, stationed at Fort Davis, declared that he would not have a laundress in his company were he again a captain. Whether

McDowell to Banning, Feb. 12, ibid., p. 27; Testimony of Ord, Feb. 17, ibid., pp. 46–47.

they were interested in ridding the army of women or in cutting this item of the military budget in preference for another they deemed more important, the anti-laundress elements won. An army circular issued in 1876 prohibited women from accompanying troops as laundresses. Despite this directive, many company commanders continued to provide laundresses with rations until 1883, when a revised order closed remaining loopholes.[5]

Shortages of qualified male stewards forced medical officers to hire women to work in the hospitals. Large numbers of female nurses had served during the Civil War; after 1865 many were employed at the frontier forts. They cleaned the post's medical facilities, washed the hospital linen, and helped doctors care for the patients. Most of them were married to enlisted personnel, and their employment was contingent on their soldier husbands' service.

The other women at the forts of Texas, from the commanding officer's wife to the lowliest servant, lived there on an unofficial basis. The officers' wives bitterly resented their lack of official status. One called the army's lack of provision for women "notorious" and recalled that "many indignant meetings were held at which we discussed the matter, and rebelled at being considered camp followers." Despite such complaints, no recognition was forthcoming from a War Department entangled in bureaucratic infighting and a Congress more interested in reducing costs than in improving the quality of life on the military frontiers.[6]

Their lack of official recognition notwithstanding, officers' wives were the elite of the post's society. Some who accompanied their husbands to Texas were accustomed to such lofty status. Others represented a different breed. One wife described the women of her husband's regiment as "a rather queer set." One had been a laundress whose husband had been promoted from the ranks. Another was "very common," and a woman of Mexican heritage did not even merit further comment. A nineteen-year-old wife, while "not highly educated," was fortunately "well-behaved." A fourteen-year-old child bride was deemed "an innocent little girl, ignorant alike of good or evil."[7]

Army wives were almost always younger than their husbands, who were themselves generally older than their bachelor comrades. The two officers' wives at Fort Inge in 1850 were seventeen and twenty-seven years old. Their husbands were twenty-four and thirty-four, respectively. The nine officers' wives at Fort Duncan in 1870 averaged slightly less than twenty-seven years of age. Their husbands were about thirty-four, about five years older on average than the commissioned men who did not have spouses. Four of the officers' wives were natives of New England and the South, and three were from the Middle Atlantic states. The

5. Sherman to Banning, Feb. 4, 1876, ibid., p. 7; Potter to Banning, Mar. 1, ibid., p. 114; Andrews to Banning, Feb. 25, ibid., p. 115; Miller J. Stewart, "Army Laundresses: Ladies of the 'Soap Suds Row,'" *Nebraska History* 61 (Winter, 1980): 434.

6. Mrs. Orsemus Bronson Boyd, *Cavalry Life in Tent and Field* (1894; reprint, Lincoln: University of Nebraska Press, 1982), p. 142.

7. Sandra L. Myres, ed., *Cavalry Wife: The Diary of Eveline M. Alexander, 1866–1867* (College Station: Texas A&M University Press, 1977), p. 36.

other two wives were from Illinois and France. Only two had been born in the same state as their husbands, reflecting the high degree of mobility that typified the lives of military families.[8]

The women who lived with their officer husbands in Texas usually adapted well to their somewhat primitive surroundings. Mrs. Lydia Lane dubbed Fort Lancaster "the worst of all the posts in Texas" before the Civil War. At the same time she admitted that "the ladies I met at the post seemed cheerful and contented." Mrs. Elizabeth Custer frequently extolled the virtues of army life. Several antebellum officers admired Mrs. Eliza Johnston's knack for adjusting to life in Texas. An avid painter, Mrs. Johnston taught her three children every morning and offered intelligent conversation to the lonely soldiers who paid her visits.[9]

Although many of the women had led sheltered lives before coming to Texas, most of them viewed the transfer as an adventure. Soon after their marriage the Lanes hired an Irishman to help Lydia prepare meals. Unfortunately, neither wife nor "cook" knew much about cooking. As Mrs. Lane recalled:

> I knew how things ought to look and taste, but did not understand just how to prepare them. For a time, I believe, we were obliged to eat soldiers' rations, —only hard tack, fried salt pork, and coffee without milk, and I honestly tried to enjoy them, set out as they were on top of the mess-chest. An empty candle-box and a bucket turned upside down, served as seats round this humble board, until we could get into the village, to make a few purchases of such articles as we needed to take up the country with us.[10]

In 1873, Lt. Hans Jacob Gasman arrived at Fort Concho with his new bride. Mrs. Gasman, who had run away from an Ursuline convent in San Antonio to wed her officer, did her best to enliven post society. "Mrs. Gasman always did the unexpected and unconventional," noted a bemused observer. In one episode that particularly delighted Concho's residents, Mrs. Gasman took note of another woman parading in front of the officers' quarters with a silk sunshade, hat, gloves, and a dainty little silver pistol. The following day Mrs. Gasman followed in the wake of her mark with a green cotton umbrella, oversized hat, cotton gloves, and full-sized revolver.[11]

Despite such incidents, the shock of being stationed at a western post with

8. Based on manuscript returns from U.S. census, 1850, Bexar County (Fort Inge); census, 1870, Maverick County (Fort Duncan).

9. Lydia Spencer Lane, *I Married a Soldier; or, Old Days in the Old Army* (1893; reprint, Albuquerque, N.Mex.: Horn and Wallace, 1964), pp. 44, 76; Elizabeth B. Custer, *Tenting on the Plains, or General Custer in Kansas and Texas* (1897; reprint, Norman: University of Oklahoma Press, 1971), 2:332; Lee to Mrs. Lee, Mar. 28, 1856, Francis Raymond Adams, Jr., ed., "An Annotated Edition of the Personal Letters of Robert E. Lee, April, 1855–April 1861" (Ph.D. diss., University of Maryland, 1955), p. 106.

10. Lane, *I Married a Soldier*, p. 24.

11. Barbara E. Fisher, ed., "Forrestine Cooper Hooker's Notes and Memoirs on Army Life in the West, 1871–1876" (Master's thesis, University of Arizona, 1963), pp. 117–21.

more dangers than amenities occasionally proved too much to overcome. Upon noting the plight of new recruits entering Texas, one veteran remarked: "With this last [group] is a bride. I am afraid she is sorry she has enlisted in the 1st Infy. She is the wife of 2nd Lt. H. Claywood [Henry Clay Wood], a civil appointment, & is the only lady in the party." An army wife commented that "few who have seen delicately nurtured city girls marry so gladly the men of their choice, have any idea of what they must endure in the army."[12]

Childbirth on the frontier could be an especially terrifying experience. Mrs. Lydia Lane recalled having little knowledge of how to care for her first child. The other women at the post helped dress the little newborn, but inadequate housing made life miserable for both mother and daughter. The plaster that had once filled the crevices between the logs of their shack had long since fallen out, allowing rain to pour into the interior. An enormous stockpile of blankets kept mother and baby dry, but, as Mrs. Lane admitted, "the situation was not pleasant for the mother of a three days' old baby."[13]

Not all women living on the Texas military frontiers handled the prospect of child rearing as well as Mrs. Lane did. Susan E. Newcomb, a resident of Civil War blockhouse Fort Davis, gave birth to her second child at age sixteen, jokingly remarking that her new infant was "the uglyest little fellow in Fort Davis." Newcomb went on to report, however, that a Miss Mira Sutherlin had taken drastic steps to solve the problem created by her pregnancy. Rumors that Mira had killed her child seemed unfounded until the grisly discovery of a dead baby in a nearby creek. Mira's claims that the child was stillborn fell on deaf ears, and she subsequently attempted suicide. Mrs. Newcomb concluded, "I pity the poor girl, but it cant be helped now she has brought a disgrace upon herself and the whole family."[14]

Despite such tragic occurrences, children, whose varied birthplaces were evidence of the many stations that had once been home to their army parents, were present at most of the forts in Texas. Although some soldiers complained that the swarms of children and their inevitable pets made things a bit crowded, most of the youngsters enjoyed the Texas forts. The younger set found plenty of things to do, including hunting, riding, singing, dancing, reading, drawing, and raising animals of virtually every sort. Of course, officers' children received special favors. At Fort Concho, for instance, Edith Grierson, the daughter of Col. Benjamin Grierson, celebrated one of her birthdays with a tea. The post band provided musical accompaniment, and two lieutenants attended the young girl's party.

Fortunately for America's future but unfortunately for children who felt that they had better things to do, most of the forts provided some form of schooling. Chaplains frequently held classes, which were segregated by race and rank. Other

12. Lee to Custis Lee, Dec. 5, 1860, Adams, "Lee Letters," p. 704; Boyd, *Cavalry Life*, pp. 134–36.
13. Lane, *I Married a Soldier*, p. 39.
14. Susan E. Newcomb Diary, Aug. 21, Oct. 25, 26, 1865, pp. 4, 13–14, BTHC.

military personnel, both officers and enlisted men, also served as teachers. Some parents taught their own children, and a few communities hired teachers to conduct public schools. Officers' children living in Texas were often sent away to boarding schools when they grew older, but the sons and daughters of enlisted personnel and laundresses were restricted to the meager post facilities.

To help with the household chores, many officers hired servants or bought slaves. Often an officer employed a married couple, the wife being responsible for domestic affairs and the husband for maintenance and general upkeep. Qualified workers were hard to find, and low wages and the frontier's lure of independence often made for an unstable term of servitude of both hired servants and bonded slaves. In part because of racial prejudices against the many black or Hispanic workers, most officers held their servants in very low esteem. "We had a succession [of black cooks] so worthless that I have never overcome my prejudice against them," wrote Mrs. Orsemus Boyd.[15]

Others won high marks in spite of such prejudice. Teresa Vielé found a black male servant trained during a naval apprenticeship. "No matter how forlorn the fare, the silver, glass, and china glistened in immaculate purity" during his faithful service. The maid Eliza who accompanied the George Custers to Texas, had joined the family in August, 1863. Greatly respected by the troops, Eliza had cooked under fire during the Civil War. "I didn't set down to wait to have 'em all free me. I helped free myself," she explained. "I was all ready to step to the front whenever called upon, even if I didn't shoulder the musket." In recognition of her faithfulness, while they were stationed in Austin, the Custers allowed Eliza to give a ball for her black friends.[16]

The scarcity of women at the western posts made even the homeliest servant the center of attention among officers and enlisted men starved for female companionship. When Eliza married a black lawyer, the Custers, always eager for the limelight, selected as her replacement the most beautiful girl they could find. As Mrs. Custer put it, that would "do more toward furnishing and beautifying our army quarters than any amount of speechless bric-a-brac or short tapestry." Most officers, however, hoped for longer and more dependable service and hired less attractive workers. Lieutenant and Mrs. Boyd congratulated themselves on having found a maidservant of such a forbidding countenance that she was "almost a grenadier in looks and manner."[17]

The instability of civilian servants led many officers to hire men from the ranks to help with the housework. These individuals, derisively called "strikers" or "dog robbers," were an unpredictable lot, some proving virtually worthless but others providing the utmost in care and devotion. Having found a striker in her husband's company after a series of inadequate women, Mrs. Orsemus Boyd re-

15. Boyd, *Cavalry Life*, p. 259.

16. Teresa Griffin Vielé, *Following the Drum: A Glimpse of Frontier Life* (1858; reprint, Lincoln: University of Nebraska Press, 1984), pp. 131–32; Custer, *Tenting on the Plains*, 2:38, 42, 69, 232–35.

17. Custer, *Tenting on the Plains*, 2:328; Boyd, *Cavalry Life*, pp. 195–96.

called that the man proved "a willing coadjutator, who joined heartily in my plans to disguise the flavor of meats by every art we could devise in the way of seasoning." On the other hand, the wife of another officer found her striker's want of skill around the home surpassed only by his ineptitude as a soldier.[18]

The use of soldiers as private servants took men away from the already depleted enlisted ranks and smacked of feudalism. The army tried to stop the practice after the Civil War, but the custom proved extremely difficult to halt. Officers in the Fourth Cavalry, for example, could hire a man from the ranks despite regulations if they could demonstrate a special need for such services. In addition to having a black civilian, the Vielés also employed a soldier as cook and a drummer boy as scullion while they were at Ringgold Barracks. Colonel Grierson, commanding Fort Concho during the 1870s, left two bondsmen and a governess to care for his wife and three children while he went east to attend one of his sick sons.

Scouts, many of whom were Indians, also constituted a large element of the post's population. The command needed reliable scouts to find hostile Indians and guide the bluecoats to their quarry. Some Indians served as scouts before the Civil War, and in 1866 a congressional measure authorizing the Department of Texas to hire two hundred Indian scouts made their presence even more common. Contemporaries depicted these men in stereotypical fashion. Delaware Indian John McLoughlin worked at Fort Mason. We have the following description of his major fault: "John loved whiskey, and when he was notified to hold himself in readiness to accompany an expedition he was certain to get drunk and hence be unable to march with the command at the appointed hour, but would always overtake it the next day. When asked why he always got drunk when ordered for field service he would invariably reply: 'May be so for thirty days get no more whiskey.'"[19]

About two hundred Tonkawa scouts and their families lived near Fort Griffin during the 1870s. Although the men were effective scouts and the women did sewing and beadwork much admired by the troops and the townspeople, the Tonkawas faced severe poverty. Reduced to begging in 1877, they received some assistance the following year when an officer secured for them the blankets and money they had been promised. Also notable were the Seminole-black scouts, recruited during the same decade and led by Lt. John Bullis. About fifty of these men, descendants of Seminole Indians and escaped slaves who had moved to the Rio Grande in the late 1840s, performed exemplary service for the army in Indian campaigns.

Although the army strove for self-sufficiency, post commanders usually hired a number of persons on a quasi-official basis. After the war, responding to often-

---

18. Boyd, *Cavalry Life*, p. 259; Myres, ed., *Cavalry Wife*, p. 57.

19. Townsend to Sheridan, Aug. 1, 1866, Letters Sent by the Office of the Adjutant General, main series, 1800–1890, NA, RG 94, 107 (microcopy 565, reel 30, vol. 43); George Price, *Across the Continent with the Fifth Cavalry* (1883; reprint, New York: Antiquarian Press, 1959), p. 91.

76

voiced complaints that the enlisted men were more commonly used as laborers than as soldiers, the army employed particularly large numbers of civilian carpenters, laborers, and masons. Other nonmilitary personnel gained employment as clerks, forage masters, painters, herdsmen, wheelwrights, wagonmasters, saddlers, blacksmiths, and teamsters. As might be expected, these men came from many cultures and backgrounds. The civilians on the post at Fort Clark in 1880 for example, included persons born in twenty-eight states and territories, the District of Columbia, and twelve foreign countries.[20]

To provide certain amenities, contract merchants were authorized to establish general stores on the military reservations. A post tradership, with a garrison providing a captive market, could be a lucrative plum. Originally a sutler secured his position by private arrangement with the regimental colonel and moved with the unit from station to station. Abuses in the sutler system led the War Department to take control in 1870. Unfortunately, officials in Washington were little better at keeping their hands clean, and scandals involving the illegal sale of such rights forced the resignation of Secretary of War William Belknap in 1876. While post commanders retained a great deal of influence in awarding the traderships and in establishing prices and hours of operation, the creation of a system of nonprofit canteens during the 1880s did much to improve conditions for enlisted personnel.

The post traders are difficult to categorize. Enlisted men claimed that they charged exorbitant prices for second-rate goods. On the other hand, liberal post administration rules regarding local traders stimulated competition. Five stores lay within a short distance of Fort Concho in 1869; "of course with the rivalry the soldier profits," commented Dr. William Notson. Yet traders often provided services that the army considered less desirable. In 1881, Fort Concho officials demanded that the post trader force five prostitutes out of their ramshackle quarters near his store. The ladies of the evening had sought refuge near his establishment after being evicted from the fort's premises.[21]

Some traders and their employees won high marks from contemporaries. A Scotsman named Shaw was chief clerk of the sutler's store at Fort Clark in 1859. A fat old man who had deserted his wife and family in England, Shaw enjoyed having a few drinks and reading Robert Burns and proved an amiable companion. Shaw owned a pet bear cub named Jacob that he kept drunk. The bear offered "a great deal of amusement" until it grew too large and had to be destroyed. Two "clever gentlemen" who "added much to the society of the post" ran the store at Fort Duncan during the 1850s. The fort's officers used the sutler's office as a

---

20. "Report of Persons and Articles Employed and Hired at Brownsville, Texas, during the month of March, 1868," William A. Wainwright Papers, BTHC; manuscript returns, U.S. census, 1880, Kinney County.

21. PMR, Fort Concho, May, 1869, p. 124; Shelby to Millspaugh, Records of the United States Army Continental Commands, 1821–1920, Fort Concho, NA, RG 393 (microfilm, Fort Concho Research Library, MF 69).

clubroom and bought a billiards table on which the two best players determined the post championship after a twenty-four-hour pool marathon.[22]

The soldiers, dependents, and civilians associated with the military's posts in Texas thus formed sizable communities. These initial gatherings of civilians attracted still more settlers able to provide an even wider range of services. Benefiting from the security of the frontier forts, hunters and farmers sold their goods to the garrison and utilized the services provided at the post. Hospitals were a particular boon in areas that had few doctors. Although the facilities were designed for military personnel, doctors could scarcely turn away the sick and injured. They charged their civilian patients fifty cents to a dollar a day.

The nearby settlers were a diverse group. Soldiers at Fort Lincoln profited from the existence of the little village of D'Hanis, although they could rarely communicate with the settlement's Alsatian inhabitants. After the Civil War several German immigrants established Bismarck's Farm about seven miles south of Fort Concho. The immigrants rented the land to Mexican tenants, and the farm sold supplies to Forts Concho, McKavett, and Chadbourne. Many retired soldiers also settled near their old posts, to the benefit of all concerned. One former sergeant, for instance, saved up enough money to purchase and settle on a thousand acres near the Red River after his retirement from the army. The old veteran sold grain to the army at reduced prices in return for military protection. Fort Richardson's officers allowed the editors of the *Frontier Echo* to use the services of the post printer in the absence of their regular printer.

Many persons of Mexican heritage lived near army posts along the Rio Grande. O. M. Knapp liked to mingle with the Mexicans near Fort Bliss and buy produce from them. Knowing but a few words of their language, he would "murder their Spanish & make them laugh, . . . but I murder far more apricots & other fruits than anything else & so am sick the next day." Teresa Vielé found Brownsville a "curious, half-breed town" with a striking mix of prosperous shops and rude huts. Charles J. Crane described Camargo, opposite Ringgold Barracks, as "very much run down." A mixture of half-bloods, blacks, whites, Mexicans, and discharged soldiers lived near Fort Clark at Brackettville, a collection of adobe houses, shacks, huts, jacales, picket stores, whiskey shops, and gambling saloons. Observing that these little towns were often dangerous, Capt. Richard Johnson charged that a murder was committed every day of the year at Eagle Pass.[23]

The settlements adjacent to many of the forts in West Texas gained even greater notoriety. A visitor to Fort Elliott wrote that nearby Mobeetie was "small but appears to be lively. Every other house is a saloon. Saw an unmistakable sign of civilization in a dog charging down street with a tin can to his tail." At Fort

---

22. Zenas R. Bliss Reminiscences, 2:83–85; Richard W. Johnson, *A Soldier's Reminiscences in Peace and War* (Philadelphia: J. B. Lippincott and Co., 1886), p. 65.

23. Knapp to Mead, June 17, 1867, Obadiah M. Knapp Papers, BTHC; Vielé, *Following the Drum*, p. 104; Charles J. Crane, *Experiences of a Colonel of Infantry* (New York: Knickerbocker Press, 1923), p. 101; Johnson, *A Soldier's Reminiscences*, p. 62.

Concho the attractions of "Over the River" (which eventually became San Angelo) lured many a soldier and buffalo hunter. The little settlement seemed to have more saloons than all other businesses combined. "No lady or child of the garrison ever ventured across the river unless accompanied by soldiers," recalled one of the fort's residents.[24]

No town could match the decadence of "the Flat," a settlement below Fort Griffin. Buffalo hunters and cowboys unrestrained by any form of government authority made "the Flat" notable even among jaded frontiersmen. Eight to ten saloons, several dance halls, and plenty of loose women made it "a veritable robber's hole," according to one account. Particularly memorable were Mollie McCabe's "Place of Beautiful Sin" and a noted prostitute called Indian Kate. It was "the toughest place I had ever seen," commented another writer. Several accounts mentioned one Lottie Deno, who suddenly appeared one day on the stagecoach from the East. Lottie lived alone near the brothels and wagered heavily in the town's card games. Remaining aloof from the baser debauchery of "the Flat," she disappeared just as mysteriously as she had come, a figure of much secrecy and speculation among her contemporaries.[25]

By the early 1880s the townspeople had seen enough. A "vigilance committee" began summarily to execute the more flagrant lawbreakers. A reign of terror swept the town, and stealing a horse seemed to cause more excitement than killing a human being. During one twelve-year span thirty-four men were killed, and eight more were found dead. Of these, eleven fell at the hands of the vigilantes. Only after the military garrison was withdrawn and the buffalo were virtually exterminated did Fort Griffin achieve a certain degree of respectability.

The inevitable clashes between the army and nearby civilians were usually minor. Post medical officers often called upon superiors to remove "lewd women" from the vicinity of a military reservation. Numerous officers sought to protect gullible troops from the hordes of gamblers and peddlers who lurked around the post at payday. They also tried to keep civilians from harassing army sentinels, while discouraging their own troopers from molesting nearby settlers or their property. In return, the more practical entrepreneurs recognized the tangible value of the military's presence and cooperated whenever possible.

More isolated locations attracted fewer civilians. Inadequate transportation, a continuing Indian menace, poor soil, and lack of water presented real barriers to agriculture in much of West Texas. The belief that most of the trans-Mississippi region was a desert also retarded settlement, especially before the Civil War. Zenas R. Bliss saw only four or five persons not related to the army in some fashion

---

24. R. H. Conlyn Diary, May 26, 1883, BTHC; Fisher, "Hooker Memoirs," p. 113.

25. "Frontier Experiences of Emmet Roberts of Nugent, Texas," *West Texas Historical Association Year Book* 3 (1927): 52; J. R. Webb, "Henry Herron, Pioneer and Peace Officer during Fort Griffin Days," *West Texas Historical Association Yearbook* 20 (Oct., 1944): 23; Edgar Rye, *The Quirt and the Spur: Vanishing Shadows of the Texas Frontier* (1909; reprint, Austin: Steck-Vaughn Co., 1967), pp. 27, 70–73; Herbert M. Hart, *Old Forts of the Southwest* (Seattle, Wash.: Superior Publishing Co., 1964), pp. 146–47.

during his two years at Camp Hudson. Similar conditions plagued development around Fort Chadbourne during the 1850s, which had no fewer than eighteen commanders within a four-year period. Soldiers dreaded assignment to such lonely positions, which offered few diversions from the monotonies of post life. On the other hand, army purists pointed out that isolation, by removing troops from the "demoralizing influence" of civilian establishments, could prove beneficial.[26]

In spite of such protestations, the presence of civilians usually improved the quality and diversity of life on the military posts. Those officially attached to the army, including laundresses and hospital workers, performed needed services and made it possible for a few enlisted men to rear families in Texas. The wives and children of the officers also played an important role in life on the military frontiers, making their own distinct contributions to society as well as allowing their husbands to continue their careers in the army. The mixed collection of servants, traders, gamblers, farmers, craftsmen, thieves, and laborers, and the families they in turn often brought with them, rounded out the inhabitants of the forts and nearby towns. The diversity of their backgrounds encompassed both good and bad, both pillars and scourges of the American scene. Most important, their presence prevented the soldiers they accompanied from becoming completely isolated from nineteenth-century American society.

26. Bliss Reminiscences, 2:185; M. L. Crimmins, ed., "Colonel J. K. F. Mansfield's Report of the Inspection of the Department of Texas in 1856," *Southwestern Historical Quarterly* 42 (Apr., 1939): 369; PMR, Camp Peña Colorado, Oct. 31, 1885, p. 68.

CHAPTER FIVE

Routine Duty

Nothing interesting to record.

—Assistant Surgeon Daniel Weisel

Them day began early on the military fron-
tiers. Before sunrise company and regimental buglers prepared for assembly at
all the Texas posts. Reveille sounded shortly thereafter. As the call ended, sleepy
details raised the United States flag and fired the fort's cannon. In the meantime,
the troops stumbled out of their bunks and dressed. For men who had slept on
hard bunks covered with thin hay bedsacks in barracks that fell disagreeably short
of providing comfort or even protection from the elements, the call for assembly
seemed early indeed.

Post commanders set the precise time for reveille at their own discretion,
and surgeons frequently contended that the day began too early. Noting the 3:30
A.M. assembly at Fort Richardson, Dr. W. H. Forwood argued that the men needed
more time for sleep. "If any officer doubts the propriety of this sanitary recommendation, let him fore go his after reveille nap for a few mornings," Forwood
advised. At Fort McKavett, S. M. Horton attributed the large number of men
on the sick lists to the early hour of the roll call, which compelled the troops
to go outside "in an early atmosphere loaded with moisture and malaria." Commanding officers generally accepted such advice and changed the hour of the
morning assembly according to season. As a result, reveille usually sounded between 5:00 and 6:00 A.M.[1]

As the soldiers formed on the parade ground, grumbling about the usual
variety of real and imagined complaints, their counterparts on officers' row, in
the laundresses' shanties, and at the off-post businesses also began to rise. Following roll call the infantrymen trudged back to their bunks for a little more sleep
before breakfast. In the meantime, the cavalry troopers and artillerymen donned
white dusters and tramped over to the stables, where a stable sergeant and his

1. PMR, Fort Richardson, May 31, 1875, pp. 136–37.

assistants issued combs, brushes, and pickets. The stable sergeant was responsible for the officers' horses, though most officers gave their steeds individual attention. Each enlisted man cared for his own horse. Having groomed their mounts, the riders watered and exercised the animals outside before returning the horses to the stables for feeding.[2]

Sick call sounded soon afterward, and ailing soldiers, accompanied by derisive catcalls from their fellow enlisted men, shuffled over to the hospital for the post surgeon's inspection. Many had very real complaints, for poor sanitation, inadequate rest, inferior shelter, and unbalanced diet took their inevitable toll. Medics rarely had time to give every patient a complete physical examination, instead issuing a dose of quinine or some form of laxative and excusing him from duty for the day. The doctors hustled the more serious cases into hospital beds for rest, special diet, and further attention. The larger posts had proper dispensaries with trained stewards; at others medicines were distributed from the surgeon's personal quarters or by persons poorly qualified for the task.

The lure of escaping duty inevitably drew malingerers. Exasperated doctors sometimes used unorthodox measures to "cure" their patients' imagined ailments. One chronic slacker claimed that rheumatism had caused one of his knees to lock. Tired of wasting time on the shirker, the post surgeon had the man chloroformed. "Just as he regained consciousness out went that leg, stiff as a poker," recalled an observer, "but too late." Subsequently the man showed "wonderful endurance and fortitude" while carrying a heavy iron ball and chain with his "stiff" leg. He was finally sentenced to the military prison at Leavenworth.[3]

The call for breakfast came between 6:30 and 7:30. A simple fare awaited the men as they filed into their separate company mess halls. The menu varied only slightly from day to day, bread, coffee, and bacon or beef constituting the usual meal. When they were available, onions or potatoes were mixed with the entree to form an unappetizing hash. The troops washed down their meal with strong black coffee. Sweets were reserved for special occasions.

Fatigue call sounded half an hour later. Before the Civil War miscellaneous work details probably claimed most able-bodied personnel at the typical post. Although extra pay accompanied some fatigue duties, the troops hated these nonmilitary tasks, pointing out that they had not joined the army to become common laborers. Military officials agreed that incessant fatigue duty hurt morale and discipline. As John B. Floyd, secretary of war from 1857 to 1860, noted, the average soldier "can but resent as a wrong the order which changes him from his legitimate vocation to that of a mere operative deprived of his wages." During his inspection of the Department of Texas in 1853, Bvt. Lt. Col. W. G. Freeman criticized the fatigue parties' lack of military bearing. The "extra duty

2. "Routine of Duty of Lt. Comdg. Co. 1st Arty.," Fort Clark Records, BTHC; PMR, Fort Griffin, Sept., 1869, p. 139.

3. Charles J. Crane, *Experiences of a Colonel of Infantry* (New York: Knickerbocker Press, 1923), pp. 126–28.

men . . . were . . . distinctly marked by their soiled clothes, their ungainly attitudes when at a halt, and their unsteadiness of gait in marching, as if the Quartermaster's brand had been placed upon them." Despite the obvious problems, the War Department never had sufficient funds to hire civilians for all the chores on the military reservations, although the number of outside employees increased after 1865.[4]

The work varied, with special attention given on Fridays and Saturdays to sprucing up the post for the regular Sunday inspection. Routine duties included hauling water, gathering wood, tending the post garden, working in the kitchen, building structures, and cleaning. The company's first sergeant usually oversaw these day-to-day affairs, carrying out the instructions of his officers, acting as foreman of work parties, and handling the mundane problems encountered by his outfit. He and his noncommissioned officers had to strike a fine balance between discipline and tyranny, efficiency and practicality. The men required firm but fair treatment; the officers sought results without open rebellion.

Securing adequate quantities of water for the garrison was one of the fatigue parties' major tasks. The nearest river or creek provided the water for inhabitants of newly occupied forts. But the indiscriminate use of the streams for washing, cooking, and watering animals quickly rendered sluggish waters unfit for human consumption. Then work parties dug wells to meet the garrison's needs. It was not uncommon, however, for sewage to seep into the wells. Then it became necessary for work details to haul water from springs and rivers several miles away in large tanks pulled by six-mule teams. The troops filled the barrels at the barracks and the officers' houses.

Inhabitants went to great lengths to keep their water cool and fresh. Porous earthenware jars, strategically placed to catch breezes, created evaporation that cooled the water inside the containers. Wet cloths wrapped around the pots helped the cooling process. Realizing the dangers of stagnant water, medical officers encouraged all inhabitants to clean the barrels and filter their water through sand and powdered charcoal. They also recommended boiling the drinking water.

With water at a premium, fire posed a tremendous threat even after the installation of water pipes at many posts during the 1880s. Some buildings contained special fireboxes fitted with axes, though not all sparks from chimneys and ovens could be eliminated. Upon hearing the dreaded fire alarm, the men hurriedly assembled bucket brigades and battled the fire hoping that high winds did not fan the blaze out of control. In 1873 an arsonist at Fort Davis started a fire that destroyed much of the adjutant's office and very nearly burned the twelve-hundred-volume regimental library of the Twenty-fifth Infantry. Another notable conflagration burned $5,000 worth of personal property at Fort Bliss; firefighters barely saved the post's corral.

The garrisons' large ovens and fireplaces, which made fires such a hazard,

---

4. Report of Floyd, Dec. 5, SW, AR, 1857, p. 12; M. L. Crimmins, ed., "W. G. Freeman's Report on the Eighth Military Department," *Southwestern Historical Quarterly* 53 (Apr., 1950): 446.

usually used wood for fuel. Work parties scoured the area around their post for
lumber or established small camps and mills in wooded regions some miles away.
Other men struggled with the post garden. In 1851, hoping that the troops could
reduce expenses by growing their own food, Secretary of War Charles Conrad
ordered each garrison to establish a garden. Inadequate water supplies and lack-
luster efforts by unenthusiastic gardeners limited the program's success, though
properly tended fields produced welcome vegetables.[5]

The men detested cleaning details above all else, especially when such duties

5. Report of Conrad, Nov. 29, SW, AR, 1851, p. 111; Report of Conrad, Dec. 4, SW, AR,
1852, p. 4.

included the company sinks. The commonly used latrine boxes had to be tight, and fresh earth and lime had to be regularly spread over the raw excreta. Members of fatigue parties were understandably reluctant to tend the ground near the privies and rebelled outright against cleaning the boxes. Unfortunately, the failure to do so created serious health problems as well as an overpowering stench. The medical officers warned that constant use had saturated the areas around the sinks. "It seems to be impossible to drive into the heads of men, that the capacity of earth for absorption, is like that of a small cup, which when filled will run over," reported one doctor.[6]

6. PMR, Ringgold Barracks, Jan. 31, 1875, p. 202.

Army surgeons faced great difficulties in implementing their sanitary recommendations. Low pay and infrequent promotion discouraged doctors from entering the service and created numerous vacancies in the two hundred–odd positions available. The shortages in personnel made it difficult for those on the scene to handle all their assignments effectively. Many of those who did serve proved to be unqualified, adding to the difficulties facing nineteenth-century men of medicine. To fill the gaps, the army hired civilians as "acting assistant surgeons." Regular officers scorned these contract surgeons, believing most of them to be quacks. In reality the civilians ranged from serious-minded individuals who tried their best to combat disease to a dentist who briefly practiced at Fort Elliott in 1887. He was found dead in a hospital outbuilding after only a month at the post. Coroners believed that overdoses of alcohol and opium, along with "exposure and starvation while on a prolonged debauch," caused the unfortunate man's death.[7]

Many frontier doctors deserved a better fate, doing much to improve the health and environment of the army's posts in Texas. Upon Assistant Surgeon S. M. Horton's report that the company sinks were "foul and unwholesome," the commanding officer at Fort McKavett acted vigorously to eradicate the condition. The provost sergeant's detail was to clean the sinks immediately after reveille; company officers were to see that orderlies threw fresh earth into the boxes four times a day and to inspect the latrines personally twice a day. The commander also required the officer of the day to inspect the sinks three times during his tour.

At Fort Concho, Dr. William N. Notson commended the commander for stressing the importance of police details. As a result of these efforts Notson pronounced the grounds clean, praised the improved appearance of the newly graveled walks, and pointed out that a once unseemly storage shed had been "converted into a neat and tasteful cottage."[8]

Beginning in 1874, the War Department authorized post medical officers to inspect sanitary conditions, the quality and preparation of rations, water supplies, and drainage and to comment on the general habits of the troops. The doctors' lengthy reports to the posts' commanding officers indicate that almost all of them performed these assignments with a special zeal. Surgeons pointed out broken windows and leaky barracks, warned of the health hazards resulting from unsanitary latrines, and called for cleaner and more careful food preparation. They also stressed the need for additional garbage details, suggested improvements in the posts' appearance, and urged fellow officers to take greater pains to see that orders were carried out. Others recommended that the men air out their bedding and demanded that the soldiers bathe regularly.

The often overzealous and usually undiplomatic criticisms of the health and

7. PMR, Fort Elliott, Jan. 20, 1887, p. 93.
8. PMR, Fort McKavett, Mar., 1874, pp. 162–63; PMR, Fort Concho, Apr., 1870, p. 165.

habits of a garrison included in such reports naturally incurred the wrath of many a post commander. Repeated references to the men's lack of discipline and refusal to execute their fatigue duties did not reflect well on the officers. Assistant Surgeon Daniel Weisel complained that, while former commanders had done well in seeing to the police of Fort Davis, it was "not done as regularly as it should" by 1872. W. H. Gardner's attack on the "dissipation and carefree habits" of the troops at Fort Davis eleven years later was also typical. "I know that many of [the men] are habitually out of their quarters a great part of each night," Gardner reported. The implication was, of course, that Colonel Grierson, the Fort Davis commander, could not control his men.[9]

Faced with accusations that they could not discipline their troops, commanding officers struck back against their accusers. A commander might demand a surgeon's transfer or assign him duty on a series of thankless post councils. At Fort Richardson, Surgeon Carlos Carvallo and Col. S. H. Starr engaged in a running skirmish in 1868. Carvallo complained that Starr refused to provide him with adequate quarters, ordered hospital stewards and cooks to attend parades and inspections to what Carvallo believed was the detriment of care for the sick, and refused to allow medical personnel who were drawn from the ranks to remain away from their units long enough to become proficient at their surgical tasks. In retaliation, a doctor might inconvenience a commander by refusing to lend hospital beds to visitors or balking at new assignments.[10]

Members of fatigue parties were probably aware of such conflicts but continued to go about their varied tasks. As they did, their comrades selected for guard duty according to regular rotation gathered outside the company barracks about 8:30 A.M. After the first sergeant's brief examination, the men, in clean uniforms and with shoes and buttons gleaming, assembled on the parade ground in front of the guardhouse. There the sergeant major inspected them and announced the day's duties before turning the post over to the new officer of the day. Members of the old guard going off duty escorted the prisoners outside. The officer of the day put the new guard through the manual of arms and then dismissed the old guard. The fresh guard thus began its twenty-four-hour vigil.

The men on guard duty performed several tasks. Some escorted the prisoners to their work details. Sentry duty claimed others, who observed activities on and off the military reservation from established posts or on patrol. The officer of the day, resplendent with sash and saber, inspected each sentry at least once during his general rounds. The sentry answered the officer's queries in strict military fashion; black troops were especially noted for their custom of responding with at least three "sirs" in every sentence. The various sentinels sounded off their post numbers every hour with the cry "____ o'clock and all's well," until the sergeant of the guard concluded with the reassuring "____ o'clock and all's well all

---

9. PMR, Fort Davis, 1872, p. 14, Mar. 31, 1883, p. 22.
10. PMR, Fort Concho, p. 204; PMR, Fort Richardson, Sept., Oct., 1868, pp. 89–94.

around." On occasion warning shots from sentries alerted the guard to possible intrusions, usually Indians in quest of the garrison's horses.[11]

The sentries were changed every two hours, and the men who were relieved returned to the guardhouse. While he was not allowed to remove any part of his uniform, a soldier could at least rest on a rude bench or chair in the guardroom. The oppressive summer heat and the bitter winter northers took their toll on members of the guard, especially at the smaller posts, where one's turn came up with distressing frequency. Discipline was often lax among the sentries. A typical breach of conduct was reported at Fort Richardson in 1874 when a drunken guard had the misfortune to shoot himself in the thumb.

Such duty had a few benefits. Upon completion of their twenty-four-hour watch members of the guard were awarded a brief period of free time. One man from the detail was selected as orderly for the commanding officer. The orderly ran errands for the commander, received his meals earlier than the rest of the garrison, and slept in his own bunk rather than spending a fitful night in the shabbily constructed and poorly furnished guardroom. Some soldiers became adept at sprucing up their uniforms; shining their buttons, accoutrements, and boots; and winning the notice of the commander.

Guard duty and fatigue details hardly prepared the military occupants of the army's Texas forts for their real functions, defending settlements and subjugating those who might threaten westward expansion. Recognizing the problem, army officials tried to introduce basic military instruction into the daily routine at the scattered posts. Yet a high rate of absenteeism among officers greatly hindered military training. Only two of the ten captains of the Eighth Infantry were with their companies during Inspector W. G. Freeman's tour in 1853; eleven line officers (far short of the thirty-six provided for by law) accompanied the Ninth Cavalry on its march to Forts Davis and Stockton in 1867. To make matters more complicated, those present for duty were not always qualified. Younger officers, even those with West Point educations, often learned the drills themselves only hours before instructing their men, and they confined the exercises to those they had just learned.

Assuming that qualified commissioned or noncommissioned officers were present; that fatigue, extra duty, and guard details had not claimed the entire garrison; and that sickness had not debilitated the command, drills began after breakfast. As a rule drills were held at the company level and lasted about an hour, though larger garrisons allowed for longer periods of battalion or regimental instruction. Many officers expressed something less than enthusiastic interest in the tedious marching and countermarching. Such opposition became particularly apparent when Texas state troops guarded the frontier. Regimental orders to the First Texas Mounted Rifleman "earnestly pressed" officers "to lay aside their

---

11. Sidney E. Whitman, *The Troopers: An Informal History of the Plains Cavalry, 1865–1890* (New York: Hastings House, 1962), p. 156; Erwin N. Thompson, "The Negro Soldiers on the Frontier: A Fort Davis Case Study," *Journal of the West* 7 (Apr., 1968): 229.

prejudices (if they entertain any) against drill and discipline and by submitting themselves to the instructions set an example which will encourage the men in their duty."[12]

Attempts to train cavalrymen could have inspired the slapstick antics of early film comics. As Teresa Vielé observed, "Drilling them into dragoons was by no means an easy or pleasant task. Without a knowledge of even the first principles of riding, they sat on their horses like a parcel of clothes-pins, and it was not an unusual thing to see a dozen dismounted at once, and lie sprawling on the ground; they were instantly up, however, and in their saddles to try it once more."[13]

Black troops, however, were cited by the officers as being particularly adept at drills. After a reshuffling of garrisons Fort Concho's surgeon proclaimed that "the drill of the new troops, colored, is in both the manual and manuevre decidedly superior." The drills also made fine entertainment. Capt. George Armes's exercises at postbellum Fort Stockton, in which his mounted troopers ferociously "beheaded" wooden posts topped with bundles of straw, must have delighted spectators and participants alike.[14]

Target practice did not become a regular part of the army's routine until a relatively late date. Although some units managed time for occasional firing practice, most officers ignored an 1872 directive that each man fire ninety rounds at the rifle range. Before that date such practice was generally considered too expensive. The annihilation of five companies of the Seventh Cavalry at the Little Big Horn in 1876 led military officials to place greater emphasis on marksmanship. By 1881 each captain in the Department of Texas was singling out his five best marksmen and encouraging them to practice for contests to determine the post team. Excused from duty while improving their skills, members of the post rifle squad then participated in department competition. The winners advanced to divisional and national shoot-offs.

Officers spent the mornings on a variety of assignments. The officer of the day inspected sentry mounts and post facilities. Personal involvement of officers in their company's daily affairs was not required, and the lack of incentives for excellence quickly challenged an officer's resolve to do a good job. During the Civil War state troops elected their junior officers, a practice that made it difficult to enforce discipline. Some commands fell into a lassitude that inhibited effective action, with the officers rarely accompanying fatigue details or maintaining direct contact with their troops. More conscientious officers made sure that their noncommissioned subalterns carried out directives as ordered. Personal visits and inspections of the men's rations and living conditions by company officers

12. Regimental Order No. 10, May 11, 1861, in James Holmsley Papers, BTHC.

13. Teresa Griffin Vielé, *Following the Drum: A Glimpse of Frontier Life* (1858; reprint, Lincoln: University of Nebraska Press, 1984), p. 223.

14. PMR, Fort Concho, Mar., May, 1869, pp. 114, 124; George A. Armes, *Ups and Downs of an Army Officer* (Washington, D.C.: Privately printed, 1900), p. 462.

could be effective morale boosters; their involvement in work details, drills, and target practice also increased the unit's efficiency, although overeager officers earned the unflattering sobriquet "dust inspectors" from their men.[15]

The enormous amount of paperwork on every post and in every company sometimes made such participation difficult. As might be expected, officers of state units guarding the frontier during the Civil War proved notoriously lax at filling out the innumerable muster calls, rosters, equipment inventories, and supply requisitions. After the war officers of black regiments complained that the lack of literate enlisted personnel made it impossible to get secretarial tasks accomplished. Obadiah M. Knapp did his own copying to make certain that it was done correctly, a burden that gave him "neuralgia in the head . . . due to too much sitting at this desk studying over orders & writing official communications &c &c." Fortunately, he and other officers in the same predicament owned copies of a handy two-dollar guide to help them do the paperwork: *Patten's Army Manual, Containing Instructions for Officers in the Preparation of Rolls, Returns, and Reports, and All Papers pertaining to the Duties of the Subsistence, Quartermaster, and Medical Departments, and the Accounts Connected Therewith.*[16]

The post adjutant, appointed by the commanding officer, assembled the reports delivered to him by the first sergeants of the respective companies. The information was sent to regimental and departmental headquarters and ultimately forwarded to Washington, D.C. Boards of survey helped the post commissary and quartermaster officers count supplies on hand and condemn those that had spoiled. A receiving board inspected newly arrived supplies. By custom junior officers, acting as recorders and secretaries, did most of the work by on such boards. Shortages of commissioned personnel sometimes forced officers to serve in several time-consuming positions at once.

A few commanders gave their junior officers additional military instruction. In 1878 a school for officers met twice a week at Fort Concho. At Fort Mason, Col. Albert Sidney Johnston conducted "a second West Point." Col. James Oakes played a similar role for Lt. Adam Kramer. "If I would be under his command for one year I belief I would learn the Regulation[s] by heart also the tacticks," noted the young lieutenant, whose military abilities were, one hopes, better than his spelling. "I have never in my life studied as hard as I have done since he is here." However, these examples were atypical; few of the officers troubled to add the study of military tactics or strategy to their routine. Popular belief held that a soldier could learn the art of war only through actual combat experience.[17]

15. Walter C. Conway, ed., "Colonel Edmund Schriver's Inspector-General's Report on Military Posts in Texas, November 1872–January 1873," *Southwestern Historical Quarterly* 67 (Apr., 1964): 581; Whitman, *The Troopers*, p. 181.

16. Knapp to Mead, Oct. 7, 1866, June 17, 1867, Obadiah M. Knapp Papers, BTHC.

17. Charles P. Roland and Richard P. Robbins, eds., "The Diary of Eliza (Mrs. Albert Sidney) Johnston: The Second Cavalry Comes to Texas," *Southwestern Historical Quarterly* 60 (Apr., 1957): 491; Brit Allan Storey, "An Army Officer in Texas, 1866–1867," *Southwestern Historical Quarterly* 72 (Oct., 1968): 250; Carter, *On the Border*, pp. 106–108.

Court-martial duty took up a considerable amount of every officer's time. These courts dealt with violations of the Articles of War (most commonly desertion, theft, and problems related to alcohol abuse) and, in the absence of local officials, civil cases. To deal with the more serious and complicated charges officers from several posts convened in general courts-martial. Frustrated by problems of travel and communication that often caused lengthy delays at the courts,

Robert E. Lee complained, "I feel I ought not to be here, & that I am of no use here. . . . When I shall get away God only knows."[18]

Garrison courts-martial handled official breaches of discipline. At these military tribunals much depended on the personalities of the president and the judge

18. Lee to Evans, Dec. 6, 1856, in Francis Raymond Adams, Jr., "An Annotated Edition of

advocate. Affairs remained formal if "some grim old field officer" presided. But participants viewed service on a court of younger, more easygoing individuals as good duty. They might eat, tell jokes, and gossip while supposedly hearing testimony and judging defendants. At least one officer held his court outdoors under a shade tree in good weather. This man saw such duty as providing a chance to catch up on household chores. He assembled a swing for his children during one trial and fished during another. Despite these often cavalier attitudes, the general and garrison courts-martial were vital in maintaining discipline. Many sentences were pronounced on an informal basis by officers and NCOs within the company. The official hearings often resulted in harsh and unjust punishments, but in some instances they did prevent bullies from making miserable the daily lives of fellow enlisted personnel.[19]

The workload of the officers varied from post to post. At Fort Concho, Lt. Calvin Esterly noted that "there is plenty to do," with daily drills and target practice plus duty as officer of the day every tenth day. His comrade at Fort McKavett, E. H. Plummer, reported that his duties were "not very arduous." Fellow West Pointer S. P. Wayman, while noting that he had "considerable duty" on Fort McIntosh's various boards, maintained that he did not find them "the bugbears they are 'cracked up to be.'" A good many officers did as little as they could.[20]

In such circumstances it was particularly important for the commander to set a good example for his junior officers. In the absence of a respected superior the post's daily routine often became chaotic. Many of the problems stemmed from efforts by some War Department officials to appoint post commanders themselves rather than allowing the army's divisional or departmental chiefs to select officers of their own choosing. One antebellum officer labeled most of the commanding officers "petty tyrants, styled by some Martinets." In 1872, Inspector Edmund Schriver concluded that the reason for the lack of organization at Fort McIntosh was that the commander and the surgeon were quartered a mile away in Laredo rather than at the post. Elsewhere, a confrontation between Lt. Col. John W. Davidson and Capt. Theodore A. Baldwin reached the White House when Mrs. Baldwin wrote a letter to President Rutherford B. Hayes accusing Davidson of drinking too heavily.[21]

---

the Personal Letters of Robert E. Lee, April, 1855–April, 1861," (Ph.D. diss., University of Maryland, 1955), pp. 223–24; Zenas R. Bliss Reminiscences, 1:15–17, BTHC; Don Rickey, Jr., *Forty Miles a Day on Beans and Hay: The Enlisted Soldier Fighting the Indian Wars* (Norman: University of Oklahoma Press, 1963), pp. 175–84.

19. Rickey, *Forty Miles a Day*, pp. 175–84; H. H. McConnell, *Five Years a Cavalryman; Or, Sketches of Regular Army Life on the Texas Frontier, Twenty Odd Years Ago* (Jacksboro, Tex.: J. N. Rogers and Co., 1889), pp. 196–98.

20. Calvin Esterly, Mar. 5, 1878, in R. C. Crane, "Letters from Texas," *West Texas Historical Association Year Book* 25 (Oct., 1949): 116; E. H. Plummer, Feb. 22, 1878, ibid., p. 124; S. P. Wayman, May 4, 1878, ibid., p. 126.

21. Sherman to Sheridan, Apr. 1, 1871, William T. Sherman Papers, Library of Congress, Washington, D.C., (microfilm, University of Texas, vol. 90, reel 45); George Crook, *General George*

Other post commanders were graded more favorably. In 1853, Inspector W. G. Freeman credited Bvt. Maj. John S. Simonsen with a "strict impartiality" that promoted "utmost harmony" among the officers at Fort Ewell. Freeman also reported that the garrison at Ringgold Barracks stood "preeminent" in appearance and grooming, thanks to the efforts of Commander Gabriel René Paul. Several officers appreciated the efforts of Fort Duncan's controversial William Shafter, future commander of U.S. troops in Cuba during the Spanish-American War. Shafter "had his own ideas about the administration of a post and always showed an intimate knowledge of what was going on," according to Charles J. Crane. Upon advising Officer of the Day Crane that some soldiers were gambling behind a woodpile, Shafter ordered Crane to allow the troops to continue but to make sure that civilians did not join the game.[22]

Whatever their officers might be doing, the troops were signaled in from their morning assignments about 11:30 A.M. While the officers went their respective ways, the enlisted men ate in the company barracks. The menu varied somewhat depending on the ability and imagination of the company cooks and the availability of vegetables but usually included stringy range beef, some kind of soup or vegetable, and bread. Of course, some problems—spoilage of food en route to the fort or the failure of a garden owing to weather, for example—were beyond the control of the men at the garrison. Careful inspections of the commissary, fastidious attention to food preparation and related facilities by officers, and wary observation of local suppliers could nevertheless mean the difference between a meal of watery soup and stale bread and one of roast beef, rice, gravy, and fresh bread. Conscientious officers and NCOs made very effort to ensure that their men were well fed; others did little to see that their orders were carried out or that the basic necessities were available.

Soldiers returned to duty about one o'clock. As in the morning, drill lasted one to two hours, and fatigue details took up the rest of the afternoon. A water break about three o'clock broke the monotony. The recall-from-fatigue signal ended the afternoon's efforts. Stable call sounded soon thereafter, and the cavalrymen groomed and fed their mounts while the foot soldiers enjoyed a few minutes of leisure time. A light supper of cold or warmed-over beef, bread, and coffee followed.

At sunset the garrison reassembled for retreat. While bad weather often canceled fatigue duty or drills, the evening dress parade was held whenever practicable. Buglers, trumpeters, and drummers serenaded the companies as they formed on the parade ground. The men went through the manual of arms, after which orders were read, roll call was taken, and the flag was lowered. A school call, if

---

Crook: His Autobiography, ed. Martin F. Schmitt (Norman: University of Oklahoma Press, 1960), p. 10; Conway, ed., "Schriver's Report," pp. 571–72; William H. Leckie, *The Buffalo Soldiers: A Narrative of the Negro Cavalry in the West* (Norman: University of Oklahoma Press, 1967), p. 165.

22. M. L. Crimmins, ed., "W. G. Freeman's Report on the Eighth Military Department," *Southwestern Historical Quarterly* 51 (Jan., 1948): 251; *Southwestern Historical Quarterly* 52 (Oct., 1949): 256; Crane, *Colonel of Infantry*, pp. 79–80, 85.

the fort had a teacher, sounded fifteen minutes after retreat. At about 8:30 P.M. tattoo signaled the men to prepare for bed. Taps were played half an hour later. By the last note lights were to be extinguished and the men in their bunks. The long day ended, quiet fell over the fort.

At Fort Davis, Assistant Surgeon Daniel Weisel's report of February, 1871, noted that "nothing worthy of notice transpired during the month." His next monthly report had a familiar laconic note: "Nothing interesting to record has occurred during the month."[23] But the colorful individualists who lived at these forts did not allow life to lose all of its minor pleasures, despite the boredom of everyday routine. Gleeful tales of odd and humorous incidents reflect the troops' determination to make the best of their frontier existence. Upon hearing that a man bitten by a poisonous snake had received liberal doses of good whiskey, one Irish private at Fort Richardson decided that a stiff drink was worth the pain of a viper's bite or a court-martial's punishment. The man skipped inspection to wade barefoot into a nearby creek with his trousers rolled above his knees. Spotting the soldier, the officer of the day dispatched a corporal to bring the fellow in. As one observer told it:

"What were you doing out there, and why were you absent from inspection, sir?" demanded the Captain. "Ah sir," was the reply. "I saw the tratement John Burns got for the snakebite, and I though it worth me while to try and get one meself."

  This was too much for even army discipline, and although jokes from enlisted men are seldom appreciated, in this case the Captain's sense of humor got the best of him, and he ordered a quart of whiskey for Paddy, with orders for him to be compelled to drink it all at once; whether the man considered it a punishment or not I cannot say.[24]

Another observer recounted the ludicrous action of an absentminded officer before his troops on parade. An avid hunter, the officer instinctively raised his sword to his shoulder to get off a couple of quick shots as a flock of geese flew low over the assembly. Realizing that his sword could hardly bring down the quarry, he sheepishly remarked: "I've lost a splendid shot. If I had my gun I believe I could bag two of those birds—I do indeed; and possibly I could have killed three!" The rows of amazed troopers roared with laughter, all rules of military bearing temporarily forgotten.[25]

One enlisted man "took to fishing on the parade ground" at Fort Richardson during the 1870s. With pole and string he sat muttering to himself for hours. Thinking the man a lunatic, his superiors granted him a medical discharge. A

23. PMR, Fort Davis, Feb., Mar., 1871, pp. 205, 209.
24. McConnell, *Five Years a Cavalryman*, pp. 110–11.
25. Randolph B. Marcy, *Border Reminiscences* (New York: Harper and Brothers, 1872), pp. 76, 79–81.

few days later the commanding officer happened across the man and asked why he was not fishing. "Your honor," the soldier replied, "I've got what I was fishing for this long time." Such events most assuredly highlighted conversation at the post for days afterward.[26]

26. McConnell, *Five Years a Cavalryman*, pp. 166–67.

During the day's activities company sergeants bore most of the responsibility for the actions of the enlisted men. Reliable veteran noncommissioned officers were vital to a company's efficiency and to an orderly routine. Still, a good officer could do much to solidify discipline, morale, and efficiency. The troops respected his almost lordly authority, especially when he tempered that authority with fairness and proper military behavior. Personal visits and inspections of the men's rations and living conditions could also be put to advantage. The officer who showed an interest in the welfare of his command set an encouraging example for all subordinates and greatly eased their tasks.

For daily affairs to run smoothly, the individuals stationed at the army's posts in Texas had to put aside personal difficulties. A spirit of professionalism, usually stemming from the example set by the commanding officer, permeated the better garrisons. On such posts officers responded quickly to complaints made informally as well as through regular channels. The wise veteran knew that his job entailed not only giving orders but also making sure that the orders were carried out. Careful appointments to boards of survey, commissary, and post adjutant were also necessary, for effective aides and advisers could solve minor problems before they disrupted the tenuous harmony of garrison life. In all, the smooth functioning of army routine depended on the efforts of both commissioned and noncommissioned officers; without their cooperation conditions at the far-flung posts deteriorated rapidly.

CHAPTER SIX

Economic Concerns

. . . a dollar or so in my pocket.

—Private Max Thayer

Money was important to everyone living on the Texas military frontiers. The army supplied enlisted men with food and clothing; officers received extra pay in lieu of such allowances. Having secured their material needs, those serving at the Texas forts then acquired a few small luxuries. To some this meant a better pair of boots or a more stylish hat. Many invested in other forms of pleasures—drink, food, or women. The size of a nearby civilian community, along with the limitations of nineteenth-century transportation, often determined the goods and services that were available to those with money. In turn, the economics of the fort exerted a tremendous influence on the financial condition of the surrounding region, for the presence or withdrawal of the army could make or break local businessmen.

Officers were the economic elite of the frontier garrisons. Some of them came from wealthy families. In the 1850 census thirty-year veteran Maj. Pitcairn Morrison was reported as owning $13,000 in real property, an estate that placed him among the wealthiest 5 percent of Texas residents. Lt. Col. Robert E. Lee, stationed in Texas during the 1850s, came from one of Virginia's most prominent families. In 1870, thirty-five-year-old Lt. William E. Kingsbury, serving at Fort Griffin, had $80,000 in real property and $15,000 in personal property. Other officers bettered their economic status through marriage. In 1870, Capt. Jacob DeGress, a twenty-seven-year-old native of Prussia, reported his total wealth as a respectable $9,527. Bertha, his twenty-four-year-old bride, was a native Mississippian who owned property totaling $40,000.[1]

The typical officer, however, depended on his army pay to make ends meet.

---

1. Manuscript returns, U.S. census, 1850, Medina County; census, 1870, Shackelford and Maverick counties; Randolph B. Campbell and Richard G. Lowe, *Wealth and Power in Antebellum Texas* (College Station: Texas A&M University Press, 1977), p. 34.

In 1848 monthly salaries ranged from $25 for a second lieutenant to $75 for a full colonel. Officers also collected extra allowances for food, fuel, forage, and quarters that virtually trebled their base pay. By 1860 the commander at Fort Quitman was receiving extra monthly pay of $36 for commanding the post, $10 for commanding a company, $11 for acting as commissary officer, and $5 for serving as post treasurer. Still, across-the-board raises of $20 a month in 1857 proved a much-needed boon to commissioned personnel.

By contrast, during the Civil War state troops in Texas fared poorly, their miserly salaries failing to keep pace with the rampant inflation that beset the Confederacy. Postwar pay scales offered some relief. Pay scales set in 1870 provided for salaries of $291.67 a month for a colonel down to $125 for a second lieutenant. Infantry officers' annual earnings were $100 less than those of their cavalry counterparts. In the postbellum era five years' experience netted the individual a 10 percent raise, and another such increase awaited ten-year veterans. Smaller bonuses rewarded those with fifteen and twenty years of service. Each officer received an extra 10 percent of his salary to pay for food. Officers forced to live off the post were awarded an extra $12 to $18 a month per room, with allowances ranging from a second lieutenant's one room to a colonel's six rooms.

While the low pay scales did not match the salaries West Point graduates might have received in private business, most officers lived in relative comfort. Bachelors often pooled their resources to form an officers' mess. Many of them hired servants; some accumulated extensive sets of furniture, including beds, tables, chairs, and even pianos. Off-post housing was inexpensive: in 1856, Col. Albert Sidney Johnston and his wife, Eliza, rented a four-room house with closets, an outhouse, and a bathhouse overlooking the San Antonio River for $50 a month.[2]

Some officers, on the other hand, faced economic problems. Fort Chadbourne's surgeon found it difficult to support his family, a servant (whom he paid $15 a month), and his brother-in-law, who lived with him while he was studying medicine. The refusal of the U.S. House of Representatives to pass an army appropriations bill in the summer of 1877 threatened officers with economic ruin. While Congress delayed, private concerns paid the commissioned personnel, exacting a 3 percent service charge. In November a special session of Congress finally resolved the impasse, which had resulted from differences between the House and the Senate over the size of the army and its continued involvement in Reconstruction.

Some officers tried to live above their means. A few gained renown for their culinary prowess and used private resources to supplement their standard fare with wine and champagne. Those who were not blessed with personal fortunes found it increasingly difficult to make ends meet as the month ended. In 1853 one surgeon estimated that his monthly expenses—clothing, horse, food, and

2. Randolph B. Marcy, *Border Reminiscences*, pp. 53–55; Charles P. Roland and Richard P. Robbins, ed., "The Diary of Eliza (Mrs. Albert Sidney) Johnston: The Second Cavalry Comes to Texas," *Southwestern Historical Quarterly* 60 (Apr., 1957): 497.

105

servant—exceeded his $25 salary by $75. Another related the woes of a fellow lieutenant who, having exhausted his money, was forced to resort to a diet of rice. During this time a friend, accustomed to the lieutenant's noted generosity but unaware of his temporary economic distress, paid the officer a visit. The host, seeking to make the best of the situation, borrowed some mustard from a fellow officer. Upon being offered the rice, the story holds, the unwitting guest refused, saying that he never ate rice. "Then help yourself to mustard," replied the host, "for if you can get anything else in this ranch, you are smarter than I am."[3]

Enlisted personnel also felt the effects of congressional frugality. During the early 1850s mounted privates received a less than princely $8 a month, and their comrades in the infantry and artillery were paid $7 a month. Sergeants received $13 a month. In 1854, Congress granted all soldiers $4-a-month pay raises and awarded those enlisting for a second time with an additional $2 a month. Each additional enlistment earned the individual another $1 a month.

The postbellum army received further salary hikes. A cavalry private could expect $13 a month during his first two years, another dollar a month being added every year for the remainder of his five-year enlistment. Sergeant majors were paid $23 a month during their first two years and $24, $25, and $26 a month during their third, fourth, and fifth years. As in the pre–Civil War years, for one's first reenlistment, $2 was added to the monthly salary, with an additional $1 a month for subsequent renewals. The bonuses, it was hoped, would reduce desertions. As a further deterrent, $1 a month was automatically withheld at 4 percent interest until discharge.

The army also provided enlisted men with food and clothing. An infantryman received a uniform allowance, which after 1865 totaled $134.99 for each three-year enlistment. Although uniforms were generally of poor quality, most soldiers limited their clothing requisitions, for unused allowances were returned to them at the time of their discharge. Veterans bought the used uniforms of men leaving the service at reduced rates, further increasing their savings. A record of these transactions was kept in the company barracks.

In addition to saving a few dollars from their uniform allowances, some enlisted men also benefited from an additional source of income. Extra-duty pay could provide a sizable supplement to the regular salary. In January, 1860, for example, the army hired a carpenter, a blacksmith, a stonemason, several wheelwrights, a saddler, a clerk, three woodcutters, and nine teamsters from the ranks at Fort Clark, paying the group a total of $164 for their work. At the same post ten years later the military employed a similar group of extra-duty soldiers, who earned from $0.20 to $0.35 a day (the former for a carpenter or a laborer, the latter for a wagonmaster, a herder, or a mason) in addition to their base salaries.[4]

A few men had left wealthy families to join the army, and they probably

---

3. Col. M. L. Crimmins, "Experiences of an Army Surgeon at Fort Chadbourne," *West Texas Historical Association Year Book* 15 (Oct., 1939): 31–33; Marcy, *Border Reminiscences*, pp. 54–55.

4. "Roll of Non-Commissioned Officers and Privates Employed on Extra Duty as Mechanics

received periodic gifts from their relatives. Others had inherited or established their own private estates. The 1850 census credited 1st Sgt. James Rochelle, stationed at Fort Inge, with $9,000 worth of real property, which placed him among the wealthiest 10 percent of the state's population. A number of noncommissioned personnel could also count on their laundress-wives to supplement (or even surpass) their regular army pay. A laundress might add $30 to $40 a month to the family income during the 1870s.[5]

Official regulations decreed that the troops were to be paid every two months. A shortage of paymasters, however, often forced the men to wait up to six months for their pay. In the meantime, clothing and tobacco became common forms of barter, and the men could usually secure credit from the post trader for limited purchases. News of the long-awaited paymaster's approach revitalized the sagging spirits of those who had undergone enforced abstinence from alcohol, tobacco, and culinary delicacies. As the paymaster set up his table, companies lined up according to their commanders' seniority. In undress uniform the men filed by the pay table, removing one white glove to sign a receipt and saluting with the other, gloved hand. Individuals then paid off their debts to the laundresses or the post sutler.

General mayhem came next. It proved impossible to clear the post of the shady characters who lurked about on payday. The soldiers, with up to six months' salary and extra-duty money burning holes in their pockets, hastened to nearby stores to buy the beer, liquor, sweetmeats, and canned goods they had gone without for several weeks. Some troops gorged themselves on the delicacies and gambling broke out all over the post. Others headed for nearby brothels, or "hog ranches."

The quality of the army ration made such outbursts understandable. In 1853 the estimated cost of a daily ration ranged from a little more than $0.16 at Fort McIntosh to just over $0.26 at Fort Belknap. Official allotments included twelve ounces of pork or bacon or twenty ounces of fresh or salt beef a day, plus eighteen ounces of bread or flour, twelve ounces of hard bread, or one and a fourth pounds of cornmeal. For every one hundred rations the army also furnished either eight quarts of peas or beans or ten pounds of rice and six pounds of coffee and sugar, plus vinegar, salt, tallow, and soap in assorted quantities. Post–Civil War regulations permitted a greater variety of foods, including mutton, dried or pickled fish, and hominy and the substitution of tea for coffee.[6]

Even the modest variety of foods provided under official regulations was rarely available at isolated stations, where bacon and beef were the staples of daily fare.

---

and Laborers," Jan., 1860, Fort Clark Records, BTHC; "Roll of Enlisted Men on Extra Duty," Fort Clark, Nov., 1870, H. B. Quimby Papers, BTHC.

5. Manuscript returns, U.S. census, 1850, Bexar County; Campbell and Lowe, *Wealth and Power*, p. 34; John R. Sibbald, "Camp Followers All," *American West* 3 (Spring, 1966): 65.

6. Abstract of Provisions Issued to Troops, Fort Clark, Dec., 1872, Quimby Papers, BTHC; Abstract of Provisions Issued to Troops, Fort Davis, June, 1872, BTHC; Table Showing Cost of Rations, Texas Forts, 1853, in Crimmins Papers, BTHC.

The typical entree was boiled meat, often combined with desiccated potatoes or beans to form what the cooks called stew. A common bread recipe called for flour, salt, and water mixed into a stiff dough one inch thick. Bakers then poured about an inch of water over the mixture, which was then covered and heated until all the water had been converted to steam. Henry Flipper recalled that "when hot and freshly made it is good and very palatable, but when it gets cold, it falls and becomes hard and soggy and a mule can't eat it." Seeking to cut expenditures, officials dumped Civil War surplus hardtack on the frontier troopers. Perhaps the kindest response to this economy measure came from Sgt. H. H. McConnell, who simply commented that hardtack "should never be used when any other kind of bread can possibly be had."[7]

Unreliable contractors hampered efforts to improve the food service. The War Department took public bids on most of the goods it bought. In theory, the contract was awarded to the bidder who achieved the best balance between quality and price. In practice, bribery and mismanagement proved all too common. One group of Texas businessmen, for example, submitted three bids for every contract. If no outside offers were lower, they would pay a small penalty, withdraw their two lowest bids, and substantially increase their profits. Suppliers frequently shipped meat with an excess of bone content. Locally purchased cattle often proved lean and tough, and even the best shipped-in meat arrived in 200-pound barrels filled with an overpowering saline brine. Poor-quality manufactured goods added to the miseries of the nation's frontier guardians. One inspector pointed out that water casks and pails purchased from one contractor were "of such worthless character that I am undecided who is the most to blame for imposing them on the Government—the vendor or the buyer!"[8]

Close inspection of such transactions was all too often lacking. Troops at interior stations routinely forwarded goods ahead without first ensuring that the supplies had not spoiled. In the fiscal year ending May 31, 1856, 10 percent of the 2,000 barrels of pork, 13 percent of the 5,500 barrels of flour, and 21 percent of the 280,000 pounds of bread delivered to the Department of Texas had to be condemned. The inspection problem was glaringly apparent when the Second Cavalry marched from Jefferson Barracks to Texas in 1855, as private contractors scoured the area ahead of the column for everything edible. After purchasing the food themselves, they promptly resold it to the troops behind, turning a neat profit

7. "Bill of Fare," Co. F, 11th Inf., PMR, Fort Griffin, National Archives, Washington, D.C., RG 94 (microfilm BTHC), p. 42; Henry O. Flipper, *Negro Frontiersman: The Western Memoirs of Henry D. Flipper,* ed. Theodore D. Harris (El Paso: Texas Western College Press, 1963), p. 7; H. H. McConnell, *Five Years a Cavalryman; Or, Sketches of Regular Army Life on the Texas Frontier, Twenty Odd Years Ago* (Jacksboro, Tex.: J. N. Rogers and Co., 1889), p. 84.

8. Charles J. Crane, *Experiences of a Colonel of Infantry* (New York: Knickerbocker Press, 1923), p. 109; PMR, Ringgold Barracks, Nov. 18, 1876, p. 341; Doug McChristian, "The Commissary Sergeant: His Life at Fort Davis," *Military History of Texas and the Southwest* 14, no. 1, p. 24; Walter C. Conway, ed., "Colonel Edmund Schriver's Inspector-General's Report on Military Posts in Texas," *Southwestern Historical Quarterly* 67 (Apr., 1964): 570.

in the meantime. The practice ended only after the regimental colonel's personal intervention.[9]

The poor transportation network that plagued Texas throughout the nineteenth century created further problems. Goods bought outside Texas had to be transported by sea, usually from New Orleans, to Galveston, Indianola, Corpus Christi, or Brazos Santiago. From these ports private contractors hauled the supplies to their frontier destinations by way of San Antonio. Each post required a staggering volume of goods. For the month of May, 1860, for example, Fort Clark's adjutant issued 3 barrels of pork, 1,500 pounds of bacon, 4,300 pounds of fresh beef, 34 barrels of flour, 348 pounds of hard bread, 221 pounds of rice, 5 barrels of beans, 381 pounds of coffee, 762 pounds of sugar, 63 gallons of vinegar, 254 pounds of soap, 3 barrels of salt, 116 pounds of desiccated vegetables, 63 pounds of candles, and 8 gallons of whiskey.[10]

The Quartermaster's Department hired private concerns to haul supplies to their final destinations. The great distances, lack of navigable rivers, and rough terrain sent shipping costs skyrocketing. In 1850, Secretary of War Charles Conrad estimated that it cost the army $48 to ship a barrel of pork to El Paso del Norte (Fort Bliss). During the fiscal year 1850–51 the War Department spent $73,000 for construction and repairs at its nineteen Texas posts. In the same period contract transportation in the Lone Star State cost more than $390,000.[11]

Officials realized that money that might otherwise be used to improve the quality of life of the soldiers was instead being spent on transportation. Seeking to reduce such costs, during the 1850s the army made several attempts, largely unsuccessful, to make greater use of the Rio Grande. The War Department also funded an attempt to establish a series of artesian wells in West Texas, an ineffective exercise that if successful might have eased travel and reduced the expenses of overland shipments. The military also sponsored a number of railroad surveys in West Texas, but not until the 1880s did the iron horses make a significant impact on freighting in Texas.

During the 1850s, in a more exotic attempt to cut shipping costs, Secretary of War Jefferson Davis persuaded Congress to purchase about seventy camels for use as pack animals in the Southwest. The fantastic sight of camels and their specially imported Arabian handlers must have amazed many a poor soldier. The

9. M. L. Crimmins, ed., "Colonel J. K. F. Mansfield's Report of the Inspection of the Department of Texas," *Southwestern Historical Quarterly,* 42 (Oct., 1938): 137–38; Roland and Roberts, eds., "Diary of Eliza Johnston," p. 474.

10. Abstract of Provisions Issued to Troops, May, 1860, Fort Clark Papers, BTHC; James A. Huston, *The Sinews of War: Army Logistics, 1775–1953* (Washington, D.C.: U.S. Government Printing Office, 1960), p. 148.

11. Report of Conrad, Nov. 30, SW, AR, 1850, p. 5; Erna Risch, *Quartermaster Support of the Army: A History of the Corps, 1775–1939* (Washington, D.C.: U.S. Government Printing Office, 1962), p. 493; Leonora Barrett, "Transportation, Supplies, and Quarters for the West Texas Frontier under the Federal Military System, 1848–1861," *West Texas Historical Association Year Book* 5 (June, 1929): 91.

great beasts proved superior to mules and oxen in every test but never gained popularity among army handlers and terrified the other animals. The project lost its most powerful sponsor when Davis left the War Department; the animals were eventually abandoned, and some were later rounded up and sold to a circus.

With its reams of paperwork and inadequate inspections, the creaking army bureaucracy and the poor road system created major supply problems at virtually every post in Texas. Inexplicably, shipments were sometimes held until win-

ter, when the lack of grass and muddy roads slowed overland movement to a crawl. In January, 1869, a surgeon blamed the supply problems at Fort Concho on "an incomprehensible want of judgement, in the arrangement of the contracts for transportation, and ignorance of the actual obstacles to travel." In March he reported that "the increased inconvenience arising from want of supplies . . . has completely exhausted the subject for words of suitable condemnation." The supplies for Fort Concho, which had left New Orleans in December, 1868, did not

arrive until the following May, despite official estimates calling for the 827-mile route to be covered in four to five weeks.[12]

Fresh vegetables proved a rare treat. While all the garrisons maintained small gardens, military duties, dry weather, and insects made regular farming problematic. Even onions and desiccated potatoes, which could be shipped and stored with a fair rate of success, were served in less than adequate amounts. One observer condemned the watery soups as "tasteless & unfit for human food." Suggested alternatives such as codfish and sauerkraut were never introduced in large amounts at Texas stations.[13]

Poorly trained cooks taken from the ranks compounded the food problems. Many called on the army to establish a special cooking school. First sergeants often tried to help the novice bakers; surgeons also joined in the culinary operations. One doctor made repeated efforts to come up with a satisfactory mixture of cornmeal and flour to increase the quantity of bread. After fruitless attempts that engaged the entire gamut of post bureaucracy, the doctor admitted defeat. "There seems to be no baker at this post who understands making satisfactory bread with the mixture of corn bread and wheat flour," he concluded.[14]

Enraged enlisted personnel often clashed with the cooks over inadequate food preparation. Upon discovering that Fort Richardson's baker had used all the hops on hand to make beer for himself and his assistants, officers drove the would-be brewer out of camp. Understandably, a good cook was a highly valued commodity. Skillful management and preparation could mean the difference between a meal of beef and potato hash, hardtack, and coffee and a more pleasing menu of roast beef, soup, potatoes, onions, warm bread, and coffee. When a company found a good cook, it tried to keep him. One sergeant recalled a "Hollander" who had been an inept soldier but a fine chef, producing "wonderful puddings and mysterious sauces" for special occasions. To ensure his continued services, the men pooled their money to augment his salary.[15]

Talented cooks also managed to save many of the company's provisions. Elizabeth Custer claimed that the ration was "so large that a man who can eat it all in a day is renowned as a glutton." Adept cooks and bakers sold or exchanged excess flour, which was rationed in particularly generous quantities. A successful hunt for wild game sometimes allowed cooks to dispose of regulation meat in a similar fashion. In 1874 at Fort Richardson, for instance, the troops brought in 8,000 pounds of buffalo meat, 20 pounds of deer meat, 200 pounds of fish, and 100 pounds of turkey. The next year hunters at Richardson killed a great number of prairie chickens, further augmenting the amount of

12. PMR, Fort Concho, Jan.–March, May, 1869, pp. 105, 109, 113, 121; Lowell H. Harrison, "Supplying Texas Military Posts in 1876," *Texas Military History* 4 (Spring, 1964): 23–24.

13. PMR, Ringgold Barracks, Aug. 12, 18, 1876, p. 310; PMR, Fort Brown, Jan., 1872.

14. PMR, Fort Elliott, Dec. 1, 1886, p. 78.

15. McConnell, *Five Years a Cavalryman*, pp. 211, 265.

food available for resale or barter. The resulting savings were placed in a special post fund used to provide a few amenities otherwise beyond the average soldier's reach.[16]

The collection and disposition of these monies varied widely among the Texas forts. At some posts each company retained its own savings, which it used to purchase its own supplies. The troopers of Company K, Ninth Cavalry, for instance, amassed four water pitchers, four castors, seventy-two teaspoons, sixty-eight knives, sixty-five forks, four mustard spoons, eleven tablecloths, and one carving knife and fork. Other officials channeled savings and receipts from taxes on sutlers or loose animals into a fund administered by the post adjutant. This system worked very effectively at Fort Richardson, where collective savings financed a comfortable reading room, well stocked with current magazines and newspapers, and also a good band. In addition, each company had hot and cold water and nice tables, constituting an unusual degree of comfort for frontier inhabitants.

Troops at other forts proved less fortunate; much depended on military necessity, management, and local conditions. Constant fatigue duty or scouting left little time for hunting or gardening and reduced the amount of savings. Efficient management was also essential. Captains in charge of separate company funds often spent the money unwisely. Those at small, isolated posts found it difficult to amass adequate savings from the regular rations. In 1887, desperate for fresh vegetables, the hungry men at Camp Peña Colorado each contributed a dollar a month of their salaries toward the purchase of such items.

Post gardens, mandated by War Department orders, provided varying amounts of produce. While such efforts at Forts Duncan and Clark yielded little, the garden at Fort Davis did fairly well. Perhaps the greatest success came at Fort McKavett. In 1868 crop failures forced cooks to substitute watercress for fresh vegetables, but during the 1870s enterprising troops built a windmill and dammed the San Saba River to irrigate their garden. Divided into seven equal portions, the McKavett fields produced onions, beets, cabbage, radishes, corn, lettuce, squash, parsley, turnips, okra, cucumbers, string beans, peas, tomatoes, and melons for the six companies and assorted staff stationed there.

Hospitals usually managed to offer the patients a more balanced diet. Several doctors and stewards maintained separate hospital gardens. To purchase better food, surgeons collected savings from their patients' rations and payments from private citizens undergoing treatment to create special funds. As a result, the fare at Fort Clark often included vermicelli or macaroni. Dinner in the Fort Griffin sick ward was composed of a meat dish (occasionally even chicken), bread, soup, and pickles, tomatoes, or bread pudding. For supper patients received a regular

---

16. Elizabeth B. Custer, *Tenting on the Plains, or General Custer in Kansas and Texas* (1897; reprint, Norman: University of Oklahoma Press, 1971), 3:506; PMR, Fort Richardson, Dec., 1874, Nov. 30, 1875, pp. 100, 161.

fare of bread, tea, and prunes, butter, or syrup. Eggs, milk, ham, and fresh fish were served when available.[17]

Even with the limited variety made possible by unit purchases, post gardens, and an occasional stay in the hospital, the average soldier had to invest some of his pay in extra food. At the small town of Dallas, for example, the troops from Fort Worth bought milk, butter, chickens, and eggs at reasonable prices. Robert E. Lee took some chickens with him to Camp Cooper. Hungry Confederate soldiers at Fort Bliss swapped coffee, soap, and bacon with nearby Mexican residents for eggs and apples. But drought, seasonal changes, and the scarcity of civilian farmers or ranchers made private purchase or trade impossible at the more isolated posts. Milk products were especially scarce after the Civil War, when many cattle were moved onto the open range in preparation for more profitable drives to the north. Mrs. Orsemus Boyd claimed that "we nearly starved" at postwar Fort Clark, where vegetables proved to be virtually unobtainable, the meat tough, the milk tainted with a disagreeable taste of garlic, and the butter oily.[18]

The post trader and the commissary offered some supplementary fare. Provisions were available for sale to officers and enlisted personnel, the variety depending on the location, the resources of the sutler, and the season. Obviously South Carolinian LeGrand G. Capers, post sutler at San Antonio, who reported $60,000 in real property in the 1850 census, could supply a greater variety of goods than could Gouverneur Morris, a New York storekeeper at Fort Inge, who reported owning $500 in real property at the same time.

In general, food supplies became more plentiful after the Civil War. In December, 1871, enlisted men at Fort Clark made purchases of hams, flour, cornmeal, tea, dried apples, tomatoes, corn, peas, and butter. Eager to spice up their Christmas fare, they also bought more exotic foods, including ten cans of oysters, twenty cans of clams, a like number of canned lobster, and thirteen cans of peaches, along with assorted jellies, jams, and cranberry sauce (in anticipation of their celebration they also remembered to buy thirteen pounds of bicarbonate of soda). Officers invested in such special items as mackerel, salmon, berries, lemon and vanilla extract, cloves, cinnamon, and Worcestershire sauce.[19]

Not all the posts were as fortunate. From Fort Concho, Dr. William Notson complained that "requisitions are regularly made yet never fulfilled. . . . Flour, coffee, tea, sugar, beans, and other articles have all been out, not perhaps at the same time, but each at some time, and at all times something." In 1872, Notson's successor, Assistant Surgeon W. F. Buchanan, reported that the commissary department's stocks included a reasonably good supply of canned goods. Three

17. "Abstract of Provisions for Hospital," Fort Clark, Jan., 1871, Quimby Papers, BTHC; PMR, Fort Griffin, 1874, p. 45; PMR, Fort Elliott, July, 1887, p. 128.

18. Mrs. Orsemus Bronson Boyd, *Cavalry Life in Tent and Field* (1894; reprint, Lincoln: University of Nebraska Press, 1982), p. 258.

19. Manuscript returns, U.S. census, 1850, Bexar County; Abstract of Provisions Sold to Enlisted Men, Fort Clark, Dec., 1871, Quimby Papers, BTHC; Abstract of Provisions Sold to Officers, Fort Clark, Dec., 1870, Quimby Papers.

years later, however, Buchanan complained that the store had no crackers, lard, sugar, syrup, mackerel, oysters, or prunes for sale. A recent shipment of peas and butter had been inedible. He also wondered why Fort Concho had received no canned pears or cherries, though he knew that other posts offered such luxuries. This, he argued, was no way to treat soldiers of the U.S. Army, especially when the troops were just returning from a grueling winter campaign.[20]

The sutler's wares also offered little attraction to the soldier on a tight budget. Post traders often used nefarious means to gain the privilege of trading on the military reserve. To ensure a return on their investments, some charged exorbitant prices for inferior goods; others sold liquor to drunken soldiers or allowed troops to put too many goods on account (at 10 percent interest per month) without permission from their company commanders. Enlisted men also accused the post's council of administration of taking bribes from sutlers in return for neglecting to establish fair prices. One sergeant complained, "In practice, [the Council members] sampled the sutler's whiskey, smoked his cigars, partook of an elegant free lunch, 'set up' for the occasion, and blandly winked at the scale of prices."[21]

The blazing Texas sun made ice an especially sought-after commodity. Seeking brief respites from the heat, some purchased ice from San Antonio, though most of the shipments melted before reaching their destinations. When rivers and streams at the northern Texas posts froze over, eager work parties packed ice in underground holes or, during the latter part of the century, specially constructed icehouses. Overheated members of the garrison quickly devoured the winter ice; the small quantity stored at Fort Griffin in 1870–71 was gone by the following May despite its almost prohibitive cost of twenty-five cents a pound. At sweltering Ringgold Barracks surgeons tried to save money toward the purchase of an ice machine. Their efforts were unsuccessful: in 1876 the War Department, wary of setting an expensive precedent, refused to provide supplementary funds for such a purchase. Not until the last years of the century were ice machines commonly supplied to Texas military posts.

With some additions to his regular ration, the careful enlisted man, who was paid $8.00 to $30.00 a month, could obtain plenty of food if he did not mind the poor quality. Prices varied widely. At El Paso pork, sugar, and coffee cost $0.50 a pound in 1850. The commissary at Fort Concho sold tobacco for $0.60 a pound. At Fort Richardson a soldier could buy a quart of milk for $0.10 in the summer and $0.25 in the winter. Butter cost $0.40 to $0.75 a pound there. For $0.50 a soldier at Fort Clark could purchase a can of tomatoes; a jar of jelly was priced at $1.25.

With their surplus funds many soldiers bought pillows to make their rough board bunks more comfortable. In the early 1870s the army helped by shipping

---

20. PMR, Fort Concho, Dec., 1870, Dec., 1872, Feb., 1875, pp. 198, 296, 170.

21. Bill Green, *The Dancing Was Lively: Fort Concho, Texas: A Social History, 1867–1882* (San Angelo, Tex.: Fort Concho Sketches Publishing Co., 1974), pp. 39–40; McConnell, *Five Years a Cavalryman*, p. 209.

in new iron bedsteads and a supply of mattresses. A large percentage of disposable income probably went for alcohol and prostitutes, though many soldiers were prudent in their spending. In 1879, Pvt. Max Thayer commented that even if he saved $10 every month he could still have "enough to pay my washing tobaco and tailors bills besides always having a dollar or so in my pocket in case of an emergincy."[22]

Military installations also had a significant economic impact on the nearby civilian residents. At the bustling seaport of Indianola the quartermaster employed a civilian clerk, a forage master, a veterinarian, a blacksmith, a carpenter, a wheelwright, a wagon master, a watchman, seven teamsters, and four laborers. Each worker received one ration a day, and the total monthly salaries of these civilians amounted to $545. Other typical figures range from $350 paid to civilian employees at Fort Davis in November, 1873, to the $12,000 paid for workers' wages and rent at Brownsville in March, 1868. The latter figure included more than 370 nonmilitary construction jobs at the new national cemetery and on renovations at Ringgold Barracks. Wages varied: an unskilled laborer received from $20 to $30 a month, while a clerk was paid $80 to $150 a month.[23]

An army post also provided civilians with other forms of economic assistance. Government contracts for beef, hay, and wood were a great stimulus for local farmers and ranchers. The army leased the grounds for its Indianola depot for $80 a month and office space for $12 a month. Pre–Civil War facilities at San Antonio included buildings rented from a Catholic church ($150 a month), space for the subsistence department ($20 a month), and a lot rented from Samuel A. Maverick ($20 a month). Maverick and a partner also leased land to the military at Forts Clark and Chadbourne.[24]

Other civilians provided goods and services. Traders competed with post sutlers and offered the garrison's personnel a wider selection. Such competition was particularly keen at Fort Richardson, where the soldiers published a newspaper, the *Flea*. There post trader J. L. Oldham advertised "Staple and Fancy Dry Goods, Groceries, Boots, Shoes, Hats and Caps. Hardware, Cutlery, Queensware, Woodware, Tinware, Yankee Notions. Hosiery and Gloves, and in Fact everything required to fill up a General Assortment of Goods suited to the necessities of Frontier Life." Not to be outdone, rival dry-goods merchant S. W. Eastin promised in the same issue that "particular attention will be paid to filling the orders of either civilian or those connected with the army, for all specialties procurable in the Northern Markets." Saloons and brothels provided entertainment. Farmers and ranchers sold food and patronized the other local establishments. Enter-

22. Heyman, "Letter from a Soldier," p. 72.
23. M. L. Crimmins, ed., "W. G. Freeman's Report on the Eighth Military Department," *Southwestern Historical Quarterly* 51 (July, 1947): 57; "Report of Persons and Articles Employed and Hired," Fort Davis, Nov., 1873, Quimby Papers; "Report of Persons and Articles Employed and Hired," Ringgold Barracks, Mar., 1868, Wainwright Papers, BTHC; General Order No. 15, July 16, 1872, Crimmins Papers.
24. Crimmins, ed., "Freeman's Report," pp. 57, 168–69.

prising children also shared in the profits. Young R. H. Flutsch ran errands for the surgeon at Fort McKavett. J. M. Hunter gathered flattened lead bullets scavenged from McKavett's target field for ten cents a pound.[25]

The economy of the army's forts obviously affected much more than the military garrison. The quality of food and clothing available to the soldiers varied greatly over time and place. Troops at one post might benefit from fresh shipments of new uniforms, a productive garden, and a good hunting season, while their comrades at another station weathered a drought in tattered uniforms. Whatever the immediate circumstance might provide, army personnel generally offered a captive market for enterprising merchants and sutlers. While purchases could be made from mail-order catalogs, the men and women who lived on the Texas military frontiers spent most of their money at local stores. As the federal government's often substantial ante increased the stakes, the military presence could prove essential to the region's economic well-being.

25. *Flea* (Weatherford), Apr. 15, 1869; "Flutsch Statement," Rathjen Papers, BTHC; J. Marvin Hunter, Sr., "Old Fort McKavett," *Frontier Times* 31 (1954): 204.

CHAPTER SEVEN

Uniforms and Weapons

. . . the costume as truly serviceable as it is unmilitary.

—Capt. Edmund Kirby Smith

Reinforced by lavishly illustrated books and western movies, the popular image of regular soldiers during the nineteenth century often brings to mind neatly clad individuals armed with the most up-to-date weapons of the time. The picture is vivid: blue-coated soldiers firing repeating rifles and six-guns at scantily clad Indian warriors carrying an array of bows, arrows, spears, tomahawks, and Winchester rifles. This vision is a far cry from reality, however. Changes in military fashion, the tremendous expense of arming and equipping even a small force, and the inbred conservatism of many army officials presented huge obstacles to efficiency and effectiveness in military weapons and uniforms. Not surprisingly, the lowly frontier regular bore the brunt of such problems.

After rations and housing, uniforms drew the heaviest criticism from nineteenth-century observers of daily military life. Realizing that neat, serviceable uniforms would encourage esprit de corps in the ranks, even the most hardened War Department bureaucrats recognized the validity of many of the criticisms. As a result, the Quartermaster Department, responsible for clothing the nation's soldiers, periodically organized boards of officers to select uniforms and articles of equipment. Particularly important were decisions made by such groups in 1851 and 1872, although less celebrated modifications were made throughout the era. In theory, these changes represented a sincere effort to improve the quality of life for the common soldier; in practice, the constant adjustments often meant confusion, waste, and needless expense.

In 1851 a board of officers completely revised uniform regulations. The frock coat was to be of dark-blue cloth with a skirt extending to midthigh. Enlisted men and company officers (lieutenants and captains) were to wear single-breasted jackets, with two rows of buttons distinguishing the higher grades. The trousers,

formerly blue gray, would be sky blue, with senior officers wearing a darker shade. Color variations in trim, collars, and piping marked the various service branches: scarlet for artillery, light blue for infantry, green for mounted riflemen, and orange for dragoons. The cap, or, more properly, shako, was of dark-blue cloth and had a leather visor with a pompon and a lower strip of material colored according to the branch of service.[1]

In addition to colors, markings distinguished rank and unit. The enlisted man wore plain yellow buttons stamped with letters (*A, I, R,* or *D*), according to service branch. Gilt buttons of a slightly larger size (one-half to seven-eighths inch in diameter) adorned the officer's jacket. Epaulets carried his badge of rank; chevrons sewed above the elbow on both sleeves of the uniform coat distinguished the corporal and the sergeant from other enlisted personnel. A noncommissioned veteran also boasted a diagonal half chevron below the elbow for every five years of service. Officers wore glittering arrays of yellow and gold embroidery; further detail identified members of ordnance, medical, engineer, quartermaster, inspector general, adjutant general, judge advocate, and subsistence departments. The regimental or company letter was emblazoned on the front of the shako. To save money, the new outfits were to serve as both dress and fatigue uniforms.

In an effort to ensure better-quality craftsmanship than had been possible under the contract system, the new patterns were crafted at government arsenals in Philadelphia and New York City and were sent out to seamstresses for finishing. Although this practice seemed guaranteed to yield a better product, the elaborate specifications of 1851 soon proved inadequate. The worsted epaulets were impractical; not surprisingly, the brass shoulder scales offered in their place were equally cumbersome. The long jacket, while well suited for foot soldiers, made sitting in a saddle uncomfortable. In 1854 shorter shell jackets previously issued to officers for stable duty replaced the longer coats as official uniforms for mounted men.

Of special importance to troops serving in Texas was the proper selection of headgear. Virtually everyone recognized that the 1851 shako was totally inadequate. Officers and inspectors complained that the small visor afforded little protection from the Texas sun, and they demanded a more suitable replacement. Thanks to the quick action of Col. William Harney, the Second Dragoon Regiment secured a special shipment of 445 floppy hats found in storage in Philadelphia. These proved superior to the official shako, but there were not enough to furnish all the troops stationed in the Lone Star State. A less than adequate replacement came in 1855 with the substitution of the "Jeff Davis" hat for the shako. Reputedly designed by Secretary of War Jefferson Davis for the mounted regiments authorized that year, the new oval hat was made of black felt and had

1. The 1851 regulations are printed in Randy Steffen, *The Horse Soldier, 1776–1943; The United States Cavalryman: His Uniforms, Arms, Accoutrements, and Equipments,* vol. 2, *The Frontier, the Mexican War, the Civil War, the Indian Wars, 1851–1881* (Norman: University of Oklahoma Press, 1978), pp. 6–15.

A VARIETY OF HEADGEAR — RANGING FROM SHAKOS AND FORAGE CAPS TO STRAW HATS AND PRUSSIAN STYLE HELMENTS — SAW USE AT NINETEENTH-CENTURY TEXAS FORTS.

a three-and-one-fourth-inch brim and a six-and-one-fourth-inch crown. The right brim was turned up; ostrich feathers decorated the new design. At about the same time yellow was adopted as the official trim for the new cavalry branch.

The stiff new Jeff Davis hat left much to be desired. One veteran claimed that "If the whole earth had been ransacked, it is difficult to tell where a more ungainly piece of furniture could have been found." In yet another futile effort to solve the problem, the army began issuing new forage caps in late 1858. The dark-blue caps resembled poor second cousins of the elegant French kepi and were often referred to as "bummer's caps" during the Civil War. In response to complaints chin straps were added to the caps worn by mounted men.[2]

Troops guarding Texas during the Civil War faced even greater obstacles in securing adequate clothing. The vast majority of those serving on the frontiers remained in state rather than Confederate service. A lucky few obtained what little provisions the state made available. Most, however, depended on private sources. Some state units were outfitted with donations of socks, shirts, trousers, and coats collected by their respective communities. Others received supplies from friends and relatives. Many had to make do with what they had brought with them upon entering military service. Generally these makeshift provisions failed to meet wartime needs, and in desperate efforts to secure proper clothing, officers detailed men to return home to pick up replacements.

Soldiers in the federal service after the Civil War fared better than their southern counterparts, though their condition could be said to have improved only in comparison to the low standards of earlier times. An inventory of quartermaster's supplies taken in June, 1865, showed that bulging warehouses included 297,000 shell jackets, 361,000 pairs of cavalry trousers, 890,000 forage caps, and more than 1 million sack coats. With Congress eager to reduce spending and army quartermaster officials eager to balance their inventories, it seemed that the Civil War surplus would be more than adequate to meet the army's needs for years to come.

Regular troops stationed in Texas rarely reached the same conclusion. To meet the needs of a one-million-man force, the army had turned to private contractors during the Civil War. While some of these businessmen had delivered high-quality products, virtually every soldier found serious flaws in the contract uniforms. The more brazen suppliers increased their profits by using cheap materials; craftier contractors turned a larger profit by making the uniforms smaller than specified by army regulations, thus reducing the amount of material used in each outfit. Defects in dyes, colors, craftsmanship, and storage took a further toll in terms of aesthetics, comfort, and durability.

---

2. Albert G. Brackett, *History of the U.S. Cavalry* (1865; reprint, New York: Argonaut Press, 1965), pp. 160–61; Steffen, *Horse Soldier*, 2:42–43; Robert M. Utley, *Frontier Regulars: The United States Army and the Indian, 1866–1891* (New York: Macmillan Co., 1973), p. 75; Gordon Chappell, *Search for the Well-dressed Soldier, 1865–1890: Developments and Innovations in United States Army Uniforms on the Western Frontier*, Museum Monograph no. 5 (Arizona Historical Society, 1972), p. 8.

By 1872 mounting shortages in the more common uniform sizes led a new board of officers to make sweeping changes in the regulation dress. Most striking were the new spiked dress helmets, similar to those popularized in Prussia. The new parade headgear bore a large metal eagle and a striking horsehair plume. The plumes matched the service colors, which had been simplified during the Civil War—yellow for cavalry, red for artillery. Infantrymen received a redesigned shako with a light-blue plume for officers and a matching pompon for enlisted personnel (the foot soldiers were not authorized to wear the spiked helmets until 1881; their plumes were white). Forage caps were trimmer than the older issues, and all troops received new broad-brimmed black felt hats. Yellow, red, and sky-blue trim distinguished the various branches of the army; officers received spectacular dress jackets with gold cords, tassels, epaulets, and brass buttons. The new garments were made at government depots across the country.[3]

Although the 1872 uniforms made for a smarter military appearance, the new outfits once again proved less than perfect. The campaign hats quickly lost their shape and disintegrated in the rain. The new jackets, based on a recommendation by a medical team in 1868, adopted a Swiss-style pleated fatigue pattern. Soldiers viewed the new coats as completely unacceptable. In 1873 one soldier described the strange garb in a letter to the military service paper, the *Army and Navy Journal:* "To the military mind the 'ruffled Blouse' is an object of utter disgust and loathing. When received, it is a shapeless mass, and when the unsuspecting votary of Mars is inducted into it, it converts him into a shapeless mass, destroying in him all resemblance to anything either in nature or art, and so transmogrifying him that his own mother would fail to recognize him."[4] In 1874 plainer sack coats, with five buttons for cavalry and nine for infantry, replaced the pleated jackets. The discarded blouses, along with the older hats and miscellaneous equipment that had remained in storage, were issued to Indian prisoners and scouts or sold for what little they could bring on the open market.

Official regulations provided for a uniform allowance for every soldier. A typical post–Civil War allowance included one overcoat, two dress coats, three woolen blouses, three fatigue blouses, seven pairs of uniform trousers, seven dark-blue woolen shirts, seven pairs of kersey trousers, three pairs of fatigue pants, a like number of overalls, nine undershirts and drawers, thirty-six linen collars, twelve pairs each of woolen and cotton socks, nine pairs of shoes, four fatigue caps, three campaign hats, two helmets, two woolen blankets, twenty-four pairs of white gloves, and three pairs of suspenders. A cavalryman was also issued a gutta-percha talma-style rain cape, which was subsequently replaced by a rubber poncho. The horse soldiers finally secured leather gauntlets in 1884.[5]

3. The regulations are printed in Steffen, *Horse Soldier,* 2:107–13. Utley, *Frontier Regulars,* p. 76; Erna Risch, *Quartermaster Support of the Army: A History of the Corps, 1775–1939* (Washington, D.C.: U.S. Government Printing Office, 1960), p. 502.

4. Quoted in Steffen, *Horse Soldier,* 2:125–27.

5. George A. Forsyth, *The Story of the Soldier* (New York: D. Appleton and Co., 1900), pp.

Uniforms came in four sizes during the Civil War, and a fifth was added in the postwar period to meet demands for larger uniforms. Since calls for certain measurements inevitably exceeded the supply, securing a decent fit became problematic even in the best of circumstances. The contractors' tendency to make clothing smaller than called for by regulations compounded the problems. Enlisted men paid fellow soldiers acting as company tailors to alter their outfits, leading the quartermaster general to blame the shortage of larger sizes on troops who allegedly ordered bigger uniforms to allow for alterations. Whatever the case, striking variations in appearance resulted. Some men preferred natty, tight-fitting garments; others opted for looser, more comfortable cuts. The constant modifications in the official pattern added to the mix. Shirts and trousers of various shades and jackets of different lengths with fading trim made for still greater diversity.

Modifications in the cloth, style, cut, and pattern of the jackets reflected fluctuations in military fashion as well as attempts to adapt uniforms to frontier conditions. Officials realized that woolen uniforms hardly suited Texas summers, and post surgeons oversaw a series of experiments in military dress. Some relief came in 1871, when the secretary of war gave troops in the Department of Texas official permission to wear straw hats and lightweight white trousers during the summer. Unfortunately, soldiers had to pay for the cooler garb with their own money. Brown canvas fatigues underwent trials during the 1880s. Cotton garments were eventually distributed to the men in Texas as well as in the Departments of Arizona and Missouri.

Cork summer helmets covered with white drill cloth were also issued. The helmet was lined with green cloth around the underside of the visor to reduce the glare; a cork washer provided circulation by separating the interior leather sweatband from the body of the helmet. Another hole at the top, covered with a screw-on perforated cap, allowed more ventilation. Better than earlier headgear, the white cork helmet still had its share of critics. Various styles of broad-brimmed hats continued to appear in the field, although the new helmets proved adequate for garrison duty.

Similar to contemporary British helmets worn in India and Africa, the new headgear undoubtedly served the needs of Texas soldiers better than had former articles of issue. Even so, changes in regulations often meant little to troops stationed along the frontiers. Plagued by budgetary constraints, Washington officials ordered post quartermasters to issue whatever supplies they had on hand before making new requisitions. While army rules stipulated that an outfit's uniforms should not include articles from different regulation patterns, such a policy proved impossible to enforce in practice. "Company K in the new uniform & M in the old," reported Col. J. K. F. Mansfield of the Fourth Artillery units stationed at Fort Brown in 1856. And of the 251 men appearing for his inspection

94–95; Fort Duncan Manuscripts, 1859, packet 14, BTHC; Steffen, *Horse Soldier*, 4:99; Utley, *Frontier Regulars*, p. 77.

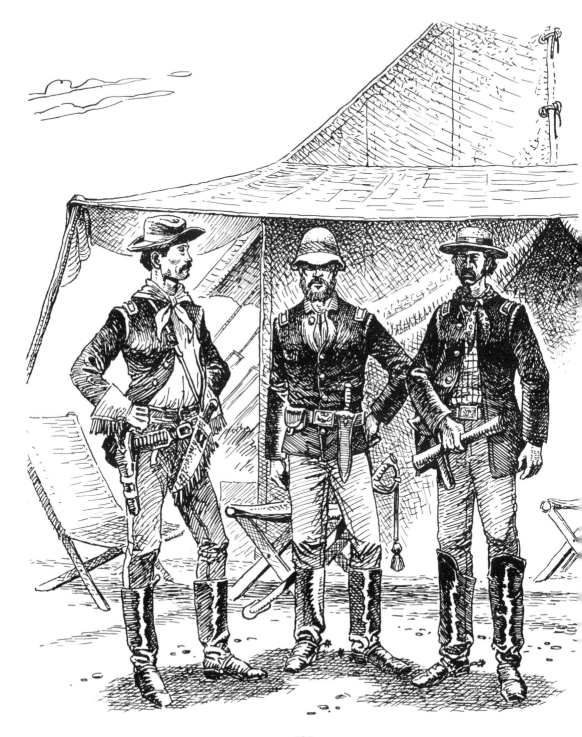

of Fort Davis later that year, 149 had no caps. Three of the six companies there also reported shortages of canteens and trousers.[6]

The hard service in Texas necessitated further changes. Most officers recognized the need for alterations in the official dress and did not demand uniformity in campaign dress. Regulation hats generally proved the first to go as soldiers purchased more serviceable wide-brimmed slouch hats on the open market. Blue or dark-gray flannel hunting shirts studded wtih pockets also served as substitutes for heavy woolen coats. White jeans occasionally replaced regulation uniform trousers. Brightly colored handkerchiefs rounded out the average soldier's daily garb, complete uniforms usually being reserved for dress parade. During the winter troops made or purchased their own mittens, heavy gloves, leggings, and other cold-weather gear, for Texas-based troops rarely received the army's winter outfits of buffalo fur.[7]

Weapons proved a similar problem for the U.S. Army. Rapid technological advances during the latter half of the nineteenth century made necessary several changes in the military's regulation arms. Again, however, questions of cost and taste presented serious considerations for Ordnance Department boards studying possible improvements. Added to these issues were problems of doctrine: What was the army's main function? Was its chief task subjugating Indians or preventing an armed invasion by a foreign power? Should it adopt expensive repeating weapons, which often jammed and used up large amounts of ammunition, or should it retain more dependable single-shot arms, which had greater range but took much longer to load and fire?[8]

In 1841 the army began production on its first percussion musket. A great improvement over the old flintlock, the 1841-model .69-caliber smoothbore musket was used well into the 1850s by foot soldiers. The pulled hammer of the weapon struck a fulminate cap, which ignited a flame in the main charge, hurling a round shot at the target. In 1855, with the aid of the designs of Claude E. Minié, a captain in the French army, the smoothbores were rifled, converted to .58 caliber, and equipped with attachments for a 22½-inch saber-bayonet. The spinning action that resulted from the rifling gave the ball greater velocity and accuracy. Older

6. M. L. Crimmins, ed., "Colonel J. K. F. Mansfield's Report of the Inspection of the Department of Texas in 1856," *Southwestern Historical Quarterly* 42 (Jan., 1939): 217; *Southwestern Historical Quarterly* 42 (Apr., 1939): 352–53.

7. M. L. Crimmins, ed., "W. G. Freeman's Report on the Eighth Military Department," *Southwestern Historical Quarterly* 54 (Oct., 1950): 210; Robert M. Utley, *Frontiersmen in Blue: The United States Army and the Indian, 1848–1865* (1967; reprint, Lincoln: University of Nebraska Press, 1981), pp. 24–25; Risch, *Quartermaster Support*, pp. 302–303; Don Rickey, Jr., *Forty Miles a Day on Beans and Hay: The Enlisted Soldier Fighting the Indian Wars, 1865–1890* (Norman: University of Oklahoma Press, 1963), p. 217.

8. Allan R. Millett and Peter Maslowski, *For the Common Defense: A Military History of the United States of America* (New York: Free Press, 1984), pp. 233–67, gives a good account.

smoothbores had an effective range of one hundred to two hundred yards; the rifled weapons were accurate at four hundred to six hundred yards.

Although the new Minié rifles were easier to load than the rifles of earlier days, they were difficult to operate under combat conditions. To load and fire his weapon, the soldier stood the rifle up and took from his pouch a cartridge consisting of a cone-shaped bullet and powder wrapped in paper. Biting open the paper, he jammed the cartridge and bullet down the barrel with the ramrod. After cocking the rifle, he placed an explosive cap beneath the hammer. Finally, he aimed and pulled the trigger. As in the percussion musket, the small explosion triggered by the hammer set off a larger explosion in the chamber, driving a small iron plug into the conical Minié ball, forcing it to expand into the rifled grooves of the bore. In the new rifle, however, the bullet spiraled out of the barrel. A good soldier might get off two or three rounds a minute.

During the Civil War the introduction of breech-loading arms and metallic cartridges greatly improved the rifleman's speed and accuracy. Fixed ammunition allowed him to load a shell directly at the breech without the gyrations required by the old muzzle-loaders. The metallic cartridges provided greater velocity and accuracy. The army converted about 50,000 of the old Civil War–issue Springfield rifles into breechloaders after the war, reducing the caliber from .58 to .50 in the process.[9]

In the meantime cavalry arms had also undergone a transformation. Mounted men carried three basic weapons: a lightweight musket or carbine, a revolver or pistol, and a saber or long hunting knife. While the edged weapons were a source of great pride to traditionalists, they usually got in the way when the men were on active duty. As time went on, more and more men left the longer weapons in the barracks in favor of shorter, handier knives.

Cavalry firearms, on the other hand, became increasingly deadly as designers built lighter and more efficient weapons. In 1847, after searching for a weapon that a man could carry and if need be fire from horseback, the army had adopted the musketoon. This piece of equipment engendered universal criticism. One inspector deemed it "utterly unreliable for almost any range." Another veteran described it as "a sort of brevet musket . . . sawed off to about two-thirds of its original length . . . [that] kicked like blazes."[10]

Carbines proved much more suitable for the horse soldiers. Particularly notable was the Sharps carbine, which had been issued to several companies by 1858. Originally a breechloader, the Sharps was altered to a .50-caliber metallic-cartridge system during and after the Civil War. Even more powerful was the Spencer carbine, developed as a .50-caliber repeater that could fire seven rounds

9. Utley, *Frontier Regulars*, pp. 72–73; Emory M. Thomas, *The American War and Peace, 1860–1877* (Englewood Cliffs, N.J.: Prentice-Hall, Inc., 1973), 71–72.

10. James E. Hicks, *U.S. Military Firearms, 1776–1956* (Alhambra, Calif.: Borden Publishing Co., 1962), pp. 72–75; Crimmins, ed., "Freeman's Report," p. 206; Zenas R. Bliss Reminiscences, 1:143–44, BTHC.

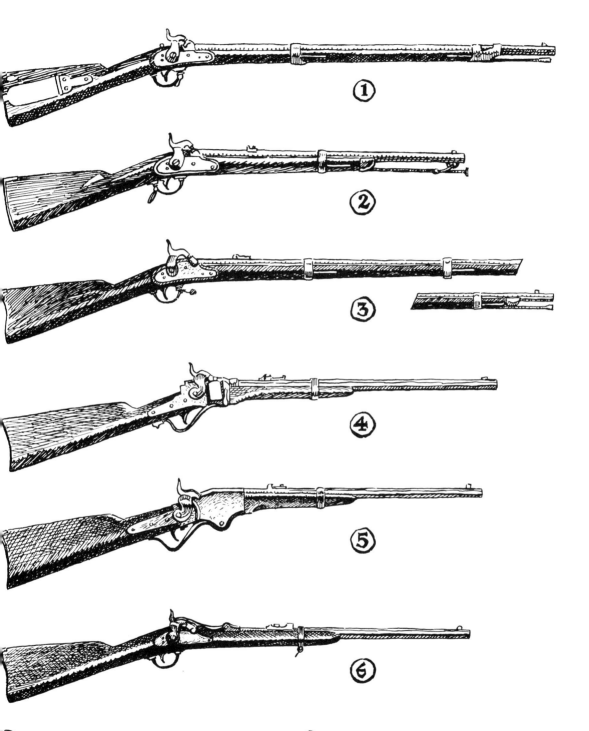

① – 1841 TYRON "MISSISSIPPI RIFLE" ; ② – 1854 SPRINGFIELD CARBINE ;
③ – 1861 SPRINGFIELD RIFLE ; ④ – 1863 SHARPS CARBINE ;
⑤ – 1865 SPENCER CARBINE ; ⑥ – 1873 SPRINGFIELD CARBINE

without reloading. On several occasions during the Civil War and the Indian Wars, dismounted troopers firing the deadly Spencer unleashed sustained and devastating volleys that mowed down surprised enemies.

Pistols also became more effective. The Colt six-shooter, issued in 1849, was popularized by Texas Rangers during the Mexican War. Using a cap-and-ball mechanism, the Colt nonetheless gave the regulars a handgun that could fire six shots in rapid succession. Some of the new cavalry units raised in 1855 received an unwieldy pistol-carbine. Featuring a removable stock, the weapon was designed to take the place of separate pistol and carbine for mounted troops. It never gained the approval of the men, however, and was soon traded in for more conventional arms.

In 1872 rapid technological change and the depletion of Civil War surplus stocks demanded that the army again consider the question of effective firearms. Under the guidance of its president, Gen. Alfred Terry, the appointed board of officers tested more than one hundred types of breech-loading systems. The resulting 1873 Springfield rifles and carbines provided the army's basic armament for the next twenty years. While the Springfield fired only a single shot, the durability and accuracy of the .45-caliber gun won much praise.[11]

At about the same time the Colt 1873 revolvers replaced the older cap-and-ball pistols. The first metallic-cartridge sidearms issued in large quantities to regular troops, the heavy .45-caliber revolvers had barrels nearly seven and one-half inches long. Army men often referred to the Colt as the "Thumb-buster"; lawmen knew it as the "Peacemaker" or "Equalizer." Unsurpassed in close combat, the piece remained the standard cavalry handgun until the 1890s.[12]

While the army opted for the single-shot rifles and carbines, growing numbers of Indians obtained newer repeating weapons, including the Winchester rifle. While most Indians had to be satisfied with whatever they could get their hands on, illegal traders (often called Comancheros) supplied significant numbers of these deadly weapons to hostile tribesmen. The prospect of swarms of Indians loosing continuous volleys against regulars armed with only single-shot firearms worried many army men, particularly after the debacle at the Little Bighorn. The Ordnance Department, however, clung to the time-tested Springfields, arguing that the single-shot weapon had one hundred yards' greater range and 50 percent more penetrating power. Ever mindful of financial considerations, advocates also pointed out that the Springfield used less ammunition and appeared less likely to jam under combat conditions. Only in 1892, with the adoption of the Krag-Jorgensen .30-caliber magazine rifle, did the army move away from the trusty Springfields.[13]

As with uniforms, however, weapons regulations could not always be fol-

---

11. Hicks, *U.S. Military Firearms*, pp. 245–51; Steffen, *Horse Soldier*, 2:51, 75–77; Brackett, *History of the U.S. Cavalry*, pp. 166–67; Utley, *Frontiersmen in Blue*, pp. 26–27.

12. Ernest Lisle Reedstrom, *Bugles, Banners, and War Bonnets* (Caldwell, Idaho: Caxton Printers, 1977), pp. 263–65; Steffen, *Horse Soldier*, 2:155.

13. Utley, *Frontier Regulars*, pp. 72–74. For a somewhat different view see Reedstrom, *Bugles, Banners, and War Bonnets*, pp. 249–58. Rickey, *Forty Miles a Day*, is also helpful.

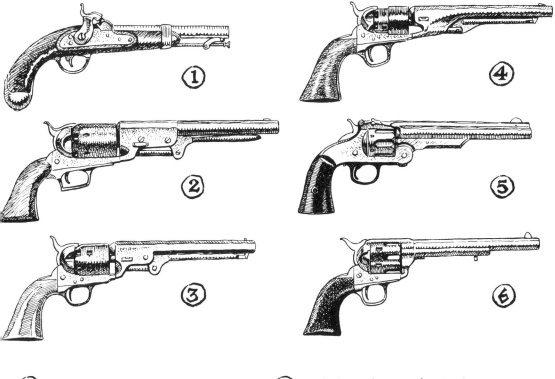

① - 1842 HORSE PISTOL
② - 1847 COLT "WALKER"
③ - 1851 COLT NAVY
④ - 1860 COLT ARMY
⑤ - 1869 SMITH AND WESSON
⑥ - 1873 COLT "PEACEMAKER"

lowed on the Texas frontiers. Inspector W. G. Freeman's report on his tour of the Lone Star State in 1853 serves as a good example. At a temporary post on the Rio Grande opposite the Mexican town Guerrero, he found Company F of the Regiment of Mounted Rifles. All sixty-nine members of the rank and file he found there had rifles, though many pieces needed repair. Yet only thirty-six had the Colt six-shooter; an equal number had older horsemen's pistols. At Fort Ewell, Freeman found other elements of the same regiment. "The three companies are not armed in the same manner," Freeman explained, "Company E having a hunting knife which is not furnished to the other two. Each soldier has a rifle, but only forty Colt's Revolver pistols are provided for a company, which does not give one per man."[14]

As might be expected, the Texans guarding the state's western and southern frontiers during the Civil War fared even worse. In 1865 two companies at Camp

14. M. L. Crimmins, ed., "Freeman's Report," *Southwestern Historical Quarterly* 52 (Jan., 1949): 350; *Southwestern Historical Quarterly* 51 (Jan., 1948): 255.

Colorado scraped together fifty six-shooters and fifty-four shotguns and adequate supplies of ammunition for both kinds of weapons. Only two rounds, however, were available for the battalion's five Enfield rifles. Four rounds could be found to fit the outfit's one Springfield rifle; the three Sharps carbines on hand had only five rounds.[15]

Similar changes and supply difficulties affected the soldier's official equipment. Belts, cartridge boxes, cap pouches, canteens, haversacks, and knapsacks provided limited capacity for ammunition, food, clothing, and miscellaneous tools. Black-leather cartridge boxes had originally been designed for paper cartridges; sheepskin lining was later added to muffle the clatter of metal after the introduction of the new cartridges. Individual alterations were made, however, as frontier infantrymen sought to redistribute weight and ease access to their ammunition. So-called prairie belts of canvas loops sewed to a leather backing were in use long before the Ordnance Department authorized their issue in 1876. The older cartridge boxes and pouches sometimes proved handy for carrying extra food, but most soldiers discarded the accoutrements as excess weight.

Particularly important to Texas-based soldiers were a good canteen and a reliable carrying bag. In 1851 the army issued wooden canteens at San Antonio on a trial basis. Shortly thereafter India-rubber canteens were distributed at Fort Gates. Further experiments followed as the army searched for a proper container. Finally, a kersey-cloth-covered tin canteen proved superior and remained the standard issue for the rest of the century. Many troopers discarded their knapsacks in favor of haversacks. Made of cloth painted black, the knapsacks underwent a chemical decomposition that over time softened the black paint into a gluelike substance.

Army footwear was of notoriously poor quality. Before the Civil War the army produced boots for the cavalrymen and shoes for the foot soldiers at its Schuylkill Arsenal, in Philadelphia. Wartime demands led the military to find civilian suppliers to fill its needs. The shoddy workmanship and inferior-quality materials that marked the contract uniforms also characterized the privately made shoes and boots, though the wartime adoption of separate patterns for left and right feet added a degree of comfort. Dissatisfied with the efforts of American private enterprise, the army began making shoes and boots at Leavenworth during the mid-1870s. Yet not until the 1890s did extensive testing produce markedly better designs. In the meantime, many soldiers opted for moccasins or individually purchased footwear.[16]

According to regulations, the infantryman's campaign gear was packed in a knapsack supported by twin shoulder harnesses. Bayonet and extra cartridges hung from a leather waistbelt. Full field equipment, including sixty rounds of

15. T. R. Havins, *Camp Colorado: A Decade of Frontier Defense* (Brownwood, Tex.: Brown Press, 1964), p. 159.

16. Sidney B. Brinckerhoff, *Boots and Shoes of the Frontier Soldier, 1865–1903*, Museum Monograph no. 7 (Arizona Historical Society).

ammunition, overcoat, gray wool blanket, rubber ground cloth, rifle, extra clothes, full canteen, and five days' rations, weighed about fifty pounds. The veteran, of course, soon reduced his burden. A blanket roll was much lighter than the cumbersome knapsack, which he left at the post with his bayonet and most of his extra clothing. Tents and the larger cooking gear were stowed on pack mules or wagons. A man might jam a few articles on the supply train if he could find room or had connections with the packers. Inevitably unnecessary articles were strewn in the column's wake as soldiers jettisoned coats, mess gear, cartridge boxes, and brass uniform adornments to reduce their loads. Discarding them, of course, meant that the men might have to purchase replacements out of their own pockets. Such were the dilemmas of the infantry.[17]

Cavalrymen faced many of the same quandaries, though the equipment differed. Little agreement about a proper cavalry saddle could be reached until 1859, when Capt. George B. McClellan, having made an intensive survey of European armies, accoutrements, and cavalry equipment, secured the adoption of the so-called McClellan saddle. The basic pattern, with minor changes in design and material, was used by the army for the next eighty-four years. The saddle included a beechwood saddletree with iron blue buckles, two thick harness leather skirts, two hickory or oak stirrups, one girth and girth strap of blue-wool webbing, a surcingle, and a crupper.

With proper care the McClellan was among the world's finest military saddles. Even so, several flaws detracted from its suitability for Texas cavalry. Many troopers believed that the saddlebags were too small. Veterans also complained about the lack of a breast strap, for the crupper and surcingle often failed to hold the saddle securely on the animal's back. The hooded stirrups, while providing protection from heavy brush and cold winter winds, posed an obstacle for an inexperienced rider, who often got a foot stuck between the stirrup and the hood.[18]

Stowing most of his belongings in his twin saddlebags and haversacks behind his saddle, the mounted soldier rolled up his blanket in front and did the same thing with his overcoat in the rear. Lariat, picket pin, drinking cup, and canteen hung from the saddle. A cartridge belt around his waist held his ammunition. His sword jangled from straps at his left hip, and his pistol rested in a leather holster on the right. A special sling across his left shoulder held his carbine, which rested muzzle down in a saddle socket just below his right leg. Full combat equipment, including five days' rations and fifteen pounds of oats, totaled about one hundred pounds.

Practicality, however, demanded certain changes in the uniform and equipment called for by official regulations. The heavy sabers seemed a needless burden and were often left in the barracks. In place of the graceful swords most troopers carried simple knives. Carbines seemed precariously balanced in saddle

---

17. Rickey, *Forty Miles a Day*, pp. 221–24, 123–28; Utley, *Frontier Regulars*, pp. 77–78.

18. Reedstrom, *Bugles, Banners, and War Bonnets*, pp. 220–23; Brackett, *History of the U.S. Cavalry*, p. 161.

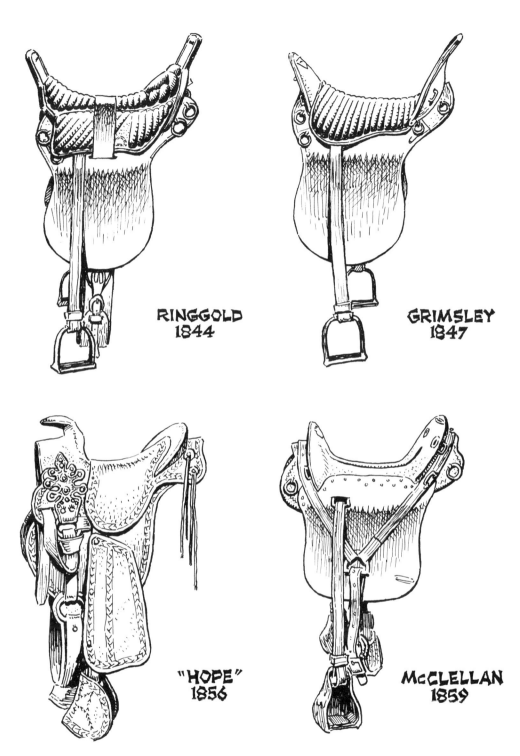

RINGGOLD
1844

GRIMSLEY
1847

"HOPE"
1856

McCLELLAN
1859

IN 1859 THE POPULAR "HOPE" OR "TEXAS MODEL," MADE BY
THE SAN ANTONIO FIRM OF RICE AND CHILDRESS, WAS RE-
JECTED IN FAVOR OF CAPTAIN GEORGE B. MCCLELLAN'S DESIGN

sockets, and soldiers complained bitterly about the difficulties of mounting with the seven-and-one-half-pound rifles slung to their backs. Trousers were tucked under calf-length boots, and overcoats or ponchos were stuffed under the saddle for extra padding.[19]

Such adjustments meant that few soldiers stationed along the Texas frontiers wore complete uniforms. They collected shirts, trousers, bags, hats, and miscellaneous gear that seemed better suited to the Texas environment than regulation equipment. Edmund Kirby Smith described his scouting garb to his mother:

> Mounted on my mule—(the dearest, gentlest, and most intelligent brute)— small but round, fat as a dumpling, with sleek coat, bright eyes and two well developed and expressive ears, actively moving in every direction and speaking as plain[ly] as an alphabet; corduroy pants; a hickory or blue flannel shirt, cut down in front, studded with pockets and worn outside; a slouched hat and long beard, cavalry boots worn over the pants, knife and revolver belted to the side and a double barrel gun across the pommel, complete the costume as truly serviceable as it is unmilitary.[20]

The official changes and alterations in uniforms and equipment during the latter half of the nineteenth century made it difficult for the army to supply every frontier soldier with every article of the most recent issue. The shortage and slowness of army transportation meant obvious problems. Financial considerations also affected the Texas troops—the army could rarely afford to buy or produce uniforms, guns, and accoutrements in quantities sufficient to supply all of its troops immediately. Instead, it purchased the new items of issue slowly, phasing out older, worn-out pieces as replacements became available. Thus one company might get new pistols before another company of the same regiment.

The army also experienced severe problems in trying to design issue articles to fit the needs of all its scattered troops. Wool jackets that seemed perfectly suitable for cool autumn evenings in the Dakotas were ludicrous to a soldier sweating in the heat at Ringgold Barracks. Seasonal uniforms were the obvious, but expensive, answer. With Congress continuously paring the army's budget, such specialization seemed an unnecessary luxury during most of the frontier period.

---

19. Rickey, *Forty Miles a Day*, p. 219; Reedstrom, *Bugles, Banners, and War Bonnets*, pp. 227–28; *Ordnance Memoranda No. 29: Horse Equipment and Cavalry Accoutrements, As Prescribed by G. O. 73, A.G.O. 1885* (Pasadena, Calif.: Socio-Technical Publications, 1970), intro. by James S. Hutchins.

20. Parkes, *General Edmund Kirby Smith*, pp. 90–91.

CHAPTER·EIGHT

Life in the Field

Very discouraging.

–Lt. Col. Robert E. Lee

The annexation of Texas in 1845 created complex problems for United States military planners. Officials soon realized that the small regular establishment could not guard each settlement along the ever-changing frontiers. In addition, the great distances between the largest bases meant that both Indians and whites could pass undetected by army patrols. Recognizing the failure of traditional defensive lines, a number of officers hoped to abandon the smaller posts and concentrate troops at important strategic points. From these central positions commanders could send regular patrols and expeditions into Indian lands. By showing the country's military might, it was believed, such columns would persuade the Indians to give up armed resistance.

In line with these theories the army launched many campaigns against hostile tribes throughout the 1850s. Yet there were not enough troops to make a distinct impression, and even mounted regiments found that catching the fleet warriors of the southern plains was a tremendously difficult undertaking. Upon learning that they were being pursued, many bands scattered, leaving little trace of their movements. Larger groups found it tempting to head for Mexico or the Indian territory, where they were generally safe from army columns. Usually the regulars came up empty-handed.

As small western columns chased their elusive foes, it became increasingly apparent that it would be politically impossible to abandon many of the army's frontier bases. Instead of being gathered at a few large posts, most troops thus continued to be scattered in small contingents across the country. In Texas complications increased as settlers pushing north and west forced more tribes across the Red River and the Rio Grande. When the Indians fought back, whites attributed every crime and depredation to them. In the face of the growing public outcry, state and federal authorities called for the vigilant pursuit of every Indian trail. "In following Indians, the pursuit must never be given up as long as men

and horses are able to pursue," read a typical order issued in June, 1861. "They should be caught at all hazards." Of course, commanders quickly found that it was much easier to give such orders than to carry them out. The violence continued, and the Indians often gained the upper hand in Texas during the Civil War.[1]

1. Zenas R. Bliss Reminiscences, 2:158, BTHC; Special Order No. 40, June 18, 1861, James B. Barry Papers, BTHC.

When Union forces reoccupied the Lone Star State in the summer of 1865, Texans shared their fellow southerners' bitter resentment against Reconstruction troops. At the same time northern officers discounted reports of frontier raids. In command of the Fifth Military District (Texas and Louisiana), a wary Philip Sheridan suspected that "the secret of all this fuss about Indian trouble is the desire to have all the troops removed from the interior." Commanding General William Tecumseh Sherman also doubted the veracity of reported Indian depredations until his dramatic inspection of Texas in 1871. Sherman and his small escort were spotted by an Indian war party about eight miles west of Fort Richardson. Fortunately for Sherman, the hidden warriors allowed his entourage to pass unscathed, electing instead to annihilate an upcoming supply train. Lucky to have retained his scalp, the commanding general learned of the attack on the supply train after reaching Fort Richardson.[2]

The aggressive Sheridan, finally convinced of the need for action, determined to strike a crushing blow. Yet demands for permission to launch retaliatory strikes into Indian-held territory at first fell on deaf ears in the Department of the Interior, where the Office of Indian Affairs demanded more time to implement peaceful policies. As Indian raids into northern Texas became increasingly frequent in the early 1870s, attempts to track down hostile tribesmen proved fruitless. Not until 1874, after several false starts, did the War Department persuade Secretary of the Interior Columbus Delano and Commissioner of Indian Affairs E. P. Smith to allow soldiers to follow the Indian war parties wherever they went.

Realizing that they might not receive another such opportunity, Sheridan, Sherman, Gen. John Pope (commanding the Department of the Missouri), and Gen. Christopher C. Augur (commanding the Department of Texas) organized no less than five columns of two hundred to seven hundred men each to strike against suspected Indian haunts in the Staked Plains. Sheridan's intentions were clear: "We will keep at them so long as we have the authority & will be sure to get them in the end." Feuds between rival officers, supply failures, and a drought made campaigning especially difficult. Yet with a few brief respites, the beleaguered troops in the field fulfilled Sheridan's intentions. The bluecoats crisscrossed the Texas Panhandle; weary Indians, denied their traditional winter homes and short of supplies, surrendered by the hundreds throughout the spring and summer of 1875.[3]

Similar complications confused military operations along the Rio Grande. By the Treaty of Guadalupe Hidalgo the United States accepted responsibility for the actions of Indians living in Texas and the Mexican cession lands. Not surprisingly, however, the fiercely independent Apache and Kickapoo tribes living along the border saw little reason to respect the international boundaries of two foreign governments. The foot soldiers who garrisoned Forts Brown, Ringgold, McIntosh, Ewell, and Duncan found themselves powerless to stop the Indians, the horse and cattle thieves, or the revolutionaries who frequently crossed the river. Although the U.S. State Department had refused Mexico's call for in-

---

2. Sheridan to Grant, Oct. 12, 1866, Ulysses S. Grant Papers, Library of Congress (microfilm, University of Texas at Austin, ser. 5, vol. 54, reel 24); Capt. Robt. G. Carter, *On the Border with Mackenzie; Or, Winning West Texas from the Comanches* (Washington, D.C.: Enyon Printing Co., 1935), pp. 80–82.

3. Sheridan to Pope, July 24, box 56, Philip Sheridan Papers, Library of Congress; Augur to Sheridan, July 28, Sept. 13, Nov. 26, 1874, Letters Sent, Department of Texas, NA, RG 393. The best secondary account is in Robert M. Utley, *Frontier Regulars: The United States Army and the Indian, 1866–1891* (New York: Macmillan Co., 1973), pp. 225–41.

ternational cooperation in policing the border in 1850, at the end of the decade Lt. Col. Robert E. Lee concluded that the army's only hope of quelling the disturbances lay in entering Mexico. Yet even Lee admitted that his command's broken-down horses and the barren terrain south of the border "would defeat my object."[4]

Conditions along the Rio Grande were no better when the regular army returned in 1865. American authorities deemed Emperor Maximilian's regime in Mexico intolerable and assembled a large force along the border in an effective display of Yankee displeasure at renewed French involvement in the New World. Yet Mexican governments established in the wake of Maximilian's fall seemed, to Washington at least, increasingly incapable of preventing Indians from crossing the Rio Grande, making raids in Texas, and then recrossing the river to their homes south of the border. In a bold move Col. Ranald S. Mackenzie led a lightning strike across the Rio Grande on the night of May 17, 1873. In a grueling ride covering 160 miles in thirty-two hours, Mackenzie's four hundred troopers and twenty-five black Seminole scouts burned Kickapoo, Lipan, and Mescalero Apache villages at Remolino, forty miles inside Mexican territory, and returned virtually unscathed on May 19.

Although most of the Indian warriors were away from their camps, Mackenzie's terrible vengeance frightened most of the Kickapoos into returning north to Indian Territory. Lipan and Mescalero raids also diminished for a time. But depredations increased as Mackenzie's raid faded from memory. In 1876, Department of Texas Commander E. O. C. Ord instructed Lt. Col. William R. Shafter to cross the border on the trail of hostile bands. Shafter's Twenty-fourth Infantry immediately began scouring northern Coahuila. Despite a mild censure from Commanding General Sherman, Ord's initiative proved popular with Texans, whose continued support in Congress was essential to an army besieged by legislative attacks.

On June 1, 1877, President Rutherford B. Hayes formally recognized the doctrine of crossings in hot pursuit. Heated opposition from Porfirio Díaz's new government seriously endangered American troops on several such expeditions into Mexico. In fact, columns led by Shafter (1877) and Mackenzie (1878) encountered Mexican troops while they were south of the Rio Grande, but fortunately, war between the United States and Mexico was averted as increased Mexican efforts combined with those of U.S. troops—particularly Lt. John L. Bullis's company of black Seminole scouts—to halt Indian raids along the Rio Grande. President Hayes revoked the "Ord Order" in 1880.

Subsequent campaigns in Texas consisted largely of cleanup operations, patrols, and larger-scale efforts to quell incursions led by the dynamic Warm Springs Apache chief Victorio. After an unsuccessful transfer of five troops of the Tenth

---

4. Jerome A. Greene, "The Geronimo Affair: International Implications of the Geronimo Campaign," *Journal of the West* 2 (June, 1972): 143; Lee to Custis Lee, Apr. 16, 1860, in Adams, ed., "Lee Letters," p. 612.

Cavalry to New Mexico, Col. Benjamin Grierson insisted that his men be recalled to Texas in 1880. Grierson deployed his Tenth Cavalry, plus strong elements of the Twenty-fourth Infantry, at water holes north of the Rio Grande in the rugged trans-Pecos region. Victorio soon became entangled in skirmishes with troops holding the army outposts. Grierson himself directed the defense at Tinaja de las Palmas, in Quitman Canyon, where twenty-three soldiers and his teenaged son Robert thwarted an Apache attempt to reenter the Lone Star State. Another Apache war party was turned back by a mobile column, again led by Grierson,

at Rattlesnake Springs. Victorio was killed later that year by Mexican troops in Chihuahua. With his death the final major Indian threat in Texas came to an end.[5]

Throughout the nineteenth century military men and their dependents viewed their Indian foes with a mixture of racism, paternalism, and respect. Many un-

5. Utley, *Frontier Regulars*, pp. 369–73.

doubtedly agreed with Mrs. Teresa Vielé, who advocated extermination. In 1867, Yale-educated O. M. Knapp offered similar views in a letter to his mother: "The quicker *every* Sioux & Cheyenne & Apache, Comanche, Navajo, & Kiowa is killed & the *whole* of these tribes *exterminated, men, women & children*, the better it will be for humanity. They ought to be dealt with the same as wild animals and butchered or starved into complete annihilation. They are so untamable and treacherous as rattlesnakes & ought to be similarly dealt with."[6] Others, however, expressed concern for the fate of these native Americans. In 1858, for example, Bvt. Maj. Earl Van Dorn complained that the temporary Indian reserve set up at Camp Cooper was too small. As he explained: "It cannot reasonably be expected that they, as wild and as free as the eagle, would voluntarily shut themselves up in such a coop, or that they would be driven there without a violent struggle. Who would?" Benjamin Grierson, a veteran of twenty-five years' service in the Indian Territory, Texas, and Arizona, expressed the view held by many moderates when he stated that "a spirit of fairness & justice should prevail" in all affairs regarding Indians. Grierson and others also pointed to repeated reductions of reservation lands as a major source of dissatisfaction and distrust among the tribes.[7]

Yet few army men trusted the theories of Indian reformers, preferring that the military carry out Indian policy. Rarely acknowledging the Indians as equals, War Department officials maintained that the Indians, whom they perceived to have childlike intellects, needed government protection against the evil influences in American society. Given time, they might become hardworking independent farmers and stock raisers. Until that harmonious relationship could be achieved, however, army men argued, Indian affairs should be removed from the Department of the Interior and returned to the War Department, where they had been administered until 1849. In addition, Indians had to be shown the futility of military resistance. Sherman concluded that "these Indians must be terribly whipped before they can appreciate kindness."[8]

Soldiers usually had little time to prepare for field campaigns. Officers hurriedly assembled their commands in response to reported sightings of their elusive foes. If they were available, medical officers and one two-wheeled ambulance per company accompanied the column. The prospect that those who were leaving might never return gave a sober tone to preparations. The grim columns departed with little fanfare. If there was a post band, the soldiers marched off to the tune of "The Girl I Left behind Me."

6. Teresa Griffin Vielé, *Following the Drum: A Glimpse of Frontier Life* (1858; reprint, Lincoln: University of Nebraska Press, 1984), p. 121; Knapp to Mead, Oct. 3, 1867, Obadiah M. Knapp Papers, BTHC; Knapp to Mother, May 19, 1867, Knapp Papers.

7. Van Dorn to Withers, Dec. 28, SW, AR, 1858, p. 357; Report of Grierson, Sept. 1, SW, AR, 1889, p. 183.

8. Sherman to Tappan, Sept. 24, 1868, William T. Sherman Papers, Library of Congress (microfilm, University of Texas, vol. 90, reel 45). Thomas C. Leonard, *Above the Battle: War-Making in American from Appomattox to Versailles* (New York: Oxford University Press, 1978), pp. 43–58, gives a penetrating analysis of officers' views of Indians.

In reality, however, although the possibility of combat always existed, veterans knew that most parties never encountered any hostile Indians. Large numbers of men were more often dispatched to the field to guard stagecoaches, supply trains, and water holes. Others built roads and telegraphs. The immediate prospect of several days or weeks without alcohol seemed the most immediate problem. Risking severe punishment, some of the men filled their canteens with whiskey instead of water. Others, having imbibed too heavily the night before departure, struggled to overcome hangovers, stubborn mules, and undisciplined horses. At least one animal usually managed to throw its load, adding to the general disorder.

Other problems arose as the departing troops took the field. The few well-conditioned companies quickly outdistanced their less-than-ready comrades. After a hot march toward the Rio Grande one writer recounted his astonishment when he observed members of a Twenty-fourth Infantry battalion turning out for additional drill. Although white troops making the same march had "arrived in camp fagged out," Maj. Charles Bentzoni's black infantrymen engaged in a one-hour drill, "completing the manuevers by a grand charge on a neighboring hill which was taken with a rush amid great cheers." The observer's classically understated comment that "the tired white soldiers looked on with distinct disapproval" undoubtedly fails to capture the true animosity surrounding the occasion.[9]

Few officers asked their men to perform such antics on reaching camp, requiring only that they find water and grazing for the animals. Guards tied the horses and mules at a spot some distance away and then just before dusk brought them nearer camp for protection and fresh forage. Other troops built fires and began preparing the evening meal. A fortunate few had bread or biscuits baked in a Dutch oven—a cast-iron pot with three legs and a flat iron cover; many had to make do with hardtack and bacon. Hunting parties added game to the routine fare when they could find it. On such occasions "frying pans were in great demand" as the hungry men boiled, broiled, or fried the meat to suit their taste. Bunkies paired off and erected their small tents, sharing their single blankets in cold weather. With luck a beautiful moon inspired a peaceful rest after the day's travails.

To everyone's chagrin sudden weather changes frequently disturbed such a tranquil scene. "We camped one night on a pretty grass plot," wrote a recent arrival. "After night there was a Texas shower, and soon there was six inches of water in our tents; and I made my first military mental note: When you see a green spot in Texas ask why, before you camp there." Torrential Texas downpours proved that few army tents were waterproof. "Probably sleeping in wet clothes, in a tent, on muddy ground is healthy, and invigorating, and all that," mused one veteran, "yet it has its discomforts, especially when one is awakened about a dozen times during the night to dodge a stream of water that has found an entrance through some seam of your tent." In addition, rainstorms seemed to encourage the mules and horses to try to break their picket lines, lending even more unwelcome excitement to the night's events.[10]

An Indian attack might also keep things lively. Occasionally an unwary guard would be found dead, the victim of his own negligence and a testimony to the skill of his opponents. Yet most night-time Indian raids were directed at the column's horses and mules rather than the troops. Few animals were safe—even Col. Albert Sidney Johnston's favorite saddle mule was stolen during an expedition to El Paso in 1849. Larger, better-organized assaults on the expedition's animals could immobilize an entire command. For this reason wary officers made doubly sure that the column's horses were hobbled and then stationed a number of men around the collected animals. During Mackenzie's campaigns in 1874 just such a tactic thwarted a major raid. A hail of fire met a group of Indians intent on

9. James Parker, *The Old Army: Memories, 1872–1918* (Philadelphia: Dorrance and Co., 1929), pp. 104–105.

10. P. M. Ashburn, *History of the Medical Department of the United States Army* (Boston: Houghton Mifflin Co., 1929), pp. 104–105; Lonnie J. White, ed., "Letters of a Sixth Cavalryman Stationed at 'Cantonment' in the Texas Panhandle," *Texas Military History* 7, no. 2 (1968): 98.

stampeding the command's horses about thirty yards outside the line. "But for the total lack of target practice in those days [we] would have emptied many saddles," recalled one participant.[11]

Whether or not the night passed peacefully, reveille sounded early the next morning; summer marches began at two or three o'clock. As the sleepy soldiers awoke, grumbling about their inadequate tents and thin bedrolls, breakfast preparations began. Meals differed, depending on circumstances. Boiled salt pork was fried or broiled. Wise veterans had soaked old hardtack in water, softening the tasteless, cardboardlike substance enough to allow them to chew it. After repacking the animals and gulping down some coffee, the column again took up the trail.

The pace and length of the upcoming march depended on the elements, the mobility of the command, and the terrain. Muddy trails or sudden northers slowed progress to a virtual standstill, especially when the column was using wagons to carry its supplies. Pack mules fared much better. Nicknamed "jugheads" by army wags, mules provided the mobility and speed essential to successful Indian warfare. The stubborn, hard-working creatures captured the heart of many a traveler. "Every few days they evinced a spirit with which I heartily sympathized, running for miles and creating a profound excitement throughout the command," wrote Mrs. Orsemus Boyd. While most officers believed that only cavalrymen could catch Indians, foot soldiers and even mounted infantry, if led by hard-driving men like Col. Nelson A. Miles, could over the long haul outperform the horse soldiers, whose grain-fed mounts required increasing quantities of food and water as the campaign dragged on.[12]

Water shortages proved a major danger in all field operations in Texas. Repeated dry camps severely reduced a column's efficiency, as long, hot marches strung out the troops and encouraged straggling. Desperately seeking to retain a few drops of moisture, some men kept buckshot in their mouths. The lack of water was particularly hard on cavalry horses. Troopers frequently dismounted and led their horses in an effort to save the animals' strength. Despite their riders' concern, hundreds of horses died on the trails. Some bunkmates shared their stronger steeds with partners whose horses had died; others subjected their footsore comrades to a withering barrage of jokes and disparaging remarks.

The problem was brought home with dramatic effect in 1877. Under the command of Capt. Nicholas Nolan, Company A, Tenth Cavalry, had been on an extended scout of the Staked Plains. Picking up an Indian trail, Nolan's men pursued it vigorously but unsuccessfully, draining their canteens while battling the heat. In the chase the guide became lost. Repeated attempts to find water proved

---

11.   Charles A. P. Hatfield, "Campaign of Col. R. S. Mackenzie . . . ," Order of Indian Wars Collection, U.S. Army History Research Collection, Carlisle Barracks, Pa.

12.   Sidney E. Whitman, *The Troopers: An Informal History of the Plains Cavalry, 1865–1890* (New York: Hastings House, 1962), p. 131; Mrs. Orsemus Bronson Boyd, *Cavalry Life in Tent and Field* (1894; reprint, Lincoln: University of Nebraska Press, 1982), p. 246.

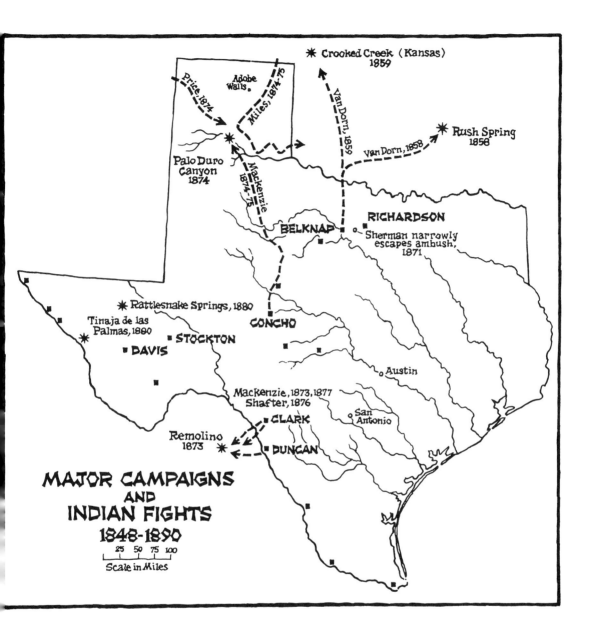

MAJOR CAMPAIGNS
AND
INDIAN FIGHTS
1848-1890

25 50 75 100
Scale in Miles

Map labels:

- ✳ Crooked Creek (Kansas) 1859
- Price 1874
- Adobe Walls
- Miles, 1874-75
- Van Dorn, 1859
- ✳ Rush Spring 1858
- Van Dorn, 1858
- Palo Duro Canyon 1874
- Mackenzie 1874-75
- RICHARDSON
- BELKNAP
- Sherman narrowly escapes ambush, 1871
- ✳ Rattlesnake Springs, 1880
- CONCHO
- Tinaja de las Palmas, 1880
- ■ STOCKTON
- ■ DAVIS
- ○ Austin
- Mackenzie, 1873, 1877 Shafter, 1876
- ■ CLARK
- ○ San Antonio
- Remolino 1873
- ■ DUNCAN

fruitless, and the thirsty troopers drank horse blood and urine in desperate attempts to stay alive. After four maddening days without water the scattered command finally stumbled to safety. Four men, twenty-three horses, and four mules had died during the terrible ordeal.[13]

13. W. Curtis Nunn, ed., "Eighty-six Hours without Water on the Texas Plains," *Southwestern Historical Quarterly* 43 (Jan., 1940): 356–64.

Nature thus posed a cruel threat to the army's movements in Texas. For that reason many leaders failed to pursue enemy trails with the tenacity and vigor necessary for success. Others simply seemed unlucky, and the size of the state posed a formidable obstacle indeed. Some columns chased Indian parties for hundreds of miles only to be forced to stop at the Rio Grande on the south or at the boundary of the Indian Territory on the north. Most of these missions were futile. The failure to develop special policies for Indian warfare was a painful reminder of the army's stagnating tactical and strategical thought. "Our horses have been on half rations, there is little grass, & the weather is inclement . . . Very discouraging," sighed Lt. Col. Robert E. Lee after sending out a pursuit party. Wirt Davis noted the return of such a detachment after a ten-day scout: "Unsuccessful as usual." "I have been on several scouts but haven't caught sight of an Indian yet," reported a recent West Point graduate in 1878.[14]

Finding an Indian camp was no guarantee of success. As the Indians accumulated repeating rifles to supplement bows and arrows, army commanders sought to balance the need for greater firepower against the necessity for quick movement. Some columns hauled light mountain cannon or Gatling guns in efforts to amass greater firepower on the battlefield. Yet moving the wheeled guns that invariably struck fear in the enemy could slow down a column and prevent it from catching the foe. Shortages of trained personnel and proper mounts further restricted the artillery's effectiveness on the Texas frontiers.[15]

When they gathered for open combat, the Indian warriors presented a sight not easily forgotten. The ponies, braves, chiefs, and colorful garb created a spectacular contrast to the Texas landscape. More often, however, combat consisted of long-range skirmishing and ambush. During such minor encounters the soldiers deployed in skirmish formation three to five yards apart. To reduce the target they presented and to take better aim, cavalrymen dismounted before the fighting began. Three troopers snapped the links attached to the left sides of their horses' bridles into the halter ring of the horse on their left, and the fourth man led all four horses to the rear. Taking advantage of trees, rocks, bushes, and slight changes in elevation, the troops scrambled for cover. They usually fired at will as officers called out distances and advised their men to aim low—abdominal hits were believed to be more likely fatal than glancing wounds to heads or arms.

On the battlefield good training was fundamental. Buglers blared out orders to the various commands. Veteran units generally performed well once the enemy had been joined, and the steadiness of a well-trained company in combat often

14. Lee to Custis Lee, Jan. 30, 1861, Adams, ed., "Lee Letters," pp. 738–39; Davis to Huntt, Aug. 27, 1867, George G. Huntt Papers (microfilm, Fort Concho Research Library, MF 14); Safford, Apr. 29, 1878, in R. C. Crane, "Letters from Texas," *West Texas Historical Association Year Book* 25 (Oct., 1949): 124.

15. Smith to Jones, July 18, SW, AR, 1852, pp. 18–19; Bliss Reminiscences, 1:143–44; Sheridan to Townsend, May 6, 1872, Sheridan Papers; Miles to Sherman, July 8, 1876, Sherman Papers, vol. 44, reel 23; Sherman to Belknap, July 12, 1870, Letters Sent by the Adjutant General, vol. 52, reel 39.

outweighed the greater mobility of Indians. Through resolute, disciplined fire small detachments often held out against much larger Indian forces. Troops that kept their lines intact could make careful advances or withdrawals, since Indian warriors usually shied away from frontal confrontations with any sizable force.

Decisive battlefield victories proved rare after long-range skirmishing had broken out. Surprise and ambush in the opening minutes of action thus provided the tactical key to success. Indian warriors carried out such maneuvers superbly. Sergeants and corporals directed 25 of the army's 146 armed encounters with Indians in Texas from 1846 to 1890, clearly illustrating the importance of small-unit combat over many years. Recognizing the army's disadvantages in this kind of warfare, the military enlisted large numbers of frontiersmen and allied Indians to serve as scouts, guides, and skirmishers. Experience showed that skillfully handled troops could turn the tables when they found an enemy camp, for hostile Indians were as negligent as white soldiers in guarding encampments against surprise attack.

Some of the most important blows struck by Texas-based troops before the Civil War were operations conducted by the elite Second Cavalry, which provided no less than sixteen Civil War generals to Union and Confederate forces. In September, 1858, in one particularly famous raid, Bvt. Maj. Earl Van Dorn led four companies of the Second Cavalry and more than one hundred Indian allies out of Fort Belknap. Moving north, the column established temporary Camp Radziminski just above the North Fork of the Red River. Upon learning of the whereabouts of Buffalo Hump's Comanches, Van Dorn conducted a forced march of ninety miles in thirty-six hours. Just after daybreak on October 1 the troops spotted the Comanche camp at Rush Spring. Van Dorn dispatched one company and the Indian auxiliaries to capture the Comanches' horse herd, taking the remaining three companies directly into the camp.

Van Dorn achieved complete surprise. As a bugler sounded the charge, cavalrymen thundered down the hills surrounding Buffalo Hump's village. Astonished warriors stumbled out of their tepees to find soldiers racing through the camp and animal herds. A melee resulted as excited troopers chased down scattered clusters of Indian men, women, and children. Fog, smoke, and rough terrain rendered leadership from a central location impossible, and the fight deteriorated into a series of bloody individual encounters. Van Dorn was wounded by an arrow. A fellow officer was killed as he and several Indian allies pursuing a fleeing band of Comanches suddenly found themselves surrounded. Lawrence ("Sul") Ross, the leader of the auxiliaries, also suffered a severe wound.

After about an hour and a half of fighting, the Comanches withdrew from the battlefield at Rush Spring. Fifty-six warriors and two women lay dead; the soldiers had burned 120 lodges, captured three hundred horses, and seized most of the food and supplies in the village. The price for Van Dorn's victory was three dead, one missing, and thirteen severely wounded. One sergeant later died, and it was initially assumed that Van Dorn would pay the ultimate price himself; an arrow had torn through his left lung and stomach. A remarkable recovery en-

abled him to return to the saddle within five weeks. A year later he inflicted another serious defeat on the Comanches at the Battle of Crooked Creek.[16]

In similar fashion Col. Ranald B. Mackenzie's Fourth Cavalry frequently managed to overcome the difficulties that beset field campaigns. When the number of raids along the Rio Grande decreased after their raid against Remolino in 1873, Mackenzie's veterans moved north to the Staked Plains to participate in the Red River offensive with men from the Fourth, Sixth, Eighth, and Tenth Cavalry regiments, as well as the Fifth Infantry and the Eleventh Infantry. Department of Texas Commander Christopher C. Augur cautioned Mackenzie not to expect success "in a day" but instructed him to follow his enemies to the limits of his endurance.[17]

Having established their base camp near Blanco Canyon, Mackenzie's hardened veterans took the field in September, leaving foot soldiers to guard the base and the supply train. Early-fall rains impeded movement, but after several skirmishes the expedition found fresh signs of the enemy at about 1:00 A.M. on September 28. Mackenzie's men halted an hour later and bivouacked until 4:00 that morning. Then they remounted and followed the trail to Palo Duro Canyon, where they found the winter camp of a large number of Kiowas, Comanches, and Southern Cheyennes. Moving as quietly as possible, the exhausted, tense troops dismounted and began a tortuous descent into the canyon. They came within about a hundred yards of an Indian sentinel before the sleepy Indian guard noticed their approach and fired a belated warning shot.

Second Lieutenant Charles A. P. Hatfield remembered that "the effect was immediate, from perfect quiet to pandemonium" in the Indian villages below. "From all the camps, indians were streaming west in noisy disorderly flight." After stumbling down to the base of the canyon, the troopers formed a skirmish line and tried to pursue the panicked Indians. Boulders and clumps of willows and cottonwoods hampered an orderly advance as long-range skirmishing continued. The Indians made good their escape with no more than five casualties; a bugler was the only soldier wounded.[18]

Despite the light casualties the attack was devastating to the Indians. Mackenzie's men sacked the village, burning all the lodges, equipment, and winter food stocks. Even more important, the bluecoats captured virtually the entire Indian pony herd. The following day the best animals were selected as rewards for the scouts and replacements for spent horses. Fearing that he could not prevent the Indians from recapturing the others, Mackenzie ordered his men to

16. Robert M. Utley, *Frontiersmen in Blue: The United States Army and the Indian, 1848–1865* (1967; reprint Lincoln: University of Nebraska Press, 1981), pp. 131–32; Van Dorn to Wife, Oct. 12, 1858, in E. V. D. Miller, ed., *A Soldier's Honor: With Reminiscences of Major-General Earl Van Dorn by His Comrades*, p. 39; Report of Twiggs, Oct. 19, 1858, in ibid., pp. 37–38.

17. Sheridan to Sherman, July 21, 1874, Sheridan Papers, box 56; Utley, *Frontier Regulars*, pp. 225–32; Augur to Mackenzie, Aug. 28, 1874, Letters Sent, Department of Texas.

18. Hatfield, "Campaign of Mackenzie"; Utley, *Frontier Regulars*, pp. 232–38.

shoot the rest of the herd, more than one thousand animals. The tribes never re-covered from their losses, and most gave themselves up in the following months.

Few fights went as smoothly for the army. Some soldiers panicked in the heat of combat, and excited officers frequently lost control of their men when the situation suddenly changed. "This poor regiment has been led by damn fools," wrote a Tenth Cavalry critic. Attempts to fan out and make contact with enemy Indians often confused the various elements of a command. Army battle doc-trine called for the scattered columns to converge at the sound of firing. Poorly disciplined soldiers, however, opened up on anything that moved, making the doctrine ineffective. In 1875, Pvt. S. S. Peters described a company's reaction to distant firing: "With vengeance depicted on their grim visaged brows," they "left three of their party rolling in the dust by the tumbling of their nags into prairie dog holes. At last we saw the enemy—a herd of frightened antelope, and a de-mure looking owl."[19]

In the meantime, life continued at the posts from which the columns had set out. The departure of an expeditionary force often proved beneficial to camp sanitation. Those remaining at the fort might clean and whitewash the barracks during their comrades' absence. On the other hand, surgeons suggested that life in the field was healthier than that in the garrison. Scouting and outpost duty meant that the men could "lead perfectly pure and simple lives" away from the grog shops and hog pens near the post.[20]

However, the absence of a large number of troops of a regular garrison meant double duty for those remaining behind. The depleted command still had to mount guards and continue work projects. Families missed their loved ones. And while the Indians never launched any full-scale attacks on the regular army's Texas posts, the prospect of hundreds of Indians swooping down on defenseless wives and children caused even the most experienced veteran to shudder. Such fears were not without justification, for small raids directed at a post's horses or commissary were common. One night in the late 1850s, thirteen Indians crossed the parade ground at Fort Quitman. In another incident fourteen arrows felled a soldier who was returning to his barracks after obtaining some alcohol from a nearby hut.

Rumors that a column had been annihilated tormented anxious dependents. Most of the families living along the frontiers had some knowledge of the brutal nature of warfare. Mackenzie's attack at Remolino, for example, came while most of the Indian warriors were away from their villages. Nonetheless, the old men, women, and children put up stiff resistance against the Fourth Cavalry's surprise assault, suffering nineteen casualties in the fight. Based on at least some element

19. L. F. Sheffy, ed., "Letters and Reminiscences of Gen. Theodore A. Baldwin: Scouting after Indians on the Plains of Texas," *Panhandle-Plains Historical Review* 11 (1938): 24; White, ed., "Letters of a Sixth Cavalryman," p. 95.

20. PMR, Fort McKavett, Feb., 1872, p. 273.

of truth, tales of Indian savagery gained wide credence. Mrs. Lydia Lane expressed the common fear of Indian mistreatment:

Woe to the hapless party that fell into the devilish hands of a band of Indians! Men were generally put to death by slow torture, but they were allowed to live long enough to witness the atrocities practised on their wives and children, such things as only fiends could devise. Babies had their brains dashed out before the eyes of father and mother, powerless to help them. Lucky would the latter have been, had they treated her in the same

way; but what she was forced to endure would have wrung tears from anything but an Indian.[21]

While few columns actually met a disastrous end in the field, life on scouting detail was usually unpleasant. Clothing and shoes disintegrated in the dusty Texas summers, grating on nerves and lowering morale. In the winter northers

21. Utley, *Frontier Regulars*, pp. 356–58; Lydia Spencer Lane, *I Married a Soldier; or, Old Days in the Old Army* (1893; reprint, Albuquerque, N.Mex.: Horn and Wallace, 1964), pp. 73–74.

took their toll. In 1874, Mackenzie's column was "frozen as tight as though we had been in the Artic regions," recalled one participant. "The tents were like boards, one solid sheet of ice." Indeed, miserable field rations, inadequate tents, and long marches in the field made standard garrison fare, leaky roofs, hard bunks, and monotonous fatigue duty seem comfortable by comparison. Whatever the degree of success or failure in the field, the troops' spirits soared as the expedition neared home.[22]

In contrast to the solemn scene accompanying their departure, troops returning from the field could expect a rousing welcome from the garrison. The post band played "When Johnnie Comes Marching Home" as a long-awaited expedition straggled in. Many a party was organized as the weary soldiers, sunburned and lips parched, exchanged stories and celebrated their safe homecoming. A waiting letter from a loved one far away might also help a lucky campaigner forget his woes. "When I returned to camp," wrote the seriously wounded Earl Van Dorn to his wife in 1858, "I found your long, kind letter telling me about my little children and yourself. This letter made me feel well again." Few had encountered any Indians; even fewer had acted with special valor—or cowardice—under fire. The great majority had simply carried out their orders as well as the country could expect.[23]

22. Carter, *On the Border with Mackenzie*, p. 507; Sheffy, ed., "Baldwin Letters and Reminiscences," p. 26.

23. Don Rickey, Jr., *Forty Miles a Day on Beans and Hay: The Enlisted Soldier Fighting the Indian Wars* (Norman: University of Oklahoma Press, 1963), p. 267; Van Dorn to Wife, Oct. 12, 1858, Miller, ed., *A Soldier's Honor*, p. 40.

CHAPTER NINE

Cultural Activities and Entertainment

. . . we managed to exist and to enjoy ourselves

—Col. Charles J. Crane

The inhabitants of Texas' military frontiers enjoyed a number of social and recreational activities. The garrison residents derived great pleasure from the mails and eagerly awaited periodicals from the East. Schools, churches, and libraries existed at the larger stations. Soldiers and civilians organized dances, balls, hops, and theatrical performances. Others opted for different forms of entertainment, drinking and gambling being two of the more popular diversions. Many took advantage of the frontier environment to raise veritable menageries of pets, and the abundance of wildlife made hunting and fishing popular. In addition, post residents celebrated holidays—the Fourth of July, Christmas, and New Year's Day in particular—with a special vigor. In all they took part in a surprisingly wide range of nonmilitary activities.

In accordance with nineteenth-century social thought, the War Department made several efforts to improve the army's "moral tone." To do so, the military sponsored various educational, religious, and cultural activities at its frontier posts. Long concerned with the high illiteracy rates among enlisted men, the army encouraged the organization of base schools during the 1850s. Official action came in 1866, when Congress ordered each permanent station to set up a school. Placing special emphasis on the new black regiments, Congress instructed regimental chaplains to oversee the education of the buffalo soldiers.

Lack of money usually prevented such noble aspirations from reaching fruition. Although Congress wanted to educate the enlisted men, it was reluctant to finance such programs. Beset by economic constraints, the army found a loophole in the congressional mandate. Since most western posts were not classified as permanent, the army was not technically obliged to provide regular schools at such forts. Instead, education was left to the discretion of the post commander or the regimental chaplain. If a teacher could be found and paid from post funds, a school was organized on an ad hoc basis. If not, the school was forgotten.

Several examples illustrate the range of educational programs. At Fort Duncan a sergeant from the Twenty-fourth Infantry was detailed as a teacher in February, 1873. During the day he taught reading, writing, and spelling to his fellow noncommissioned officers; in the evenings anyone who cared to attend school was welcome. One month later, however, the school closed with the transfer of two of the three companies that had been stationed there. At Fort Griffin in 1868 and 1869 a quartermaster sergeant gave free lessons at one end of the commissary. The man tacked white sheets to the hardwood benches to make them more comfortable and opened classes with a song. Unfortunately, the selfless teacher proved to be a selfish sergeant, deserting with $25,000 in army funds.[1]

Other educational efforts achieved greater success. In January, 1874, chaplains opened a school for enlisted personnel at Fort Brown, assembling a selection of spelling, reading, writing, and history books. The school began at 6:00 P.M. and boasted 80 scholars from the post's 259-man garrison. The officers, wives, and children at Fort Worth learned French from a traveling gentleman, who also found time to teach music, drawing, and dancing. The instructor at Fort Concho reported that "all officers, their wives, and the men . . . not only show but feel a deep interest in the subject of education."[2]

Such cooperation was essential, for most post teachers also held classes for children during the day. Some set aside separate hours for children of enlisted men and officers, or for black and white children. The pupils, however, often proved inattentive and bored with scholarly pursuits. A civilian instructor at Fort Davis recalled one particularly restless young schoolboy named Willie:

> Willie was usually looking out the window. A Mexican, a burro, a rattling old wagon, any thing drew his attention from his books. In desperation I tried to shame him once. I said, "Willie, there is never any thing interesting to be seen from that window. If ever a man comes by with a hand organ and a monkey you have my permission not only to look out but to *jump* out and follow him."
>
> Not many days after that an awful commotion occurred in the school. The children rushed out through windows and doors pell-mell. Was the house afire? Could I escape? As I went out I heard a sound dear to my childhood. The impossible had happened. Never before, never since has a man with a hand organ appeared in Fort Davis. I followed in the procession. There was no more school that day.[3]

Along with efforts to improve education, the War Department and Congress encouraged the propagation of Christianity among the frontier regulars. In

1. PMR, Fort Duncan, Feb., Mar., 1873, NA, RG 94 (microfilm, BTHC), p. 298; Sallie Reynolds Matthews, *Interwoven: A Pioneer Chronicle* (1936; reprint, El Paso: Carl Hertzog, 1958), pp. 50–51.

2. PMR, Fort Brown, Jan., 1874; Starr to Eliza, Jan. 6, 1850, Samuel Henry Starr Papers, BTHC; Shelby to Mullins, Apr. 20, 1881, Records of the United States Army Continental Commands, 1821–1920, Fort Concho, NA, RG 393 (microfilm, Fort Concho Research Library, MF 69).

3. M. B. Anderson Reminiscences, pp. 6–7, BTHC.

1838, Congress had funded chaplains to guide the men at fifteen military bases. The post's council of administration selected the chaplain, who received four daily rations, fuel and living allowances, and a monthly salary of $40. Forts McKavett, Belknap, and Bliss and the military reservation of San Antonio had chaplains at one time or another under the antebellum system. Men of the cloth likewise accompanied Confederate regiments to the western stations during the Civil War, and after the war Congress expanded the program, funding thirty post chaplains and one chaplain for each of the four black regiments. Clergymen were paid $1,500 a year. Of course, even thirty-four chaplains could scarcely serve all of the more than two hundred military stations in the country.

Among the army's chaplains Episcopalians predominated, especially before 1861, when southern officers held a particularly large number of commissioned appointments. The first rabbi was not enlisted until the Civil War; only seven Roman Catholic priests were selected from 1872 to 1898. Henry V. Plummer became the first black clergyman commissioned by the regular army in 1884. Responsible to the adjutant general, chaplains performed their regular clerical duties, preaching, burying the dead, visiting the sick, operating schools, and performing marriages and baptisms on the military frontiers. In addition, they were frequently called on to carry out a number of miscellaneous tasks, including those of post librarian, gardener, post treasurer, manager of the commissary and bakery, and defense counsel at courts-martial.[4]

The men charged with these responsibilities displayed varying degrees of interest, dedication, and effectiveness. From Fort Bliss the chaplain of the Second Texas Mounted Rifles complained: "I have a great deal to do here as a preacher. I get between the boys and ruin, and use every effort to keep them back. . . . I am a thousand miles away, among the dissipated, the profane, the skeptical; standing up for God *almost* alone." Military men debated the merits of the chaplain program and referred informally to all chaplains as "padres." Lt. Gen. Philip Sheridan believed them necessary, but Gen. E. O. C. Ord voiced a typical criticism when he wrote that, while good chaplains "would be useful," "not more than one in ten" met the necessary standards.[5]

An army chaplain's influence on the daily lives of his charges depended largely on his religious prowess and his ability to get along with other officers. The Reverend Norman Badger served as post chaplain at Fort Concho from 1871 to 1876. Hampered by the lack of a regular chapel, Badger vainly tried to reach the members of his garrison at improvised meeting places, including the mess hall, the hospital, the post trader's bar, and his own quarters. Attendance varied from a high of twenty-eight to a low of three, the decline apparently stemming from Bad-

---

4. Carol Schmidt, "The Chaplains of Fort Concho," pt. 1, *Fort Concho Report* 16 (Spring, 1984): 33; Earl F. Stover, *Up from Handymen: The United States Army Chaplaincy, 1865–1920* (Washington, D.C.: Office of the Chief of Chaplains, 1977), 3:2–3, 53–57, 88.

5. Martin H. Hall, ed., "A Confederate Soldier's Letter from Fort Bliss, July 6, 1861," *Password* 25 (Spring, 1980): 18; Testimony of Sheridan and Ord, 44th Cong., 1st sess., H. Rept. 354, ser. 1709, pp. 20, 45.

ger's bitter personal disputes with the less than saintly Commander Grierson. On the other hand, Badger's successor, George Dunbar, settled in more comfortably. Dunbar maintained better relations with Grierson, and their children and wives enjoyed each other's company. Dunbar also recognized the unique environment in which the military clergy operated. "We have as nice and orderly Sunday services as you would find anywhere, but they have to be short, rather less than an hour," he reported to his mother. "It would seem queer to you to have uniforms and jingling sabres in church, but that we always have here."[6]

In line with attempts to improve the "habits" of enlisted men, frontier officials made strenuous efforts to establish libraries, which might be housed in tents, extra offices, or special buildings. Reading material came from private donations and loans, company funds, regimental collections, and special appropriations from the quartermaster general ($22 per company in August, 1879). Arrangements and holdings differed greatly. Two hospital tents housed Fort Duncan's volumes, which ranged from 120 to 355 books, depending on the number of units stationed there. In 1875, Fort Concho's collection reached 720, "embracing several valuable works and a large quantity of light literature." In August, 1879, the post had subscriptions to daily newspapers published in Chicago, Cincinnati, Saint Louis, Louisville, and New York. The Concho library also subscribed to twenty-seven magazines, including the *Army and Navy Journal* and *Army and Navy Gazette, Harper's Weekly, Home Journal, Illustrated London News, London Punch, Scientific American, Atlantic Monthly,* and *Scribner's.*[7]

Although regular schedules called for the mail to arrive once or twice a week, bad weather and mismanagement often held up postal service. Members of the garrison enthusiastically awaited the arrival of mail, which formed "part of the little excitement on this isolated post," a Fort Concho surgeon reported. Between mail deliveries in 1867, the residents of Fort Belknap read every available scrap of printed material. "Every old newspaper and novel were read and re-read and loaned until worn out." The well-traveled Elizabeth Custer recalled that "even advertisements were scanned." While mail deliveries caused "absolute contentment" among recipients, a disappointing arrival could be extremely painful to those whose high hopes of receiving a letter or parcel were dashed. Lt. Samuel H. Starr informed his wife that a recent arrival of the mail had fallen into the latter category: "But one letter came by it and no papers; so everybody is as badly disappointed as myself, and I received—blanc [*sic*]. . . . I am alone, all alone."[8]

6. Schmidt, "Chaplains," pt. 1, pp. 29–30; pt. 2, *Fort Concho Report* 16 (Summer, 1984): 35–37; Badger to AG, Jan. 31, Aug. 31, Sept. 30, 1874, Jan. 31, 1875, Appointment, Commission and Personal Branch, Letters Received 3046–1876 (microfilm, Fort Concho Research Library, MF 13); Bill Green, *The Dancing Was Lively: Fort Concho, Texas: A Social History, 1867–1882* (San Angelo, Tex.: Fort Concho Sketches Publishing Co., 1974), pp. 76–78.

7. Grierson to QMG, Aug. 1, 1879, Records of U.S. Army Continental Commands, MF 69; PMR, Fort Duncan, May, 1875, Mar., 1877, pp. 170, 258.

8. PMR, Fort Concho, Jan., 1873, p. 81; O. M. Knapp to Mother, Jan. 12, Obadiah M. Knapp Papers, BTHC; H. H. McConnell, *Five Years a Cavalryman; Or, Sketches of Regular Army Life on*

Soldiers and dependents found solace in indoor games and activities. At least two officers were amateur painters. Several commands used surplus post funds to purchase billiard tables, which might be set up in the sutler's store or in a spare office. Post canteens established on a nonprofit basis at selected forts during the 1880s attracted enlisted men lucky enough to serve at such stations. Checkers, chess, and backgammon provided further entertainment. Others wrote letters to friends and family, a practice encouraged on at least one post by the provision of free stamps and stationery purchased with surplus company funds.

In 1867, not satisfied with such routine diversions, "the boys" at Fort Belknap, led by Sgt. H. H. McConnell, published a handwritten weekly paper called the *Little Joker.* "No printing press then being near by, . . . the copy would circulate until it was worn out, and afforded much amusement to officers as well as men," he later remembered. In February, 1869, having been transferred to Fort Richardson, the enterprising McConnell published the first of six issues of the *Flea,* which featured post news and advertisements. "Its success was immense," reported the editor, for "having had the cheek enough to send copies all over the country for 'exchanges,' the regularly established journals thought it a good joke, and our exchange list at once became quite large."[9]

Amateur theatricals were also extremely popular. In 1856 the soldiers at Fort McIntosh organized a theatrical company and earned rave reviews from spectators hungry for entertainment. At Duncan the chaplain, to procure funds for music books for the chapel, directed a variety show, with performances on January 5 and 6, 1880. Perhaps stemming from these shows was the "dramatic troupe" organized by the men of Company B, Eighth Cavalry. The post surgeon deemed their opening performance "very good," with healthy attendance and music courtesy of the Twenty-fourth Infantry band. "Second performance by 8 Cavalry dramatic troupe very poor," however, sighed the same critic after the following night's production.[10]

To the delight of all who had tired of seeing clumsy soldiers parading in female costumes, women and children took an active part in productions. In December, 1877, the officers' children gave a "dramatic entertainment" at Fort McKavett, with roles ranging from Prince Diamond to Little Bo Peep. More spectacular were the theatricals put on by the adults at Fort Clark. At a garrison swollen by rumors of war with Mexico, the Fort Clark performers organized several shows during the 1870s. "We soon found that a good paying audience could readily be commanded," one actress recalled. Money raised by the amateur group renovated

---

the *Texas Frontier, Twenty Odd Years Ago* (Jacksboro, Tex.: J. N. Rogers and Co., 1889), pp. 89–90; Elizabeth B. Custer, *Tenting on the Plains, or General Custer in Kansas and Texas* (1897; reprint, Norman: University of Oklahoma Press, 1971), 2:410; Starr to Eliza, Feb. 8, 1854, Starr Papers.

9. McConnell, *Five Years a Cavalryman,* pp. 60, 173.

10. M. L. Crimmins, ed., "Colonel J. K. F. Mansfield's Report of the Inspection of the Department of Texas in 1856," *Southwestern Historical Quarterly* 42 (Jan., 1939): 238; PMR, Fort Duncan, Jan. 20, 21, 1880, pp. 55–56.

the garrison hall, bought Christmas gifts for the children of the enlisted person-nel, and supported famine-relief efforts in Ireland.[11]

Dances also enlivened post society. "Much lenience has been allowed the soldiers in their festivities," wrote one doctor, who had observed "music dancing and exhibition in the quarters of the men, once or twice during each week." Mrs. Luda Avery Johnston, the wife of Sgt. William M. Johnston, remembered that company hops were a Friday night fixture at Fort McKavett during the late 1870s. Civilians living near army posts also gave dances, drawing not only soldiers but settlers from thirty miles away. While any occasion would do, they made a special point to hold a dancing party to commemorate the dedication of a house.[12]

The officers and their wives held their own dances. New arrivals had to be welcomed with a proper "hop"; of course, the new companies responded in kind in honor of their hosts. Turkey, venison, bear meat, ham, smoked buffalo tongue, quail, salmon salad, preserves, jellies, rolls, coffee, and even *real mince pies* made many of these affairs especially memorable. A newly wedded officer and his bride also merited a gala celebration. A "Complimentary Hop Tendered to Lieuten-ant & Mrs. Ellis, 8th Cavalry, by the Officers of the Garrison, Fort Clark," in late December, 1879, included a bewildering variety of dances—lanciers, waltz, quadrille, schottische, Dan Tucker, and galop being listed among the evening's activities.[13]

A good band lent a flair to the parties. Each antebellum regiment had its own band, which was customarily stationed at the unit's headquarters. In its cost-cutting measures after the war, however, Congress refused to fund such musical groups. Congress "has done a wrong thing," complained one disgruntled soldier. "The expence is but smal to the Government and it is a great pleasure to both Officers and Soldiers to have a Band." To the delight of all concerned, most regi-ments continued to sponsor their own bands through collections and subscrip-tions even without congressional appropriations.[14]

Individual musicians also performed at the army's bases. The strains of gui-tars, banjos, and violins frequently wafted from company quarters. Lt. Col. George Buell played the fiddle. A captain at Fort Griffin owned a music box valued at $500. "It was a Godsend to us," recalled another officer, who enjoyed playing the expensive gadget. Others brought pianos to the frontier, and men like Colonel

---

11. "Children's Dramatic Entertainment," Dec. 27, 1877, Texas Letters of Benjamin H. Grier-son (microfilm, Fort Concho Research Library, MF 17); Mrs. Orsemus Bronson Boyd, *Cavalry Life in Tent and Field* (1894; reprint, Lincoln: University of Nebraska Press, 1982), pp. 283–84.

12. PMR, Fort Concho, Feb., 1870, p. 158; N. H. Pierce and N. E. Brown, *Free State of Menard: A History of the County* (Menard, Tex.: Menard News Press, 1946), p. 117.

13. Capt. R. G. Carter, *On the Border with Mackenzie: Or, Winning West Texas from the Co-manches* (Washington, D.C.: Enyon Printing Co., 1935), p. 341; "Complimentary Hop . . . ," Dec. 31, 1879, Fort Clark Records, BTHC.

14. Brit Allan Storey, "An Army Officer in Texas, 1866–1867," *Southwestern Historical Quar-terly* 72 (Oct., 1968): 250.

Grierson (who was a former music teacher) persuaded their children to take up an instrument.[15]

Not all diversions were so genteel. The temptations of strong drink were evident at every military post in Texas. Soldiers drank everything they could get their hands on, from imported French champagne to homemade whiskey. At one post a man could purchase a canteen of a clear white mixture known as "pine-top" or "white-mule" whiskey for $3 to $5. Rum sold for $.20 to $.25 a gallon after the Civil War. A soldier could buy his choice of beverage at the sutler's store, the post canteen, a civilian grocery store or saloon off the post or a private still. Spectacular binges marked paydays, and a bad supply of Louisiana rum caused mayhem at Fort Belknap in 1867. From the top of the forage house one soldier shouted that he had been on a balloon ride. Another was discovered trying to lasso a grasshopper.

Plagued with such abuses, the army made concerted efforts to reduce alcohol consumption among enlisted personnel. Since attempts at complete prohibition before the Mexican War had only caused the men to turn to private sources, the War Department concentrated on restricting the quantity and inspecting the quality of the liquor that was sold. During the Civil War state troops usually ignored orders to abstain. Temperance movements occasionally took hold at frontier garrisons, sometimes temporarily reducing the number of arrests. On a larger scale, in the late 1880s the Women's Christian Temperance Union persuaded the government to forbid the sale of hard liquor to enlisted men on military bases. Eventually, beer and light ales were prohibited as well, although troops managed to secure alcohol despite the official bans.

Gambling was tremendously popular among the frontier soldiers in Texas. Card games included poker, three-card monte, seven-up, and blackjack. Dice games such as craps were also common. Although gambling was illegal, post commanders generally resigned themselves to its pervasive appeal. They did, however, seek to prevent professional gamblers from taking the unwitting soldier's money. In 1861 an order was issued to Texas state troops that "if any gamblers come to the posts or about them to filch the troops of their earnings [you] will order them to stop their gambling or require them to leave at once."[16]

Horse racing might have more serious implications. The challenge between Bumble Bee and Gray Eagle created tremendous excitement among the officers gathered at a Fort Mason court-martial session in the mid-1850s. Ladies wagered gloves and handkerchiefs; officers ventured baskets of champagne or pay. However, authorities frowned on these races, which wore out animals intended for service against Indians. This was especially true during the Civil War, when Texas

15. PMR, Fort Griffin, Oct., 1869, p. 143; M. K. Kellogg, *M. K. Kellogg's Texas Journal, 1872,* ed. Llerena Friend (Austin: University of Texas Press, 1967), pp. 89, 91; Susan Miles, *Fort Concho in 1877* (San Angelo, Tex.: Bradley Co., 1972), p. 39; John Creaton Papers, p. 6, BTHC.

16. General Order No. 19, June 18, 1861, General Order No. 40, Sept. 18, 1861, James B. Barry Papers, BTHC.

officials made repeated efforts to regulate the morality of state troops. Authorities expressed their particular displeasure that one officer in the First Mounted Regiment had built a racetrack despite clear orders to the contrary.

Other soldiers opted for pleasures of the flesh. Army regulations prohibited married men from enlisting, and soldiers in the ranks who hoped to wed had to secure their commanding officers' approval. These obstacles to matrimony, combined with normal human proclivities, led many to fulfill their sexual desires with prostitutes or camp followers. Although nineteenth-century mores prevented open homosexuality between soldiers, such relationships also existed. The most famous case was that of a Mrs. Nash, company laundress for the Seventh Cavalry. "Old Nash" was a skilled midwife and had at least four relationships with enlisted men. After Nash's death outsiders were shocked to learn that "Mrs. Nash" had been a man.[17]

In addition to reading, amateur theatricals, drinking, gambling, and sexual activities, members of frontier garrisons found amusement in keeping pets. Mrs. Teresa Viélé raised a fawn, two goats, chickens, a parrot, several mockingbirds and orioles, doves, and what she called a "tiger cub." After the Civil War an enlisted man at Fort Belknap kept a young buffalo, which he named The Philosopher, in front of the old commissary building. Cats, chickens, squirrels, and prairie dogs proliferated at virtually every military post, but dogs were the most popular pets. At Fort Belknap in 1854 one officer reportedly owned thirty-five dogs. At Fort Davis in 1885 the surgeon reported that "a great number of worthless curs" created "a perfect pandemonium." Faced with exploding animal populations, some post commanders tried to restore order by levying taxes on dogs or decreeing that all stray animals were to be killed.[18]

Hunting and fishing were also extremely popular. Benjamin Grierson believed that "all the officers & ladies here [at Fort Concho] have what may be called *fishing on the brain*." Daytime excursions to nearby fishing or swimming holes allowed dogs and children to play and men and women to gossip. The danger of Indian attack notwithstanding, hunters combed the area around each fort seeking buffalo, deer, antelope, bear, turkey, rabbit, and quail. The garrison's best marksmen went out frequently to bring in fresh meat. Some organized elaborate hunting parties. During the 1870s one such safari from Fort Duncan included seven scouts and a cook. The six-mule wagon carried bread, bacon, flour, salt, onions, sugar, candles, potatoes, lanterns, soap, pepper, snakebite antidote, kettles, ovens, coffeepots, blankets, forage, and ammunition.[19]

17. Patricia Y. Stallard, *Glittering Misery: Dependents of the Indian Fighting Army* (Fort Collins and San Rafael, Colo.: Old Army Press and Presidio Press, 1978), pp. 53–60.

18. Teresa Griffin Viélé, *Following the Drum: A Glimpse of Frontier Life* (1858; reprint, Lincoln: University of Nebraska Press, 1984, p. 133; McConnell, *Five Years a Cavalryman*, pp. 64, 132; PMR, Fort Davis, Apr. 30, 1885, pp. 83–84; James Parker, *The Old Army: Memories 1872–1918* (Philadelphia: Dorrance and Co., 1880), p. 215.

19. Grierson to Alice, May 8, 1875, Texas Letters of Benjamin Grierson, MF 16; Zenas R. Bliss Reminiscences, 1:40–41, 2:162–63, 5:129–30, BTHC.

Others preferred quieter trips into the surrounding countryside. Women and children took innumerable tours through the nearby areas. Seizing rare opportunities for privacy, officers and their wives or girlfriends liked to go on romantic horseback rides. Such excursions offered those who worked behind desks the chance to keep physically fit, in preparation either for more rigorous duties in the field or simply for the long trek to the next station. Paymaster Albert Sidney Johnston took the opportunity afforded him by his travels to study the state's flora and fauna. Lt. Philip Sheridan, who later won the enmity of Texans by joking that "if I owned hell and Texas I would rent out Texas and live in hell," dabbled in ornithology while he was stationed at Fort Duncan in the 1850s. One Confederate stationed at Fort Bliss sent his father some clover seed he had gathered. The amateur agronomist had found that his horse liked the clover better than corn and urged his father to begin planting it on the family farm.[20]

Holidays provided the men and women of the army posts with a special cause for celebration. Most commanders called off fatigue duties and drill on July 4, Christmas, and New Year's Day. The typical Independence Day celebration was a particularly gala affair that attracted settlers from throughout the region. July 4 baseball games were common, particularly near the end of the century. Some outfits fielded excellent teams, which practiced after retreat and played on Sundays and holidays. Races—between men, mules, and horses—also attracted tremendous interest. "We had one of the liveliest entertainments that was ever held in this section of the country," wrote an officer about Fort Stockton's 1882 jamboree. "The usual expenditures of gunpowder and whiskey" marked Fort Brown's festival in 1871. That night the officers' party "revived the drooping soul" of many commissioned men and local dignitaries with ample servings of the regimental band's fine music and roast beef, and chilled champagne.[21]

Christmas was another festive occasion. Using savings from the hospital and company funds, cooks prepared special Christmas meals and sweets for company and hospital tables. Some officers presented their men with sheep or pigs, and the resulting spread could be quite impressive. A typical company table boasted several roasted pigs and chickens, doughnuts, eggnog, potato salad, lobster salad, cakes, fruit, and raisin pudding. At Fort Concho, Col. and Mrs. Wesley Merritt, having no children of their own, put up a tree in their quarters and invited the youngsters of the garrison to join them for a party. Not surprisingly, many soldiers topped off the day's celebration with liberal doses of beer and whiskey. "During the Christmas holidays drunkenness was prevalent," remarked a diarist, "and

20. William Preston Johnston, *The Life of Albert Sidney Johnston, Embracing His Services in the Armies of the United States, the Republic of Texas, and the Confederate States* (New York: D. Appleton and Co., 1878), pp. 174–75; Philip Henry Sheridan, *The Personal Memoirs of Philip Henry Sheridan* (1888; rev. ed. New York: D. Appleton and Co., 1902), 1:30–31; Taylor to Taylor, Oct. 2, 1861, Martin H. Hall, ed., "The Taylor Letters: Confederate Correspondence from Fort Bliss," *Military History of Texas and the Southwest* 15, no. 2 (1970): 59.

21. George A. Armes, *Ups and Downs of an Army Officer* (Washington, D.C.: Privately printed, 1900), p. 505; PMR, Fort Brown, July, 1871.

desertions very numerous, and I began to have an insight into the thousand and one ways and means that a soldier will indulge in to get whiskey."[22]

On New Year's Day officers and their wives held open house for fellow commissioned personnel and local citizens. Cakes and champagne figured prominently in the day's events. The women borrowed furniture, dressed in their best finery, and proudly displayed their finest possessions as the visiting went on until dark. Bachelors eagerly made the rounds up and down officers' row, seizing the opportunity to sample the delicacies offered by the wives and to flirt with the daughters. Enlisted men enjoyed their own parties and the day's rest from regular duty.

Sporadic leaves also broke some of the monotony of life at the frontier forts. Such absences were granted irregularly, depending on the availability of substitute military personnel and the whim of the commanding officer or department official. Some of those who received time off elected to remain at their post and relax; others visited friends, relatives, or locations far afield. Especially popular with the ambitious political set was the nation's capital. Some, of course, never returned from their leaves and were eventually classed as deserters.

The inadequate transportation system posed almost insoluble difficulties to those on a tight time schedule. O. M. Knapp's experience appears to have been typical. With seven days' leave from Fort Bliss, Knapp headed for Albuquerque. The journey, however, took ten days. Upon arriving, Knapp explained his dilemma to the ranking officer and spent a carefree week enjoying that New Mexico city. "It is the first time I ever ran any risk of the kind," he reasoned. "I have always stuck to duty but it is peace times now, my play spells have been few and now I am going to make the most of it."[23]

Mexican border towns attracted large numbers of U.S. soldiers throughout the nineteenth century. Troops stationed along the Rio Grande ventured into Nuevo Laredo, Piedras Negras, Matamoros, or Juárez at least once during their tours of duty. Reflecting the prejudices of race, religion, and culture common to many Americans of the period, most observers considered Hispanics lazy and immoral. The gambling and dancing south of the border received mixed reviews. Few, however, left Mexico with fond memories of their inevitable trips to the bullfights. Lt. J. J. Brereton remembered the animals as being "mostly cows, all nearly paralyzed from fright, and without the slightest intention of injuring any of the men who danced around them."[24]

Unfortunately, leaves could not be granted as often as soldiers would have liked. They could not go hunting and fishing every day, nor were there dances every evening. The most common form of entertainment was a quiet visit with other members of the garrison. Officers and their families spent countless hours

---

22. Armes, *Ups and Downs*, pp. 460, 508; Barbara E. Fisher, ed., "Forrestine Cooper Hooker's Notes and Memoirs on Army Life in the West, 1871–1876" (Master's thesis, University of Arizona, 1963), p. 122; McConnell, *Five Years a Cavalryman*, p. 42.

23. Knapp to Mead, Feb. 18, 1867, Knapp Papers.

24. Brereton, Jan. 4, 1878, in R. C. Crane, ed., "Letters from Texas," *West Texas Historical Association Year Book* 25 (Oct., 1949): 112.

sitting on their front porches. Trying to reduce the glare from the parade ground for those who sat on his porch, one officer at Fort Bliss planted oats in front of his house. They were well tended until it was discovered that rattlesnakes enjoyed the cool shade afforded by the plants. Some places inevitably became favorites; at Fort Concho, for example, Capt. Theodore A. Baldwin's porch was an especially popular gathering point.

Visitors and family helped overcome the frontier soldier's loneliness. Almost without exception residents welcomed visitors with open arms and eager hospitality. At a Texas Ranger camp near Menard, Mrs. D. W. Roberts invited pretty local girls to stay with her while her husband was away on patrols. She realized, as did George and Elizabeth Custer when they hired their servant girl, that dashing young men would flock to see the attractive house guests. On one typical September night at Fort Concho, Colonel Grierson's wife Alice watched as two young lieutenants played whist with her oldest son, Robert, and his cousin Helen. After some effort Alice convinced her younger sons that they could not go with their older brother Robert on his projected overnight hunting trip. The disappointed youngsters settled for their own card game in the kitchen.

The size and composition of a garrison could mean the difference between miserable boredom and a pleasant social life. The lack of entertainment became especially demoralizing at the smaller, more distant posts. Mrs. Orsemus Boyd, a temporary victim of the overwhelming depression that often engulfed the residents of a small fort, found Fort Duncan, a two-company post during her residence, "inevitably dull." From Fort Chadbourne, George Steuart complained that "there is nothing to do here, and I think the government ought to pay us more, and give us a leave of absence . . . in recompense for our remaining here, and being cut off from all society and all the comforts & enjoyment of a civilized life."[25]

Frontier life in Texas could become tedious indeed. Poor weather or blistering heat prohibited outside recreation. "During the day our costumes were the lightest and airiest that could be devised," wrote Mrs. Boyd. "But when evening came—and no woman ever ventured out of doors until after sunset—we arrayed ourselves in pretty white dresses, and started forth to enjoy the breeze, whose never-failing, grateful presence was compensation for the day's intense heat." Col. Charles J. Crane voiced similar views when he called Ringgold Barracks "the hottest place I had ever seen." Yet, he said, despite the heat, "we managed to exist and to enjoy ourselves."[26]

The desire to make the best of the difficult conditions at the frontiers of Texas permeates the letters and diaries written by contemporaries. "We had no amusements outside of the Post but what we could invent with our limited means, and had to resort to almost every device to kill time," wrote Zenas R. Bliss of antebellum Fort Davis. Yet rather than passively accepting their isolated condi-

25. Boyd, *Cavalry Life*, p. 285; Steuart to Mary, Aug. 16, 1854, George H. Steuart Correspondence, Eberstadt Collection, BTHC.

26. Boyd, *Cavalry Life*, p. 266; Crane, *Colonel of Infantry*, pp. 98, 102.

tion, the men of the garrison built a racetrack and a makeshift theater. Others showed comparable determination by going to school after having worked all day or going to the library to read a newspaper or a popular novel. Those who preferred outdoor activities also took advantage of the situation to hunt or to study the flora and fauna.[27]

27. Bliss Reminiscences, 1:309.

While life on the Texas frontiers may seem bleak from a twentieth-century perspective, the men and women who lived on the frontier forts relished life as much as did the city dwellers of the East. Although they were far removed from more traditional urban amusements, it should be remembered that most of them came from rural backgrounds and were accustomed to the less elaborate forms of entertainment pursued at the military bases. Thus, the majority of them adapted to the situation and found many ways to relax and enjoy themselves.

CHAPTER TEN

Post Society

. . . a bond of something sentimental.

—Sgt. John B. Charlton

Members of a fort's garrison were a disparate group whose relationships reflected a mixture of military custom and harsh frontier realities. Among the enlisted men "bunkies" became close comrades and confidants, sharing each other's joys and miseries. Soldiers usually mingled with other members of their own company, and rivalries between regiments, branches of service, and racial groups were common. The men had little social contact with their officers, the army's rigid hierarchy precluding associations between commissioned and enlisted personnel. Officers were the elite of post society, and the hierarchy of rank was assiduously observed. Similar divisions split the women and children of the garrison, although women at the forts enjoyed a higher status than the nineteenth-century norm. Despite internal bickering, the members of the garrison came together in the face of external threats. The menace of death, disease, Indian attack, or natural disaster strengthened the ties that bound together the diverse elements of a frontier post.

Whether formally or informally, every soldier was paired off with a fellow enlisted man. In the field they shared blankets, rations, and cooking chores. Not surprisingly, these close associations often developed into warm friendships, bunkies relating to each other stories and personal secrets they withheld from everyone else in the army. In the cavalry the four troopers who tied their horses together on dismounting might develop strong ties. "Between us there was a bond of something sentimental, perhaps," recalled Sgt. John B. Charlton, "a sort of 'fought-bled-and-if-need-die-together' tomfoolery which led us into many a foolhardy escapade."[1]

On a broader level the company provided the basis for organized society

1. Robert G. Carter, *The Old Sergeant's Story: Winning the West from the Indians and Bad Men in 1870 to 1876* (New York: Frederick H. Hitchcock, 1926), p. 108.

for enlisted personnel. As one observer put it, each company was in many respects a "club," whose members ate, drilled, and slept together. Encountering many of the same problems, they pooled their savings from their rations to buy books, extra food, and recreational items. They marched as a unit and shared the same hardships. As individuals they understood that their safety depended on their actions as a group in combat and on patrol. Aware of this mutual dependence, the average soldier took great pride in his company.[2]

Of course, this sentiment did not prevent dissension in the unit. Veterans hazed new recruits unmercifully. The wide range of backgrounds and personalities represented in every company and the arduous life at every frontier station strained relations in even the most disciplined unit. Gossip and scandal were common, and fights often broke out. Most of an individual's possessions were hung in the open on pegs above or beside his bunk, and the presence of a few thieves

2. James Parker, *The Old Army: Memories, 1872–1918* (Philadelphia: Dorrance and Co., 1880), p. 17.

fostered additional distrust. "Dog robbers," or officers' servants, were particularly resented by their peers, who commented scornfully that they "gobble up all the 'crumbs' of whatever kind that fall from his [the officer's] table."[3]

Sectional and national rivalries also threatened company harmony. Southerners fought northerners, and easterners battled westerners over politics and long-held prejudices. Disputes between foreign-born soldiers fired additional hostilities. A member of the Sixth Cavalry described deteriorating relations stemming from the Franco-Prussian War:

> Army "scrimmages" occurred between the German and French soldiers in the command, and although the latter were few in numbers they made it up in an excess of patriotism. But the Germans had the best of it; the majority of the band was from the "Fatherland," and the "Wacht am Rhine" and other of their national airs were played morning, noon and night, to the disgust of the "enemy." The Frenchmen would get together and sing the "Marseillaise," and occasionally blows were struck, but not much damage was done, and finally the officers prohibited the playing of the aggravating tunes.[4]

Relations among a regiment's companies could be even more strained. The army's small size meant that only three or four companies served at a typical post. Lack of familiarity bred distrust among units. En route to Camp Colorado in 1856, for example, a conflict arose between the men of Earl Van Dorn's Company A and those of Theodore O'Hara's Company F, though both companies belonged to the Second Cavalry Regiment. The men of Company A, largely drawn from the area around Mobile, Alabama, bragged about Captain Van Dorn's abilities. Tired of the constant boasting, the Kentuckians of Company F poked fun at the Alabamans' southern drawls. A huge fight finally broke out, resolved only after nine of the contestants were placed in leg irons.

Despite these differences, troops belonging to the same regiment closed ranks against outsiders. The men of a regiment, after all, shared military tradition, uniform insignia, and a single commander. Animosities between the different service branches compounded the jealousies. Infantrymen resented cavalrymen and dragoons, and the mounted troops wholeheartedly reciprocated. Proud of their status, jealous of the real or imagined preferential treatment accorded other outfits, enlisted men from different regiments usually went their separate ways. The uneasiness even extended to women and children. One Tenth Cavalry officer's daughter recalled that "we scorned the infantry children and we fought other cavalry youngsters who dared claim greater honor for their own regiment."[5]

3. H. H. McConnell, *Five Years a Cavalryman: Or, Sketches of Regular Army Life on the Texas Frontier, Twenty Odd Years Ago* (Jacksboro, Tex.: J. N. Rogers and Co., 1889), pp. 12, 107, 211; James Larsen Memoirs, BTHC, p. 219.

4. McConnell, *Five Years a Cavalryman*, pp. 220–21.

5. Barbara E. Fisher, ed., "Forrestine Cooper Hooker's Notes and Memoirs on Army Life in the West, 1871–1876" (Master's thesis, University of Arizona, 1963), p. 146; Don Rickey, Jr., *Forty*

Friction between blacks and whites was especially pronounced. Many whites objected to the presence of blacks in the army. Some predicted that blacks would be overcome by their allegedly all-consuming passion for the white women of the garrison. Others believed that blacks made poor soldiers. One surgeon blamed the inefficient policing of his post on the black garrison and concluded that "the impracticality of making intelligent soldiers out of the mass of negroes is growing more evident . . . every day." Fearing that appointment to a black regiment reflected badly on their professional competence and aware that shortages of literate noncommissioned officers in these units would increase their clerical duties, many officers dreaded the prospect of commanding black troops. A few resigned rather than serve in what they believed were racially inferior outfits.[6]

The evidence, however, clearly shows that blacks performed well along the Texas frontiers. Morale was high and the incidence of alcoholism low in black units. Desertion was significantly lower among black regiments than among white outfits. In 1867, for example, one-fourth of the entire U.S. Army deserted; during the same year only 4 percent of the black troops deserted. Furthermore, blacks did well in combat: fourteen of their number were awarded the Congressional Medal of Honor during the Indian Wars.

Most officers who led the black regiments reported favorably on their men. Assigned to the Twenty-fourth Infantry upon his graduation from West Point in 1877, Charles J. Crane admitted that "though I had not desired the colored infantry . . . I have never regretted my service in that regiment." Others credited the troops with showing special interest in drill and training. They "never complain of their food, except when ordered to do so," wrote an officer at Ringgold Barracks. O. M. Knapp believed that the men were "too much interested in the Garrison School to find time for mischief."[7]

Entrance into the army did not guarantee blacks equal treatment. The army strongly opposed integrated facilities, and blacks often received more severe punishment for infractions than did whites. Tired of the repeated violations of their civil and military rights, some black troops struck back at their persecutors. In Texas the most serious of these outbreaks occurred at Fort Stockton in 1873. Pvt. John Taylor, Company K, Twenty-fifth Infantry, reported sick to Dr. J. A. Cleary, the post surgeon. Cleary prescribed some medicine but did not excuse Taylor from duty. When Taylor reported sick a third time, Cleary had him placed in the post guardhouse as a malingerer. Taylor died the following day, and Cleary and a visiting surgeon were unable to find the cause of death. Outraged, most of the black troops stationed at Stockton signed a petition blaming Taylor's death on Cleary. Many reportedly discussed mutiny. Court-martial proceedings against those in-

---

Miles a Day on Beans and Hay: The Enlisted Soldier Fighting the Indian Wars (Norman: University of Oklahoma Press, 1963), pp. 75–87.

6. PMR, Fort Concho, Nov., 1869, NA, RG 94 (microfilm, BTHC, p. 147); Jack D. Foner, *Blacks and the Military in American History: A New Perspective* (New York: Praeger Press, 1974), p. 60.

7. Charles J. Crane, *Experiences of a Colonel of Infantry* (New York: Knickerbocker Press, 1923), pp. 59, 115; Knapp to Mead, Jan. 12, 1867, Obadiah M. Knapp Papers, BTHC.

volved in the alleged conspiracy began immediately, and everyone implicated in the affair was sentenced to prison terms of five to fifteen years.[8]

Social life at the Texas forts was segregated by rank as well as by race. Black troops held dances, white troops held dances, and officers held dances. The guest lists for such affairs had few names in common. Each group frequented different bars and saloons off the post; often their children attended school at different hours. Those who violated these practices faced criticism or even social ostracism by their peers.

Segregation of society according to rank also extended to military duty. While many officers hired strikers from the ranks, such men rarely possessed the characteristics of typical enlistees. Officers had little contact with the enlisted men on duty. Sergeants and corporals handled much of the company's paperwork, as well as the drills and fatigue parties. This practice, while freeing an officer of tedious detail, further reduced his knowledge of internal company affairs.

Not all officers fell into such malaise, however. Many displayed sincere regard for the welfare of the men in their commands. Securing a shipment of fresh vegetables might win the everlasting loyalty of hungry soldiers tired of tough beef and desiccated potatoes. Others earned the devotion of their troops through their personal magnetism or feats of gallantry in battle. The enlisted men also appreciated the efforts of those who conducted marches and scouts with a minimum of waste. Good officers sought, and usually received, the respect of their men. They did not, however, attempt to bridge the social barriers beyond an occasional compliment, often grudgingly given and grudgingly received, or a Christmas gift of a pig or a sheep.

The harsh punishment meted out by officers to soldiers under arrest undoubtedly increased social tensions. Drunkenness, petty theft, and desertion were the most common offenses, although frontier troops occasionally committed crimes ranging from murder to "neglect of duty" and "highway robbery." Pvt. George Perry lifted a jar of candy from a saloon; Richard Talbot stole a dollar from a civilian. Pvt. William Harvey, in charge of prisoner labor gangs, allowed his charges to become drunk. Zenas R. Bliss, commissary officer at Fort Inge, had to pay $80 out of his own pocket to cover the theft of coffee and sugar stores. Only later did he discover that his commissary sergeant had done the deed.[9]

Desertion was the most common major offense. Dissatisfied with the low wages and hard manual labor of military life, anxious to escape possible charges relating to other crimes, or simply using their enlistments as free trips to the West, about one-third of those who joined the army deserted. At Fort Griffin, for exam-

8. Clayton Williams, *Texas' Last Frontier: Fort Stockton and the Trans-Pecos, 1861–1895*, ed. Ernest Wallace (College Station: Texas A&M University Press, 1982), pp. 170–71.

9. PMR, Fort Richardson, Dec., 1874, pp. 107–11; William H. Leckie, *The Buffalo Soldiers: A Narrative of the Negro Cavalry in the West* (Norman: University of Oklahoma Press, 1967), p. 98, 151; Zenas R. Bliss Reminiscences, 2:32, BTHC.

ple, 98 men deserted during the first ten months of 1871. The commanding officer at San Antonio congratulated Lt. Adam Kramer for leading 289 recruits from Carlisle, Pennsylvania, to Texas with only five desertions.

Punishment was almost inevitably severe. Minor crimes drew fines or a stint in the guardhouse. A noncommissioned officer might lose his stripes. Pvt. John Curtis, Ninth Cavalry, received two months' hard labor for telling his sergeant to "go to Hell"; William Tolliver was sentenced to six months in the guardhouse for taking a nap on duty. Records for 1874 at Fort Richardson indicate that at the 450-man garrison 221 soldiers were tried for 412 offenses. General and garrison courts-martial handed down eleven acquittals, meted out imprisonment for terms totaling just under twenty years, and levied fines of $1,671.50. Until the 1880s such fines supported the Old Soldiers' Home in Washington, D.C.[10]

Other authorities resorted to corporal punishment. Although the army officially banned flogging in 1861, deserters and criminals might be "bucked" (wrists bound to ankles) and gagged, spreadeagled, or tied up by their thumbs. A convicted soldier often had to carry a heavy wooden rail on his shoulders. A hardened thief might be sentenced to have his head shaved, be stripped of his coat and hat, and be forced to walk the parade ground in front of the assembled command before being thrown off the base. A deserter endured similar punishment, with a severe whipping, a walk through the post wearing only a heavy wooden barrel, and the mocking strains of "The Rogue's March" added to his penalty.

Although the American civilian penal system dispensed similarly harsh punishment during the nineteenth century, some observers questioned the military value of such methods. They particularly galled Texans who volunteered during the Civil War. In those units the fiercely independent southerners bitterly resented attempts to enforce military discipline. One Texan seemed unable to believe the regimen at Fort Bliss. "One of us can't cross the river without a written pass," he complained, "and after nine o'clock at night, if one of us is caught over the guard line we are taken up and put in the guard house, if we have not the pass word or a written pass!"[11]

Like the enlisted men they commanded, officers were torn between the camaraderie often associated with military life and the nagging divisions that beset the frontier garrisons. To save money or to fight loneliness, bachelor officers pooled their money to hire cooks and formed mess groups. They also attended "hops" and dinners given by their peers. Some had fought together in the Mexican War or the Civil War; most had attended West Point. They came from upper- or middle-class Protestant homes and shared a northern European heritage. They commiserated with each other about the low pay and difficult life. Practical jokes were

---

10. Leckie, *Buffalo Soldiers*, p. 98; PMR, Fort Richardson, Dec., 1874, pp. 107–11; Rickey, *Forty Miles a Day*, pp. 98–99.

11. Martin Hardwick Hall, ed., "The Taylor Letters: Confederate Correspondence from Fort Bliss," *Military History of Texas and the Southwest* 15, no. 2 (1972): 55.

frequent; even the commanding officer might become the target of a prankster's antics. The realization that they had to depend on their fellow officers during scouts and fights drew them still closer.

Yet discontent was common among officers. Housing shortages created the biggest source of conflict among commissioned personnel. Officers selected their quarters on the basis of seniority, generating great antipathy among those who had been "ranked out" of their homes. The feeble efforts of less-qualified officers also disgusted the abler men, who sought to distance themselves from mediocre officers socially as well as professionally. On court-martial duty at Fort Brown in 1856, Robert E. Lee skipped his meals rather than eat with a "crowd of uninteresting men."[12]

Differences in age and experience further divided the commands as aging Civil War veterans clashed with newcomers eager for promotion. A study made in 1877 indicated that it would take the average second lieutenant twenty-four to twenty-six years to reach the rank of major; he could expect another ten-year wait before becoming a colonel. Some blamed favoritism for their failure to achieve higher rank and bitterly resented those who did secure promotion. The lack of a West Point background segregated some. Petty slights, whispered insults, or shifts in positioning during evening and Sunday dress parades engendered jealousy and bitterness. Attacks on the sobriety of fellow officers also fueled post antagonisms.

The animosity caused by inadequate housing, the lack of advancement, and geographical isolation affected familial relations among all social groups. Denied entrance to most professions in nineteenth-century America, some army wives undoubtedly transferred their own ambitions to their husbands' careers. Through their husbands' rise through the ranks, they too gained increased self-esteem and social status. Of course, men had their own egos and often neglected their wives in their quests for promotion. Alice Grierson complained to husband Benjamin that "if only a little of your energy could be transferred to me, I doubt if you would be any the worse, and I might be all the better."[13]

Problems between wives and husbands at the Texas forts were not limited to ambition or the search for proper shelter. Transfers and shifts from post to post and house to house made it difficult for a married couple to establish roots. The emphasis placed on marriage during adolescence could also prove an obstacle, in that few unions achieved the bliss portrayed in popular literature. As a result, neither party was fully prepared for the hardships and struggles that face any marriage. Taught that it was their own fault if they were unhappy, wives had few outlets for their anger and resentment. Their pent-up frustrations might affect their marriages and sanity. The discomforts and dangers of childbirth further

12. Lee to Mrs. Lee, Nov. 15, 1856, Francis Raymond Adams, Jr., "An Annotated Edition of the Personal Letters of Robert E. Lee, April, 1855–April, 1861" (Ph.D. diss., University of Maryland, 1955), p. 207.

13. Barbara Welter, *Dimity Convictions: The American Woman in the Nineteenth Century* (Athens: Ohio University Press, 1976), p. 8; Alice to B. Grierson, Sept. 23, 1883, Texas Letters of Benjamin Grierson (microfilm, Fort Concho Research Library, MF 17).

complicated women's lives on the frontier. Fearful of the problems of bearing and rearing a child in such posts, army wives resorted to various means of preventing unwanted pregnancies, including sexual abstinence and rudimentary birth control. Abortion, while uncommon, was not unknown on the military frontiers.[14]

Although perceived as weaker than their husbands, women had the primary responsibility for rearing and educating the children. In addition, women were viewed as lending moral tone to a post. The popular culture of the period portrayed women as society's moral guardians, and many females took this responsibility quite seriously. The commander's wife generally took a strong hand in setting the post's social standards and gave offenders quiet warnings to reform. Ostracism awaited those who did not.[15]

Society also dictated that the proper wife remained at home while the husband entered the industrial, business, professional, or military world. Few opportunities for work presented themselves to officers' wives in Texas, and the elite did not overtly challenge this doctrine. By contrast, laundresses often made more money than their soldier husbands. While such work remained within the accepted sphere of women's activity, it probably led to higher status for the wife in the typical army marriage than she would have had in civilian life.

The scarcity of women at the frontier posts further enhanced their status. Soldiers placed women, especially the wives of officers, on pedestals. By virtue of their few numbers, such women could expect and demand better treatment from their spouses and from males on the post than could most contemporary females. "The most profane soldier holds his tongue in a vise when he is in the presence of a woman," explained Libbie Custer. Another wife reported that army women "always receive attentions which no woman in citizen life is accustomed when no longer young. . . . Gray-haired ladies at an army post dance at the hops with as much enjoyment as the younger ones, and they are always invited by the men, young and old, to do so as a matter of course."[16]

The relatively high status accorded women also made it possible for them to become more involved in social activities than was the norm elsewhere during the period. Some accompanied their husbands to the sutler's store for entertainment or a game of billiards. Others sponsored benevolent causes. They also ex-

---

14. Anne Firor Scott, *The Southern Lady from Pedestal to Politics, 1830–1930* (Chicago: University of Chicago Press, 1970), pp. 11, 23, 27, 42, 57–58; Starr to Eliza, Jan. 25, 1850, Samuel Henry Starr Papers, BTHC; Susan E. Newcomb Diary, pp. 48, 96, BTHC; Mary P. Ryan, *The Empire of the Mother: American Writing about Domesticity, 1830–1860*, Women and History No. 2/3 (New York: Institute for Research in History and The Howarth Press, 1982), pp. 2–3.

15. Smithers to Grierson, June 3, 1883, Texas Letters of Benjamin Grierson, MF 17; Charles P. Roland and Richard P. Robbins, ed., "The Diary of Eliza (Mrs. Albert Sidney) Johnston: The Second Cavalry Comes to Texas," *Southwestern Historical Quarterly* 60 (Apr., 1957): 493.

16. Elizabeth B. Custer, *Tenting on the Plains, or General Custer in Kansas and Texas* (1897; reprint, Norman: University of Oklahoma Press, 1971), 2:353, 400; Lydia Spencer Lane, *I Married a Soldier; or, Old Days in the Old Army* (1893; reprint, Albuquerque, N.Mex.: Horn and Wallace, 1964), pp. 83–84.

erted a strong influence on the men of the garrison, who sought to gain their favor. Finally, the frequent and extended absences of their husbands on military service gave them added independence. Although other garrison members looked after their material needs, army wives frequently carried out duties not considered to be in the average woman's domain.[17]

This is not to imply that women were treated as equals (prostitutes, for example, were often censured while their patrons went unpunished). In the end the vast majority of wives followed their husbands, giving up their own friends and ambitions in the process. Furthermore, it should be noted that not all the women at a garrison were accorded the same respect. Although the harsh life and common experiences shared by all women created certain bonds, a huge social gulf divided officers' wives from the company laundresses and hospital workers. Like their husbands, they generally attended their own social functions and stayed within their peer groups. Officers' wives dominated genteel social life with their gala balls and dinners; the wives of enlisted men attended dances and parties that upper-class observers considered less respectable.

Many soldiers refused to bring their wives and families with them to Texas. Some feared that life at the frontier bases would prove too rigorous; others recognized that the lack of educational opportunities past grade school would retard their children's advancement. Economic constraints forced others to leave their families at home. Few men, however, forgot their families during such separations. "If there is a tie on earth that binds me to it, and makes me feel that it is not all a miserable dream, it is my wife and children," wrote Earl Van Dorn to his wife Carrie. "Your disinterested love breathed even through the faint medium of a letter, comes to me like the babbling of some sure fountain to the ear of a weary traveler of the desert." Colonel Grierson, whose wife had gone east for a visit, promised to send her money for a new dress upon the paymaster's arrival, "so that you may not be eternally done or dressed up in drab. . . . If I was near enough to you I would give you one of the longest strongest sweetest and best kisses you ever had or ever got from me or anyone else."[18]

Despite the tensions and the class and racial differences that beset soldiers and dependents at Texas posts, outside influences tended to unify the army's diverse elements. Most military personnel, for example, blamed their financial and military woes on Congress. Low pay and poor living conditions could be attributed to congressional parsimony. Frontier soldiers also censured the national legisla-

17. Custer, *Tenting on the Plains*, 1:176–77, 2:399–400; Sandra L. Myres, *Westering Women and the Frontier Experience, 1800–1915,* Histories of the American Frontier (Albuquerque: University of New Mexico Press, 1982), pp. 211–12.

18. Patricia Y. Stallard, *Glittering Misery: Dependents of the Indian Fighting Army* (Fort Collins and San Rafael, Colo.: Old Army Press and Presidio Press, 1978), pp. 61–62, 92; E. V. D. Miller, ed., *A Soldier's Honor: With Reminiscences of Major-General Earl Van Dorn by His Comrades* (New York: Abbey Press, 1902), p. 337; Grierson to Alice, May 8, 1875, Texas Letters of Benjamin Grierson, MF 16.

ture for its failure to give the army complete control of Indian affairs. The continued presence of the Department of the Interior in these matters, they believed, prevented the military from dealing effectively with the government's Indian wards.

The less than cooperative spirit that many Texas civilians displayed toward the regular troops further united the army against what it perceived to be a common foe. On an individual level, relations between soldiers and civilians on the Texas frontiers might be rather amicable. Soldiers patronized the local merchants and saloons. At some social events the two groups mingled well, and off-duty troopers thrived on the companionship of congenial civilians. Likewise, civilians appreciated the services of the post doctor and chaplain. Grateful for the protection against Indian attack provided by the regulars, General Order No. 5 of the newly formed Texas state troops proclaimed that "there was no exultation over the surrender of the Troops of the old 8th Infantry" after secession in 1861.[19]

Not all Texans, however, were as appreciative. The Union's victory over the Confederacy and subsequent occupation of the South during Reconstruction bred additional distrust. Hatred of northerners and jealousy of the often haughty officers led numbers of civilians to shun the armed forces, particularly while memories of the recent civil conflict remained fresh. This further distanced the regulars from Texas citizens. Others simply disliked the federal government's presence in their daily lives. On a frontier where civilian authority was often weak, officers sometimes used their troops to preserve order. The army made repeated efforts, for example, to stop Texas cattlemen from ranging their animals in Indian Territory during the 1880s. In such cases officers might be sued in civil court by those they had arrested.[20]

Soldiers venturing into saloons and gambling houses near their posts sometimes paid for their visits with their lives; blacks found themselves special targets of abuse. Several buffalo soldiers were lynched; their murderers often went unpunished by local juries. Wary troops of all races realized the dangers and entered the villages in groups for self-preservation. Others tried to prevent trouble by looking out for one another. "It was a rule among the soldiers," wrote a civilian at Eagle Pass, "that when one of their men got too much to drink and got too boisterous to have him taken home to the post." Col. William Shafter took special pains to prevent civilians from discriminating against his black foot soldiers. Shafter demanded that his men who were guarding the segregated stagecoaches be allowed to use cooking facilities at the way stations and to ride the coaches back to their posts at the end of their duty.[21]

Soldiers sometimes sought revenge against those who had killed or harassed their comrades. Minor brawls could become armed riots. The men of Company

19. General Order No. 5, May 13, 1861, James B. Barry Papers, BTHC.

20. Drum to Comm. Div. of Mo., June 11, 1884, Letters Sent by the Office of the Adjutant General (main series), 1800–1890, NA, RG 94, 407 (microcopy 565, vol. 72, reel 57); McKeever to Augur, May 23, NA, RG 94, 407 (vol. 75, reel 58).

21. Jesse Sumpter Papers, pp. 33–34, BTHC; Paul H. Carlson, "William R. Shafter Commanding Black Troops in West Texas," *West Texas Historical Association Year Book* 50 (1974): 108–109.

B, Sixth Cavalry, stole out of camp at Fort Richardson after receiving word that one of their members had been killed in a Jacksboro brothel. Fearful of a major attack, the civilians also turned out. A bloody confrontation was averted by an officer who had a private conversation with the more moderate civilian leaders.

Conflicts also arose between regulars and Texas Rangers. Although both federal soldiers and state Rangers were engaged in defending the Texas frontiers, their methods and appearance varied markedly. The uniformed bluecoats appeared in sharp contrast to the informal Rangers, who dressed according to individual taste. In general the Rangers had more mobility but less discipline than the regulars. While some examples of army-Ranger cooperation can be found in campaigns against Juan Cortina (1859–60) and in Ranger Capt. L. H. McNelly's Rio Grande crossings (1875), the two groups generally operated independently of each other.

The marked differences between soldier and Ranger created a good deal of rivalry. Ranger Capt. John ("Rip") Ford claimed that, while he disliked criticizing the army, the regulars simply "did not understand and appreciate the Indians' mode of fighting." Texas citizens usually sided with the Rangers. Not surprisingly, regulars also found fault with their rivals. By shooting first and asking questions later, maintained army men, the Rangers stirred up more trouble than they were worth. Gen. E. O. C. Ord, commanding the Department of Texas, noted that only regular troops "under discreet commanders" should operate along the Rio Grande. "If the President wants war he can get it by calling out Texas volunteers," claimed Ord.[22]

Conflicts with civilians thus unified the men and women of the army's Texas forts. The ever-present danger of disease and death had a similar effect. On average, between 1849 and 1859 the soldier stationed in Texas was ill more than three times a year. During this period 703 soldiers died, a mortality rate of about 3.5 percent. After the Civil War improved medical skills, better sanitation, and the increased numbers of men serving on Texas' healthier western frontiers rather than along the Rio Grande reduced the casualty figures. At Fort Davis, for example, from 1869 to May, 1872, the annual death rate was about six per thousand, and the yearly illness figures were only about 60 percent of total manpower. Occasional outbreaks of disease, however, could still debilitate an entire command. The surgeon at Fort Concho reported that more than half the garrison was taken sick during May, 1877.

As in every other nineteenth-century army, disease rather than combat caused the vast majority of military casualties. Before the Civil War doctors reported more cases of fever than of any other ailment. Malaria was particularly common, especially in the lowlands; 27 percent of the 66,486 illnesses and injuries reported in the Department of Texas from 1849 to 1859 were diagnosed as malaria, or intermittent fever. Fortunately, liberal doses of quinine limited to 6 the fatalities attributed to this fever during the same period. The great killer, by contrast, was

22. Ford, *Rip Ford's Texas*, p. 221; Ord to Sherman, Oct. 25, 1877, vol. 46, reel 24, William T. Sherman Papers, Library of Congress (microfilm, University of Texas).

the dreaded yellow fever. Recurring outbreaks of this terrifying ailment struck the Texas coast throughout the nineteenth century and did not spare soldiers or their dependents. During the summer of 1867 the surgeon at Galveston, a post with a mean strength of 185, reported 204 cases of yellow fever resulting in 81 deaths.

Digestive disorders also plagued the troops in Texas, outstripping even fevers as the most common afflictions at some of the western posts. Diarrhea, constipation, and dysentery were the most common of these ailments. Of the digestive problems, cholera, an intestinal disorder spread by unsanitary practices and filth, proved the most fatal. Cholera struck Texas during the years 1848 through 1854

and again in 1865 and 1867. The epidemic of 1849 was probably the most disastrous, infecting six hundred of San Antonio's fifteen hundred inhabitants who had not fled the city and killing more than half of those who contracted the disease.

Other afflictions also made their presence felt. At Fort Griffin between 1867 and 1871 physicians diagnosed ninety-eight different ailments ranging from boils to snakebites. Scurvy was particularly troublesome in Texas. Respiratory ailments— catarrh (the common cold), bronchitis, pleurisy, pneumonia, and tuberculosis— struck military and civilian personnel. Rheumatism, headaches, delirium tremens,

gonorrhea, and syphilis posed additional health hazards. Wounds and injuries, including sprains, cuts, and bruises incurred during regular duties as well as during service in the field, also accounted for a sizable number of cases reported by post surgeons.[23]

Several problems handicapped those attempting to combat the health problems. A shortage of doctors forced the army to hire large numbers of civilian contract surgeons. Even with these additions some posts lacked medical personnel. In a not unusual report, Inspector W. G. Freeman found that six of the eighteen Texas posts he visited in 1853 were without resident physicians. While some post surgeons were fortunate enough to have one or two assistants after 1865, the army never had enough medical personnel to meet its needs.

The troubled state of American medicine during the period compounded the problems. Racked by public and private quarrels and outdated procedures, the profession underwent a series of convulsions that damaged medical programs. Even the best-educated doctors who had passed the army's three-day qualifying examination found that limited facilities and shortages of medical instruments and trained assistants frustrated their efforts. Although the hospitals were often the best structures on the base, sanitary conditions remained poor.

The quality of medical knowledge also left much to be desired. Smallpox vaccinations were administered routinely; however, the bacteria responsible for cholera was not isolated until 1883, and antiseptics were not commonly used in the army until about the same time. Anticontagionists dominated army medical thought through the early 1870s. Military doctors, like their civilian colleagues, attributed malaria and yellow fever to odors or gases stemming from nearby marshes. The surgeon at Fort Brown, for instance, declared that the "exceeding unpleasant and by no means sweet scented effluence arising from the lagoon" caused the severe cases of fever at that post. No wonder, then, that Mrs. Albert Sidney Johnston expressed something less than joy upon the arrival of one Dr. Smith to treat her ill husband. "God forbid that any of us should be sick again while he is with us," she wrote in her diary.[24]

Nonetheless, most physicians did their best to reduce the lurking dangers of illness and death. Attributing many health problems to excessive drinking, the typical frontier doctor also pointed out the links between overindulgence and illness. Many of them struggled to improve sanitation, and postbellum doctors encouraged the men to bathe regularly. They issued quinine and whiskey liberally to treat colds. By 1876, the surgeon general had made sprays and carbolized dressings and sutures articles of issue. Some posts, such as Fort Elliott, seemed remark-

23. James O. Breeden, "Health of Early Texas: The Military Frontier," *Southwestern Historical Quarterly* 80 (Apr., 1977): 362–82; David A. Clary, "The Role of the Army Surgeon in the West: Daniel Weisel at Fort Davis, Texas, 1868–1872," *Western Historical Quarterly* 3 (Jan., 1972): 62–64.

24. PMR, Fort Brown, June, 1869, Apr., 1872; Stanhope Bayne-Jones, *The Evolution of Preventive Medicine in the United States Army, 1607–1939* (Washington: D.C.: Office of the Surgeon General, 1968), p. 114; James A. Huston, *The Sinews of War: Army Logistics, 1775–1953* (Washington, D.C.: U.S. Government Printing Office, 1960), p. 255; Roland and Robbins, ed., "Johnston Diary," p. 493.

ably free from disease. Reports for November, 1886, show that, of its garrison of 7 officers, 185 enlisted men, and 27 Indian scouts, there were just 9 admissions to the hospital, only 2 of which were disease-related.[25]

Yet death remained a very real threat on the military frontier, striking soldier and civilian alike with little regard for rank or privilege. Typhoid fever struck down Col. Benjamin Grierson's thirteen-year-old daughter Edith. William J. Worth, commander of the Department of Texas and New Mexico, died in the cholera epidemic of 1849. Surgeon William N. Notson's poignant comment in the June, 1869, medical record at Fort Concho contains a note that the month "opened with especial sadness, by the loss of an infant child. That it was the first born

25. PMR, Fort Richardson, Dec., 1874, pp. 111–12; PMR, Fort Concho, Oct., 1870, Nov. 24, 1877, p. 291; PMR, Fort Griffin, Dec., 1874, pp. 33–34; PMR, Fort Elliott, Apr. 2, 1887, pp. 104–105.

to an officer at Fort Concho, and the first death in an officer's family, perhaps may be the apology for the introduction of personal matters in the Record. Otis Rockwell Notson, died June 1st 1869."[26]

The common threats of death and disease united the men, women, and children who lived in the frontier forts. The shared dangers and threats from civilian authorities, Indians, and personal tragedy gave them a common bond that proved just as important as military custom in shaping the post's social life. One wife's description of this society seems particularly fitting: "Their failures, their fights, their vacillations, all were before us, and it was an anxious life to be watching who won and who lost in those moral warfares. You could not separate yourself from the interests of one another. It was a network of friendships that became more and more interwoven by common hardships, deprivations, dangers, by isolation and the daily sharing of joys and troubles."[27]

26. PMR, Fort Concho, June, 1869, p. 125, Sept. 9, 1878, p. 329.
27. Custer, *Tenting on the Plains*, 2:400–401.

CHAPTER ELEVEN

The Passing of the Military Frontiers

L arge numbers of United States troops garrisoned the Texas frontiers throughout most of the nineteenth century. Laundresses, scouts, dependents, and civilian workers joined the soldiers in occupying the far reaches of the Lone Star State. Overcoming recurring shortages of water, building materials, manpower, and money, these individuals pushed the limits of recognized settlement relentlessly forward. Beset by sagging morale and decreasing numbers, the Indians of Texas slowly gave way to the vast resources of the United States.

In the 1880s and 1890s, having eliminated the threat of Indian attack, the U.S. Army gradually abandoned most of its Texas posts. The circumstances were different from those that had forced its withdrawal from Texas at the onset of the Civil War, when Indian attacks were still common. Despite Gov. Sam Houston's opposition, on February 1, 1861, the Texas secession convention had adopted the ordinance of secession by a vote of 166 to 8, forcing the federal government to abruptly withdraw its regulars from Texas. Several officers later blasted Georgia-born Brig. Gen. David E. Twiggs, commanding the Department of Texas, for giving up so easily. Other officers complained about the failure of higher authorities to keep them informed of the deliberations. "I was as isolated as though I had been on the highest peak of the Rocky Mountains," recalled one post commander. Similarly, Lt. William Bell had "heard but little talk" regarding the state of political affairs among fellow officers, idle threats about secession having been common for years.[1]

Confusion reigned supreme among the Federal troops stationed in Texas to protect the state's frontiers and now faced with the difficult task of returning to

1. Zenas R. Bliss Reminiscences, 2:191, 3:238, BTHC; William H. Bell, "Ante Bellum: The Old Army in Texas in '61," *Magazine of History* 3 (Feb., 1906): 81–82.

Union territory. Some resigned or cast their lots with the Confederacy. Early transfers of authority generally proceeded peacefully, as the troops in West Texas marched through San Antonio to the various coastal ports. The troops kept their small arms and, despite the pleas of San Antonio officials, who begged them to avoid the city, marched through the old Spanish town in full dress uniforms with flags flying and bands playing on their way to the Union. The spirit of cooperation was short-lived, however, and elements of the Eighth Infantry who were attempting to withdraw were subsequently interned.

Four years later the Texans who had replaced the Federal troops on the frontiers during the Civil War were themselves told to withdraw from their positions. The state troops, militia, and home-guard units patrolling the western part of the state had undergone terrible deprivations during the later stages of the war. Special Order No. 39, issued by Lt. Col. J. B. Barry to the commanders of Camps McCord and Colorado on May 27, 1865, noted the plight of the poorly supplied frontiersmen: "As they have not drawn any pay for fifteen months, it is nothing more than due them than to make an equal distribution among them of all public property you have, allowing each company to retain their company property."[2]

With the regular army's reoccupation of Texas came renewed offensive campaigns to quell the Indians. Ranald S. Mackenzie and E. O. C. Ord, with the aid of William Shafter and the Twenty-fourth Infantry, helped crush Indian raiders along the Rio Grande near Forts Clark and Duncan. Benjamin Grierson's splendid Tenth Cavalry achieved the same goal west of the Pecos River. Farther north, campaigns into the Texas Panhandle and present-day Oklahoma forced the fierce plains warriors out of Texas and onto reservations in Indian Territory. Most prominent were the efforts of the Second Cavalry, with an officer corps that read like a scorecard of Civil War generals; Mackenzie's hardened Fourth Cavalry; the Sixth Cavalry and the Eighth Cavalry, operating in the scorched Staked Plains; and Nelson A. Miles's rugged Fifth Infantry.[3]

By the early 1880s the regulars' task had been greatly eased with the construction of the Southern Pacific Railroad, which Gen. William Tecumseh Sherman admitted had "revolutionized" the Texas frontiers "more completely than all the Posts we have built in the last 36 years." Indian resistance crumbled as the railroads carried increasing numbers of civilians to the frontiers and enabled the army to concentrate its scattered garrisons against local outbreaks. Although political considerations made organized withdrawal difficult, the army gradually abandoned many of its remaining Texas outposts—McKavett and Duncan in

2. Special Order No. 39, May 27, 1865, in Thomas R. Havins, *Camp Colorado: A Decade of Frontier Defense* (Brownwood, Tex.: Brown Press, 1964), p. 165.

3. Robert M. Utley, *Frontiersmen in Blue: The United States Army and the Indian, 1848–1865* (1967; reprint, Lincoln: University of Nebraska Press, 1981), pp. 70–77, 125–41; Robert M. Utley, *Frontier Regulars: The United States Army and the Indian, 1866–1891* (New York: Macmillan Co., 1973), pp. 147–68, 225–42, 353–78.

1883, Stockton in 1886, Concho in 1889, and Ringgold and Brown in 1906.[4]

News of the impending withdrawal of a frontier garrison brought cries of protest from local citizens. Anxious to avert financial loss, some appealed to their congressmen to stop the army's planned moves. Others argued that Indians still posed a threat. Upon the abandonment of Fort Richardson in 1878 the Jacksboro *Frontier Echo* warned: "There is nothing to prevent the turbulent [warriors] in the Indian camps at and near Fort Sill from visiting this and adjoining counties, and spreading death and devastation on all sides." Five years later inhabitants of the Fort McKavett area faced the same prospect when the army ordered that post's evacuation. "There were a few optimists who said the soldiers would be back in a few months and the town would grow on to be the biggest in West Texas," recalled one resident, "but there was a noticeable undercurrent of uneasiness. It was all in all a pretty gloomy town."[5]

Transfers also worried the soldiers and their dependents. Rumors of possible moves regularly swept through every post, dominating all conversations. Word that the fort that had become home was to be abandoned often came on short notice. In a frenzy of activity families packed their clothing and most prized possessions. The War Department paid for the transfer of one thousand pounds of personal effects per officer. But with space on army wagons limited and personal finances strained, families could not always take all their possessions with them to their next home. They sold what they could not transport at auctions open to fellow army personnel and local citizens.

The army's presence had altered not only the Texas landscape but also its native animal life. One doctor reported that the animals had grudgingly given way to "the advance of civilization." The prairie dogs, he noted, had finally vacated the parade ground, although a few gophers and beavers remained. Indeed, soldiers hunted and killed great numbers of the animals that inhabited Texas. More significant to this destruction, however, was the passive aid the army gave to professional hunters in the form of supplies and shelter at the army bases. Yet the military did not, as a deliberate policy, participate in the wholesale elimination of animal or plant life. In fact, several officers protested the wanton slaughter of the buffalo.[6]

The changes wrought by the army were not always permanent. The shortage of water and the poor soil sometimes forced the civilians who had come to the western outposts to pull up stakes along with the army; the country seemed

---

4. Sherman to Sheridan, Oct. 3, 1882, Mar. 7, 1883, William T. Sherman Papers, Library of Congress (microfilm, University of Texas, vol. 95, reel 47).

5. *Frontier Echo* (Jacksboro), Apr. 12, 1878; N. H. Pierce and N. E. Brown, *The Free State of Menard: A History of the County* (Menard, Tex.: Menard News Press, 1946), p. 66.

6. PMR, Fort Concho, Mar., 1872, NA, RG 94 (microfilm, BTHC, p. 257). For army opposition to the buffalo slaughter, see Sheridan, endorsement of Nov. 3, 1873, box 10, Philip Sheridan Papers, Library of Congress; Sheridan to Townsend, Oct. 31, 1879, box 58, Sheridan Papers; Belknap to Secretary of Interior, Nov. 14, Letters Sent by the Secretary of War, vol. 73, reel 66; Potts to Sheridan, June 22, Letters Sent by the Secretary of War, vol. 69, reel 63.

too forbidding without the support of the troops. With their departure from once-thriving posts like Griffin, McKavett, and Quitman, nature reclaimed the land. In 1867, Sergeant McConnell described Fort Belknap, abandoned since 1859: "When it was occupied by settlers and the fort filled with troops I have no doubt it was, as I was informed it had been, the prettiest frontier post in Texas, but now desolation reigned supreme. Sand, sand everywhere; dead buffalo lying on the parade ground; a few ancient rats and bats looked on us with an evil eye for disturbing their repose."[7]

Yet the army's role in changing the cultural and physical landscape should not be underestimated. The population of Texas, about 213,000 in 1850, had increased tenfold by 1890, when more than 2.2 million people lived in the Lone Star State. Despite the army's shortcomings in Indian warfare, the military presence had improved security, attracted settlers, and injected welcome sums of money into local economies. The soldiers patronized stores, saloons, and brothels near the posts. Significant numbers of civilians found employment as clerks, scouts, guides, and laborers for the War Department. Local freighters, contractors, farmers, and ranchers also found the army a good market for their wares. In addition, owners received payments for land and buildings used by the troops. As one veteran explained, "If we didn't actually kill many Indians, who shall say Fort Richardson was not a potent factor in 'settling up the country.'"[8]

Supplies, furniture, wagons, and animals discarded by departing troops were welcome additions to the sparse holdings of the typical settlers. After the army's departure, eager scavengers quarried the wood and stone left behind at military buildings. The soldiers and their dependents also introduced a degree of culture to the state. The education, newspapers, books, and music they brought with them would otherwise have been beyond the reach of most Texas pioneers. Soldiers also left extensive systems of roads and telegraphs. Between 1878 and 1881, for example, troops in the trans-Pecos region established more than 1,000 miles of wagon roads and strung 300 miles of telegraph lines. Between April, 1875, and April, 1876, the military had put up 1,218 miles of telegraph wire across the state. In addition, the army vigorously supported and guarded railroad construction, which fundamentally altered frontier conditions.[9]

When their enlistments expired, many soldiers elected to remain in the Lone Star State. One such individual was Sanco Mazique. Born a slave in South Carolina in 1849, Mazique enlisted in the army in 1875. After a brief stint at Jefferson Barracks, Missouri, he was transferred to Fort Concho. Upon his discharge he settled in the San Angelo area and became a cook. Pat Conway, a native of County

---

7. H. H. McConnell, *Five Years a Cavalryman; Or, Sketches of Regular Army Life on the Texas Frontier, Twenty Odd Years Ago* (Jacksboro, Tex.: J. N. Rogers and Co., 1889), p. 67.

8. Ibid., pp. 160–61, 297; Bliss Reminiscences, 5:235–36.

9. Joe B. Frantz, "The Significance of Frontier Forts to Texas," *Southwestern Historical Quarterly* 74 (Oct., 1970): 204–205; *Frontier Echo* (Jacksboro), Jan. 11, 1878; L. Tuffly Ellis, ed., "Lieutenant A. W. Greely's Report on the Installation of Military Telegraph Lines in Texas, 1875–1876," *Southwestern Historical Quarterly* 69 (July, 1965): 85.

Clare, Ireland, joined the U.S. Army in 1883. The Irishman served a five-year term in the cavalry and a three-year stint in the infantry, stationed at Ringgold Barracks, Fort Concho, and Fort Davis. After his second enlistment expired, he settled in Tom Green County, where he worked as a custodian, jailer, and manager of the county poor farm.[10] Lt. John Bell Hood was another of those who hoped to make Texas his home: "During my long service in Texas I had had occa-

10. *San Angelo Standard Times*, May 3, 1934.

sion to visit almost ever[y] portion of that extensive and beautiful territory, and was able to form an idea of the future prosperity of that State. So deeply impressed had I become with its vast and undeveloped resources that I had, just prior to the war, determined to resign and make it my home for life."[11]

Many soldiers invested heavily in Texas real estate. At least seven officers

11. John Bell Hood, *Advance and Retreat: Personal Experiences in the United States and Confederate States Armies* (New Orleans, La.: G. T. Beauregard, 1880), p. 16.

stationed at Fort Davis from 1882 to 1884 bought land in West Texas. Lt. John L. Bullis acquired title to more than 53,000 acres in Pecos County alone. While he was at Fort Concho, Benjamin Grierson bought a 5,800-acre tract between the North and South Concho rivers in the belief that frontier life might enable his two younger sons to avoid the manic depression that had stricken his older boys. Grierson also claimed about 45,000 acres in Jeff Davis, Brewster, and Presidio counties, as well as 126 lots in the little town of Valentine.[12]

Of course, not all soldiers wanted to remain in Texas. Eager to escape their enforced seclusion on the frontiers, many officers regularly sought transfers to more congenial surroundings. Those seeking promotion might hope for a staff appointment in Washington, D.C. Large numbers of enlisted men deserted their units for greener pastures in the West or more traditional surroundings in the East. Others opted to honor their three- or five-year obligations and then seek the more independent life of civilians. "All I have to do is plod along take things easily and in 1883 shake the army and all its associations and be a citizen once more," was one private's rationale.[13]

Army officials believed that enlisted personnel who had saved carefully should have ample funds with which to start a new life upon discharge. One post–Civil War savings plan allotted an enlisted man $110 to spend on himself during his three years as a foot soldier. Under this scheme the man would save $10 a month from his salary, retain $25 of his clothing allowances, and gain $21 in interest on his savings. If he followed the program, he could accumulate $406 during his three-year military stint.

A few soldiers indeed saved money. One cavalryman, George West, deposited $350 from 1882 to 1886 and upon discharge received $72 in retained pay and $81.27 on his unused uniform allotment. He would have amassed an even greater sum had he not been fined $75 for three separate incidents of sleeping on duty. Most enlisted men, however, saved little or no money and had to make their way as civilians without help from the army. They received stage fare to the nearest paymaster, where they settled their accounts. A few death and disability pensions were awarded widows or those who had suffered incapacitating injuries as a direct consequence of military duty. Yet these compensations proved extremely small ($8 a month for total disability during the 1870s) and very difficult to secure. Recognizing the bleak future a discharged soldier could look forward to, companies kept respected old veterans on their rolls rather than force them into the abject poverty of civilian life. Congress created an Old Soldiers' Home, or Military Asylum, in 1851; in extraordinary cases old veterans might be retired with full pay by special congressional legislation. Only in 1885 did Congress create a

---

12. Bruce J. Dinges, "Colonel Grierson Invests on the West Texas Frontier," *Fort Concho Report* 16 (Fall, 1984): 6–7.

13. Thayer to Mother, Jan. 7, 1879, Max L. Heyman, Jr., "A Letter from a Soldier in Texas," *Panhandle-Plains Historical Review* 27 (1954): 72.

regular retirement list by which thirty-year veterans received 75 percent of their pay and allowances.

Army service provided other benefits. The varied experience they acquired on the Texas frontiers—scouting, hunting, building, cleaning, and cooking—proved useful to many former soldiers in civilian life. Many troops took advantage of educational opportunities while they were in the army. For the period of 1875–78, for example, Chaplain George M. Mullins reported that more than 160 of his soldier-scholars in the Twenty-fifth Infantry had learned to read and write. Indeed, the military became a particularly important means for black troops to gain respect in the black community, which held soldiers in much higher esteem than did white society.

Many commissioned officers continued their military careers during the Civil War. Robert E. Lee joined the Confederacy and brilliantly fended off Union threats against Richmond for three years with his ragtag Army of Northern Virginia. Fellow Confederate John Bell Hood, who had hoped to settle down in Texas, lost an arm and a leg in the war. Philip Sheridan, who saw duty in antebellum Texas and the Civil War, closed his illustrious military career as commanding general of the U.S. Army from 1883 to 1888. Maintaining his sense of the dramatic to the end, George Armstrong Custer, who served in Reconstruction Texas, died at the Little Bighorn in 1876.

Other officers tried civilian life. Many feared that their frontier duties, far removed from the mainstream of American society, might be detrimental to the future of their children. When offspring needed advanced schooling, soldiers secured transfers to eastern posts or left the army for private business. Some used their West Point training to become professional engineers. The non–West Pointers probably had a more difficult time finding suitable employment; Benjamin Grierson's failure to become a successful rancher is an example.

Dependents of military personnel also explored various careers after leaving Texas. Many of the soldiers' sons followed their fathers into the military. A good number of their daughters followed their mothers' example and married soldiers. Others decided that military life was not for them. As Robert Grierson, the son of Col. Benjamin Grierson, explained to his mother in 1885: "I am now very glad that I didn't go into the military service. I have much more freedom than an officer. When my day's work [as a ranch manager] is done I'm my own commander." Officers' wives generally returned to the East, to more "civilized" surroundings. Teresa Vielé divorced her soldier husband, taking her son with her to Paris, where she opened a "literary salon." After her husband's death at Little Bighorn, Elizabeth Custer moved to New York City, where she assiduously promoted his public image in a series of publications.[14]

14. Grierson to Mother, June 10, 1885, Texas Letters of Benjamin Grierson (microfilm, Fort Concho Research Library, MF 17); Sandra L. Myres, "Ladies of the Army—Views of Western Life," in *American Military on the Frontier: Proceedings of the Seventh Military History Symposium* (Washington, D.C.: Office of Air Force History, 1978), p. 145.

The harsh realities of army life on the Texas frontiers left their mark on everyone who served there. Despite the achievements of black troops, segregation remained firmly entrenched in the army. In addition to the physical difficulties — poor food, low pay, inadequate quarters — the isolation took a heavy psychological toll on soldiers of all races. The loneliness of a frontier post could overwhelm veterans of the bloody excitement of the Mexican and Civil wars. Infrequent promotion and inglorious duties took away whatever glamour the army could offer. Even the generally light-hearted books written by Elizabeth Custer have poignant reminders of the internal conflicts that beset those who struggled "to gain mastery over themselves." In one episode she recalled her ambitious husband, frustrated by the lack of advancement, pacing nervously across the floor of their quarters, muttering, "Libbie, what shall I do?"[15]

Others voiced similar complaints. The lack of companionship could prove especially severe at the smaller posts, as well as among pioneers who had pushed far ahead of fellow settlers. Susan E. Newcomb, who had lived in one of the rude blockhouses erected by civilians during the Civil War, complained, "I would like to be placed where I could go to preaching once in a while." The Texas frontier, she believed, "surely is the last place on earth for a woman to live, or any one else." While she was still married to Lt. Egbert L. Vielé, Terese Vielé commented bitterly, "Little does the casual observer at West Point know of the after existence of its graduates, and their lives of exile and privation on the frontier, passed in lonely seclusion from the world, a stranger to its luxuries."[16]

Like some individuals in every other society, a few could not continue the struggle that is life. Upon hearing of the death of his only living relative, a soldier at Fort Elliott bought some strychnine at a local store and went to a saloon, where he took some of the poison. Fortunately, a fellow trooper saw him and rushed him to the hospital, where a surgeon pumped out his stomach and saved his life. In 1875 a company clerk at Fort Richardson got drunk soon after being paid and vomited in the orderly room. The soldier methodically cleaned up the mess, took off his boots, and went into an adjoining room. There he calmly loaded a rifle, put the muzzle in his mouth, pulled the trigger with his toes, and blew his head off.

The military frontier in Texas took its toll in other ways as well. From 1848 to 1890, 52 regulars died in combat against Indians; 111 more were wounded, and many of them subsequently died of their wounds. Significantly more (about 650 from 1849 to 1859 alone) died of noncombat-related injuries or diseases.[17] Whatever the cause, the Quartermaster's Department took care of the dead. During the 1850s bodies were interred in the post cemeteries; the army paid for coffins,

15. Elizabeth B. Custer, *Tenting on the Plains, or General Custer in Kansas and Texas* (1897; reprint, Norman: University of Oklahoma Press, 1971), 2:408.

16. Susan E. Newcomb Diary, June 22, 1867, BTHC; Teresa Griffin Vielé, *Following the Drum: A Glimpse of Frontier Life* (1858; reprint, Lincoln: University of Nebraska Press, 1984), p. 174.

17. Combat casualties compiled from Adjutant General's Office, *Chronological List of Actions, &c., with Indians from January 15, 1837 to January, 1891* (n.p.: Old Army Press, 1979).

headboards, and funeral expenses of enlisted personnel. Those who died in combat were often buried where they fell. With the establishment of the national cemetery system in 1862, bodies were shipped to the centralized cemeteries for burial. As scattered frontier forts were abandoned, the army exhumed the remains at the old post cemeteries for reburial at the national sites.

The death of an army man forced his dependents to leave the military posts that had become their temporary homes. Some, accustomed to the relative independence they had enjoyed on the Texas frontiers, had trouble adjusting to the more rigid standards of mainstream society. The difficulties of returning to the East from a far-flung outpost compounded the grief of those who had recently lost loved ones. A contemporary noted the plight of the wife of Capt. Benjamin H. Arthur, who was trying to make her way back to friends soon after her husband's death. Forced to stay in a tent at Fort Mason while she tried to arrange for transportation, Mrs. Arthur gamely hung on to her case of reptiles, snakes, centipedes, and tarantulas preserved in alcohol, mementos of her life at a Texas fort.

Despite such obstacles, those who lived at the army stations managed to carve out a tolerable existence. Most adapted to frontier conditions and put aside

negative perceptions of Texas and the West that had once troubled them. Newly wed Mrs. Lydia Lane reported being "treated with great consideration" at Fort McIntosh. Although Fort Stockton was hot and offered no opportunities for fishing and few for hunting, Zenas R. Bliss concluded that the congenial society there made for a "remarkably pleasant" stay during the 1870s. In a nostalgic look at

her past, Mrs. Orsemus Boyd remarked that, "despite many more prosaic draw-backs," the simple pleasures of garrison life "made me quite willing to live and die in Texas."[18]

18. Lydia Spencer Lane, *I Married a Soldier; or, Old Days in the Old Army* (1893; reprint, Al-

In sum, most of those who lived on the Texas military frontiers from 1848 to 1890 had made the best of their situation. Not all of them had enjoyed life at the frontier forts, but not all had been unhappy. They had carved out a life on the lonely frontiers enlivened with entertainment and social activities. The soldiers had spent most of their time not chasing Indians or outlaws but building habitable places to live in an often inhospitable environment. They had made significant contributions to Texas' growth. In return, many had been struck by the land, the opportunities, and the spirit of independence that still gripped the one time republic. Teresa Vielé concluded that "any attempt to estimate her [Texas'] future must fall short of reality."[19] Faced with transfer from Texas to Kansas, Sgt. H. H. McConnell described the sentiment of the men of his company:

> The prospective move was hailed by delight by most of the officers, but was generally regretted by the men, to whom Texas had become endeared in a thousand different ways. Many of the soldiers had married, others had formed attachments and friendships more or less permanent; nearly all the men who had been discharged from time to time had settled in the country, and many of them were doing well.
>
> Furthermore, there is an ethnological fact that no one ever leaves Texas after they have been here a certain length of time. They either can't or don't want to, or it may be as the old settlers used to say, "having once drank Red River water, it was not possible to go back"; the fact remains, few people seem to come here with a view of staying, but they do stay and have stayed until nearly three millions are here, and there are "more to follow."[20]

History has proved McConnell an excellent prophet.

---

buquerque, N.Mex.: Horn and Wallace, 1964), p. 27; Bliss Reminiscences, 5:188–91; Mrs. Orsemus Bronson Boyd, *Cavalry Life in Tent and Field* (1894; reprint, Lincoln: University of Nebraska Press, 1982), p. 295.

19. Vielé, *Following the Drum*, p. 240.
20. McConnell, *Five Years a Cavalryman*, p. 231.

Bibliographic Essay

Texas is fortunate in that many of the sites of its nineteenth-century military installations have been at least partly restored. The collective efforts of federal, state, and county governments, together with private individuals and historical associations, have preserved much of the flavor of daily life for the twentieth-century visitor. In hopes of rekindling some of this spirit, I have visited most of the sites discussed in this book. Fort Davis, among the more memorable of these sites, offers spectacular glimpses of the Davis Mountains as well as reconstructed post–Civil War buildings. Fort Richardson also has well-restored structures. The stark realism of Forts Griffin, McKavett, Phantom Hill, and Lancaster is striking, and brief strolls through the summer heat at these old posts can give the visitor a good feel for the hardships of nineteenth-century military life.

Forts Concho, Stockton, and Bliss offer fine museums and buildings, though their inner-city locales can prove distracting. The desolate areas around Fort Quitman and Camp Hudson are somber reminders of nature's powers. Forts Clark and Belknap, now a private residential community and a county park, respectively, are examples of contemporary uses of the old frontier forts. The rugged vistas at Palo Duro Canyon help the present-day automobile tourist understand the adversities of camp life and frontier combat.

A rich variety of sources dealing with life on the Texas military frontiers from 1848 to 1890 is available in both manuscript and printed form. Of the archival collections, those at the Barker Texas History Center, University of Texas, Austin, and the National Archives, Washington, D.C., are indispensable. The Barker Center collection is especially strong in presenting a nonmilitary perspective; the National Archives, with massive holdings of nineteenth-century government papers, offer unparalleled avenues for study of the internal affairs of the U.S. Army. The Order of Indian Wars Collection in the U.S. Army History Research Collection, Carlisle Barracks, Pennsylvania, is another excellent source for studying the American soldier during the later nineteenth century; I covet more time to utilize this strong collection more fully.

Fortunately, many of the papers relevant to daily life at the Texas forts have been microfilmed. The Barker Center and the John Gray Library, Lamar University, Beaumont, Texas, have microfilms of several key National Archives collections. The Perry-Castañeda Library, University of Texas, has extensive microfilm holdings of materials in the Library of Congress. The Fort Concho Research Library, San Angelo, Texas, also has microfilms of materials from the National Archives regarding Forts Concho and Chadbourne. Since the microfilm editions are especially convenient to Texans, they are noted below whenever possible.

Several good secondary accounts give brief histories of the individual military posts in the United States. Robert W. Frazer, *Forts of the West: Military Forts and Presidios and Posts Commonly Called Forts West of the Mississippi River to 1898* (Norman: University of Oklahoma Press, 1965) is still the best overall study. Herbert M. Hart, *Old Forts of the Southwest* (Seattle, Wash.: Superior Publishing Co., 1964), and Herbert M. Hart, *Pioneer Forts of the West* (Seattle, Wash.: Superior Publishing Co., 1967), are less authoritative but have more comprehensive maps. For Texas forts Joseph H. and James R. Toulouse, *Pioneer Posts of Texas* (San Antonio, Tex.: Naylor Press, 1936), is too often overlooked; Arrie Barrett, "Western Frontier Forts of Texas 1845–1861," *West Texas Historical Association Year Book* 7 (June, 1931): 115–39, has good detail on the western outposts. The beautifully illustrated *Frontier Forts of Texas*, coord. Col. Harold B. Simpson (Waco, Tex.: Texian Press, 1966), has longer essays on selected posts. Gerald S. Pierce, *Texas under Arms: The Camps, Posts, Forts & Military Towns of the Republic of Texas, 1836–1846* (Austin, Tex.: Encino Press, 1969), includes descriptions of more than 160 sites. Several private bastions are covered by Leavitt Corning, Jr., in *Baronial Forts of the Big Bend: Ben Leaton, Milton Faver, and Their Private Forts in Presidio County* (San Antonio, Tex.: Trinity University Press, 1967).

Collections of brief primary descriptions of the Texas forts are also available. The most comprehensive is in Military Division of the Missouri, *Outline Descriptions of the Posts in the Military Division of the Missouri, Commanded by Lieutenant General P. H. Sheridan, Accompanied by Tabular Lists of Indian Superintendencies, Agencies and Reservations, and a Summary of Certain Indian Treaties* (1876; reprint, Bellevue, Nebr.: Old Army Press, 1969). A series of inspectors' reports have also been published. Robert W. Frazer, ed., *Mansfield on the Condition of Western Forts, 1853–54* (Norman: University of Oklahoma Press, 1963), deals largely with points farther west. The following articles deal with antebellum Texas: M. L. Crimmins, ed., "W. G. Freeman's Report on the Eighth Military Department," *Southwestern Historical Quarterly* 51 (July, 1947): 54–58; ibid., 51 (Oct.): 167–74; ibid., 51 (Jan., 1948): 252–58; ibid., 51 (Apr.): 350–57; ibid., 52 (July): 100–108; ibid., 52 (Oct.): 227–33; ibid., 52 (Jan., 1949): 349–53; ibid., 52 (Apr.): 444–47; ibid., 53 (July): 71–77; ibid., 53 (Oct.): 202–208; ibid., 53 (Jan., 1950): 308–19; ibid., 53 (Apr.): 443–73; ibid., 54

(Oct.): 204–18; and M. L. Crimmins, ed., "Colonel J. K. F. Mansfield's Report of the Inspection of the Department of Texas in 1856," *Southwestern Historical Quarterly* 42 (Oct., 1938): 122–48; ibid., 42 (Jan., 1939): 215–57; ibid., 42 (Apr.): 351–87. The postwar forts are described in Walter C. Conway, ed., "Colonel Edmund Schriver's Inspector-General Report on Military Posts in Texas, November 1872–January 1873," *Southwestern Historical Quarterly* 67 (Apr., 1964): 559–83.

A large body of secondary literature is available to those interested in the history of individual forts. For Fort Belknap, see Earl Burk Braly, "Fort Belknap on the Texas Frontier," *West Texas Historical Association Year Book* 30 (Oct., 1954): 83–114; and Barbara A. Neal Ledbetter, *Fort Belknap Frontier Saga: Indians, Negroes and Anglo-Americans on the Texas Frontier* (Burnet, Tex.: Eakin Press, 1982). Several studies examine Fort Bliss: Matthew H. Thomlinson, *The Garrison of Fort Bliss, 1849–1916* (El Paso, Tex.: Hertzog and Resler, 1945), describes the garrisons; Richard K. McMaster, "Records and Reminiscences of Old Fort Bliss," *Password* 8 (Spring, 1963): 18–32, is a good study; a later work is Leon C. Metz, *Fort Bliss: An Illustrated History* (El Paso, Tex.: Mangan Books, 1981). Allan C. Ashcraft's fine article "Fort Brown, Texas, in 1861," *Texas Military History* 3 (Winter, 1963): 243–47, examines that post. Thomas R. Havins, *Camp Colorado: A Decade of Frontier Defense* (Brownwood, Tex.: Brown Press, 1964), discusses the occupation of Camp Colorado by Federal and Confederate troops.

Several accounts describe Fort Concho. These include Herschel Boggs, "A History of Fort Concho" (Master's thesis, University of Texas, 1940); J. Evetts Haley, *Fort Concho and the Texas Frontier* (San Angelo, Tex.: San Angelo Standard-Times, 1952); Susan Miles, *Fort Concho in 1877* (San Angelo, Tex.: Bradley Co., 1972); and Greg Melton, "Trials by Nature: The Harsh Environment of Fort Concho, Texas" (Master's thesis, Abilene Christian University, 1981). Rupert N. Richardson, "The Saga of Camp Cooper," *West Texas Historical Association Year Book* 56 (1980): 14–34, and Mike Cox, "Old Fort Croghan," *Texas Military History* 5 (Spring, 1965): 15–19, examine two other posts. Fort Davis is covered in B. Scobee, *Fort Davis, Texas 1583–1960* (El Paso, Tex.: Hill Printing Co., 1963), and Robert M. Utley's splendid *Fort Davis National Historic Site, Texas,* National Park Service Historical Handbook Series no. 38 (Washington, D.C.: U.S. Department of the Interior, 1965). William T. Field, "Fort Duncan and Old Eagle Pass," *Texas Military History* 6 (Summer, 1967): 160–71; James M. Oswald, "History of Fort Elliott," *Panhandle-Plains Historical Review* 32 (1959): 1–59; and Col. M. L. Crimmins, "Fort Elliott, Texas," *West Texas Historical Association Yearbook* 23 (Oct., 1947): 3–12, add to our understanding of these forts.

For Fort Griffin, Carl Coke Rister, *Fort Griffin on the Texas Frontier* (Norman: University of Oklahoma Press, 1956, reprint, 1969), should be consulted. Sandra L. Myres, "Fort Graham: Listening Post on the Texas Frontier," *West Texas Historical Association Year Book* 59 (1983): 33–51; George Ruhlen, "Fort Hancock—Last of the Frontier Forts," *Password* 4 (Jan., 1959): 19–30; and Cornelia and Garland Crook, "Fort Lincoln, Texas," *Texas Military History* 4 (Fall, 1964): 145–61, are excellent accounts. M. L. Crimmins studies McKavett in "Fort McKavett, Texas,"

Southwestern Historical Quarterly 38 (July, 1934): 28–39. For Fort Phantom Hill see Carl Coke Rister, "The Border Post of Phantom Hill," *West Texas Historical Association Year Book* 14 (Oct., 1938): 3–13; and John H. Hatcher's later "Fort Phantom Hill," *Texas Military History* 3 (Fall, 1963): 154–64.

Other good secondary works examine Forts Quitman, Richardson, and Stockton. George Ruhlen, "Quitman: The Worst Post at Which I Ever Served," *Password* 11 (Fall, 1966): 107–26, deals with the isolated post in far West Texas. Donald W. Whisenhunt, *Fort Richardson: Outpost on the Texas Frontier*, Southwestern Studies, Monograph 20 (El Paso; Tex.: Texas Western Press, 1968), is a model study. Clayton Williams's *Texas' Last Frontier: Fort Stockton and the Trans-Pecos, 1861–1895*, ed. Ernest Wallace (College Station: Texas A&M University Press, 1982), is an exhaustive account.

Reports of post surgeons are indispensable to an understanding of the soldiers' daily lives at the forts. Included in the Post Medical Returns (National Archives, Record Group 94), the reports for Texas posts are on microfilm at the Barker Texas History Center. Containing detailed postbellum reports concerning virtually every aspect of post life, the returns proved to be the most valuable source for this book. Good medical reports can also be found in S. Exec. Doc. 96, 34th Cong., 1st and 2d sess., vol. 18, ser. 827; and S. Exec. Doc. 52, 36th Cong., 1st sess., vol. 13, ser. 1035. Primary observations by medical officers are found in Rupert N. Richardson, ed., "Report of the Post Surgeon at Fort Phantom Hill, for 1852," *West Texas Historical Association Year Book* 1 (June, 1925): 73–77; David A. Clary, "'I Am Already Quite a Texan': Albert J. Myer's Letters from Texas, 1854–1856," *Southwestern Historical Quarterly* 82 (July, 1978): 25–76; and William W. Notson, "Fort Concho, 1868–1872: The Medical Officer's Observations," ed. Stephen Schmidt, *Military History of Texas and the Southwest* 12, no. 2, pp. 125–49. For longer primary accounts see Maria Brace Kimball, *A Soldier-Doctor of Our Army: James P. Kimball, Late Colonel and Assistant Surgeon-General, U.S. Army* (Boston: Houghton Mifflin Co., 1917); and Rodney Glisan, *Journal of Army Life* (San Francisco: A. L. Bancroft and Co., 1874).

Good secondary studies of army medicine and doctors are also available. Both P. M. Ashburn, *A History of the Medical Department of the United States Army* (Boston: Houghton Mifflin Co., 1929), which includes some primary documents, and Stanhope Bayne-Jones, *The Evolution of Preventive Medicine in the United States Army, 1607–1939* (Washington, D.C.: Office of the Surgeon General, 1968), should be consulted. James O. Breeden's "Health of Early Texas: The Military Frontier," *Southwestern Historical Quarterly* 80 (Apr., 1977): 357–98, is invaluable. Individual doctors are the subjects of Col. M. L. Crimmins, "Experiences of an Army Surgeon at Fort Chadbourne," *West Texas Historical Association Year Book* 15 (Oct., 1939): 31–39; David A. Clary, "The Role of the Army Surgeon in the West: Daniel Weisel at Fort Davis, Texas, 1868–1872," *Western Historical Quarterly* 3 (Jan., 1972): 53–66; and Paul J. Scheips, "Albert James Myer, an Army Doctor in Texas, 1854–1857," *Southwestern Historical Quarterly* 82 (July, 1978): 1–24.

Army chaplains also closely observed daily life at the Texas forts. Scattered letters can be found in Appointment, Commission, and Personal Branch, Letters Received 3046–1876 and 5221–1880, National Archives, Record Group 94 (microfilm, Fort Concho Research Library, MF 13). Carol Schmidt, "The Chaplains of Fort Concho," *Fort Concho Report* 16 (Spring, 1984): 27–32; ibid. (Summer, 1984): 31–40, is a good study. For more general accounts see Herman A. Norton, *Struggling for Recognition: The United States Army Chaplaincy, 1791–1865* (Washington, D.C.: Office of the Chief of Chaplains, 1977); and Earl F. Stover, *Up from Handymen: The United States Army Chaplaincy, 1865–1920* (Washington, D.C.: Office of the Chief of Chaplains, 1977).

Officers frequently recorded their thoughts and recollections about life on the military frontiers of Texas. Many have been published or microfilmed; others remain in archival collections. While they sometimes tend to fanciful exaggeration, their accounts of both commissioned and noncommissioned personnel were indispensable to the present book. Zenas R. Bliss's Reminiscences, typed and bound in five volumes at the Barker Texas History Center, cover both pre- and post–Civil War aspects of garrison and camp life. They should be a fundamental part of any research on this topic. For the years 1848 to 1860, Francis Raymond Adams, Jr., "An Annotated Edition of the Personal Letters of Robert E. Lee, April, 1855–April, 1861" (Ph.D. diss., University of Maryland, 1955), is excellent. The Samuel H. Starr Papers (Barker Texas History Center) are also good.

Among published accounts the following are valuable: John Bell Hood, *Advance and Retreat: Personal Experiences in the United States and Confederate States Armies* (New Orleans, La.: G. T. Beauregard, 1880); Richard W. Johnson, *A Soldier's Reminiscences in Peace and War* (Philadelphia: J. B. Lippincott and Co., 1886); E. V. D. Miller, ed., *A Soldier's Honor: With Reminiscences of Major-General Earl Van Dorn by His Comrades* (New York: Abbey Press, 1902); and Philip Henry Sheridan, *Personal Memoirs of Philip Henry Sheridan*, 2 vols. (1888; rev. ed., New York: D. Appleton and Co., 1902). Also available are Randolph B. Marcy, *Border Reminiscences* (New York: Harper and Brothers, 1872); George Price, *Across the Continent with the Fifth Cavalry* (1883; reprint, New York: Antiquarian Press, 1959); George Crook, *General George Crook: His Autobiography*, ed. Martin Schmitt (Norman: University of Oklahoma Press, 1960). W. Stephen Thomas, *Fort Davis and the Texas Frontier: Paintings by Arthur T. Lee, Eighth U.S. Infantry* (College Station: Texas A&M University Press, 1976), offers another perspective.

For the post-1865 period the Obadiah M. Knapp Papers and the William Wainwright Papers (both at the Barker Texas History Center) are valuable. The Fort Concho Research Library has microfilm copies of the George Gibson Huntt Papers (MF 13–15) and the Texas Letters of Benjamin Grierson (MF 16, 17). Especially valuable among the published collections are R. C. Crane, ed., "Letters from Texas," *West Texas Historical Association Year Book* 25 (Oct., 1949): 110–26; Wayne Daniel and Carol Schmidt, eds., "From the Memoirs of Alfred Lacey Hough," *Fort Concho Report* 15 (Spring, 1983): 3–19; George A. Armes, *Ups and Downs of an Army Officer* (Washington, D.C.: Privately printed, 1900); and Capt. R. G. Carter, *On the Border with Mackenzie; Or, Winning West Texas from the Comanches*

(Washington, D.C.: Eynon Printing Co., 1935). Other accounts include Charles Judson Crane, *Experiences of a Colonel of Infantry* (New York: Knickerbocker Press, 1923); Frank D. Reeve, ed., "Frederick E. Phelps: A Soldier's Memoirs," *New Mexico Historical Review* 25 (July, 1950): 187–221; ibid. (Oct., 1950): 305–27; David S. Stanley, *Personal Memoirs of Major-General D. S. Stanley, U.S.A.* (Cambridge, Mass.: Harvard University Press, 1917); George A. Forsyth, *The Story of the Soldier* (New York: D. Appleton and Co., 1900); Anson Mills, *My Story*, ed. C. H. Claudy, 2d ed. (Washington, D.C.: Press of Byron S. Adams, 1921); James Parker, *The Old Army: Memories, 1872–1918* (Philadelphia: Dorrance and Co., 1929); and Brit Allen Storey, "An Army Officer in Texas, 1866–1867," *Southwestern Historical Quarterly* 72 (Oct., 1968): 242–52.

Among secondary works Francis B. Heitman, *Historical Register and Dictionary of the United States Army*, 2 vols. (1903; reprint, Urbana: University of Illinois Press, 1965), gives a brief service record of every officer of the period. Robert McHenry, ed., *Webster's American Military Biographies* (New York: Dover Publications, 1978), is also useful. Selected biographies can be found in Robert G. Hartje, *Van Dorn: The Life and Times of a Confederate General* (Nashville, Tenn.: Vanderbilt University Press, 1967); Charles P. Roland, *Albert Sidney Johnston: Soldier of Three Republics* (Austin: University of Texas Press, 1964); William Preston Johnston, *The Life of Albert Sidney Johnston, Embracing His Services in the Armies of the United States, the Republic of Texas, and the Confederate States* (New York: D. Appleton and Co., 1878); Carl Coke Rister, *Robert E. Lee in Texas* (Norman: University of Oklahoma Press, 1946); Edward S. Wallace, "General William Jenkins Worth and Texas," *Southwestern Historical Quarterly* 54 (Oct., 1950): 159–68; Escal F. Duke, "O. M. Smith – Frontier Pay Clerk," *West Texas Historical Association Year Book* 45 (1969): 45–57; Paul H. Carlson, "Baseball's Abner Doubleday on the Texas Frontier, 1871–1873," *Military History of Texas and the Southwest* 12, no. 4, pp. 235–43; John Highland, "Sheridan's 'Hell and Texas Remark,'" in "Notes and Documents," *Southwestern Historical Quarterly* 45 (Oct., 1941): 197–98; Bruce J. Dinges, "Colonel Grierson Invests on the West Texas Frontier," *Fort Concho Report* 16 (Fall, 1984): 2–14; Ernest Wallace, *Ranald S. Mackenzie on the Texas Frontier* (Lubbock: West Texas Museum Association, 1964); and Paul H. Carlson, "William R. Shafter Commanding Black Troops in West Texas," *West Texas Historical Association Year Book* 50 (1974): 104–16. Robert M. Utley, "'Pecos Bill' on the Texas Frontier," *American West* 6 (Jan., 1969): 4–13, 61–62, also covers Shafter.

The manuscript returns for the U.S. census from 1850 to 1880 provide personal information on officers and enlisted men, as well as army dependents. Especially valuable are the economic data (listed through 1870), the place of birth, and the age, given for each individual. Collected information can also be found in the Records of the U.S. Regular Army Mobile Units, 10th U.S. Cavalry, National Archives, Record Group 391 (microfilm, Fort Concho Research Library, MF 78). Robert F. Bluthardt, "The Men of Company F," *Fort Concho Report* 15 (Summer, 1983): 3–9, provides a detailed study of the men of a single unit.

Accounts by enlisted men of their experiences are somewhat less accessible.

H. H. McConnell, *Five Years a Cavalryman; Or, Sketches of Regular Army Life on the Texas Frontier, Twenty Odd Years Ago* (Jacksboro, Tex.: J. N. Rogers and Co., 1889), should be used with care but is nonetheless a real treasure. The James Larsen Memoirs, the Jesse Sumpter Memoirs (both in the Barker Texas History Center), and Robert G. Carter, *The Old Sergeant's Story: Winning the West from the Indians and Bad Men In 1870 to 1876* (New York: Frederick H. Hitchcock, 1926), are also useful. James A. Bennett, *Forts and Forays: A Dragoon in New Mexico*, ed. Clinton E. Brooks and Frank D. Reeve (Albuquerque: University of New Mexico Press, 1948), gives an excellent account of the enlistment process.

Letters from enlisted men are published in Max L. Heyman, Jr., "A Letter from a Soldier in Texas," *Panhandle-Plains Historical Review* 27 (1954): 70–72; Jacob Howarth, "Letter, Experiences of an Ex-Soldier," *West Texas Historical Association Year Book* 11 (June, 1926): 3–7; Rex E. Greaves, "A Glimpse of Life in the 'Old Army' on the Frontier," *Military History of Texas and the Southwest* 10, no. 1 (1972): 51–54; George H. Shirk, "Mail Call at Fort Washita," *Chronicles of Oklahoma* 33 (Spring, 1958): 14–35; and Lonnie J. White, ed., "Letters of a Sixth Cavalryman Stationed at 'Cantonment' in the Texas Panhandle," *Texas Military History* 7, no. 2 (1968): 77–102. The soldiers' newspaper, the *Flea*, Apr. 15, 1869, is also valuable. Information on a few individuals can be gleaned from the *San Angelo Standard Times*, May 3, 1924.

Good secondary works are Don Rickey, Jr., *Forty Miles a Day on Beans and Hay: The Enlisted Soldier Fighting the Indian Wars* (Norman: University of Oklahoma Press, 1963; reprint, 1985); Jack D. Foner, *The United States Soldier between Two Wars: Army Life and Reforms, 1865–1898* (New York: Humanities Press, 1969); Sidney E. Whitman, *The Troopers: An Informal History of the Plains Cavalry, 1865–1890* (New York: Hastings House, 1962); and Bill Green, *The Dancing Was Lively: Fort Concho, Texas: A Social History, 1867–1882* (San Angelo, Tex.: Fort Concho Sketches Publishing Co., 1974). A. B. Bender, "The Soldier in the Far West, 1848–1860," *Pacific Historical Review* 8 (June, 1939): 159–78; and Edward M. Coffman, "Army Life on the Frontier, 1865–1878," *Military Affairs* 20 (Winter, 1956): 193–201, offer more general accounts. Edward M. Coffman's excellent *The Old Army: A Portrait of the American Army in Peacetime, 1784–1898* (New York: Oxford University Press, 1986) was published too late to be of use in the present work.

Works dealing with various aspects of daily life should also be consulted. Unpublished primary sources at the Barker Texas History Center include the Fort Clark Records, the Fort Duncan Records, the Fort Elliott Papers, and the Fort Clark Miscellaneous Collection (the last is on microfilm). Both the Col. M. L. Crimmins and the Eberstadt collections (Barker Texas History Center) offer valuable materials. The Charles S. De Montel Papers include an 1856 map of Fort Lincoln. Published works such as Ernest R. Archambeau, ed., "Monthly Reports of the Fourth Cavalry 1872–1874," *Panhandle-Plains Historical Review* 38 (1965): 95–154, offer additional insights. Mary Sutton, "Glimpses of Fort Concho through the Military Telegraph," *West Texas Historical Association Year Book* 32 (Oct., 1956): 122–34; and Carol Schmidt, comp., "Day by Day," *Fort Concho Report* 11 (Winter, 1979): 5–7, are useful. Good secondary works should be consulted as well: Stanley S. Graham, "Duty, Life, and Law in the Old Army, 1865–1900," *Military History of Texas and the Southwest* 12, no. 4, pp. 273–81; Doug McChristian, "The Commissary Sergeant: His Life at Fort Davis," *Military History of Texas and the Southwest* 14, no. 1, pp. 21–32; David C. Ambrose, "The Major Reasons for Army Desertions at Fort Davis, Texas, 1882–1885," *Password* 45 (1972): 38–45; Wayne Daniel, "100 Years Ago," *Fort Concho Report* 15 (Summer, 1983): 1–2; and "None So Beautiful," *Fort Concho Report* 16 (Winter, 1984–85): 36–37.

Black troops have been the subject of many studies. Lt. Henry Flipper's memoirs are in Henry O. Flipper, *Negro Frontiersman: The Western Memoirs of Henry O. Flipper*, ed. Theodore D. Harris (El Paso: Texas Western College Press, 1963). Donald R. McClung, "Second Lieutenant Henry O. Flipper: A Negro Officer on the West Texas Frontier," *West Texas Historical Association Year Book* 47 (1971): 20–31, is a secondary account. Other valuable studies are Jack D. Foner, *Blacks and the Military in American History: A New Perspective* (New York: Praeger Press, 1974); Arlen L. Fowler, *The Black Infantry in the West, 1869–1891* (Westport, Conn.: Greenwood Press, 1971); and William H. Leckie, *The Buffalo Soldiers: A Narrative of the Negro Cavalry in the West* (Norman: University of Oklahoma Press, 1967; reprint, 1985), John H. Nankivell, comp. and ed., *The History of the Twenty-fifth Regiment United States Infantry, 1869–1926* (1927), and William G. Muller, *The Twenty Fourth Infantry Past and Present* (1923), have been reprinted in the Regular Regiments Series (Fort Collins, Colo.: Old Army Press, 1972). A shorter account is that by Frank M. Temple, "Discipline and Turmoil in the Tenth U.S. Cavalry," *West Texas Historical Association Year Book* 58 (1982): 103–18. Erwin N. Thompson, "The Negro Soldiers on the Frontier: A Fort Davis Case Study," *Journal of the West* 7 (Apr., 1968): 217–35, is particularly good. Kenneth Porter, "The Seminole Negro-Indian Scouts, 1870–1881," *Southwestern Historical Quarterly* 55 (Jan., 1952): 358–77, fills another gap.

Good sources document women on the Texas military frontiers. Valuable collections in the Barker Texas History Center include the Emily K. Andrews Diary, the Mattie Belle Anderson Reminiscences, and the Laura Clarke Papers. The S. P. and S. E. Newcomb Papers (also at Barker Center) include materials from both husband and wife. Barbara E. Fisher, ed., "Forrestine Cooper Hooker's Notes and Memoirs on Army Life in the West, 1871–1876" (Master's thesis, University of Arizona, 1963), is an excellent study. Teresa Griffin Vielé, *Following the Drum: A Glimpse of Frontier Life* (1858; reprint, Lincoln: University of Nebraska Press, 1984), is outstanding. Officers' testimony regarding laundresses is in H. Rept. 354, 44th Cong., 1st sess., ser. 1709.

Other good books include Sandra L. Myres, ed., *Cavalry Wife: The Diary of Eveline M. Alexander, 1866–1867* (College Station: Texas A&M University Press, 1977); Lydia Spencer Lane, *I Married a Soldier; or, Old Days in the Old Army* (1893; reprint, Albuquerque, N.Mex.: Horn and Wallace, 1964); Elizabeth B. Custer, *Tenting on the Plains, or General Custer in Kansas and Texas*, 3 vols. (1897; reprint, Norman: University of Oklahoma Press, 1971); Mrs. Orsemus Bronson Boyd, *Cavalry Life in Tent and Field* (1894; reprint, Lincoln: University of Nebraska Press, 1982); and Ellen McGowan Biddle, *Reminiscences of a Soldier's Wife* (Philadelphia: J. B. Lippincott Co., 1907). Charles P. Roland and Richard P. Robbins, eds., "The Second Cavalry Comes to Texas: The Diary of Eliza (Mrs. Albert Sidney) Johnston," *Southwestern Historical Quarterly* 60 (Apr., 1957): 463–500; and Mrs. Robert Lee Howze, "Recollections of Old Fort Bliss," *Password* 3 (Jan., 1958): 30–34, are other useful records. Civilian perspectives can be seen in Mrs. William L. (Cora Montgomery) Cazneau, *Eagle Pass or Life on the Border* (1852; reprint, Austin, Tex.: Pemberton Press, 1966); and Sallie Reynolds Matthews, *Interwoven: A Pioneer Chronicle* (1936; reprint, El Paso, Tex.: Carl Hertzog, 1958). Another account is Mrs. D. W. Roberts, *A Woman's Reminiscences of Six Years in Camp with the Texas Rangers* (Austin, Tex.: Von Boeckmann-Jones Co., n.d.).

An extensive range of secondary literature deals with nineteenth-century American women. For this book the following works were invaluable: Sandra L. Myres, *Westering Women and the Frontier Experience, 1800–1915,* Histories of the American Frontier (Albuquerque: University of New Mexico Press, 1982); Sandra L. Myres, "Romance and Reality on the American Frontier: Views of Army Wives," *Western Historical Quarterly* 13 (Oct., 1982): 409–27; and Sandra L. Myres, "The Ladies of the Army—Views of Western Life," *American Military on the Frontier: Proceedings of the Seventh Military History Symposium* (Washington, D.C.: Office of Air Force History, 1978). Miller J. Stewart, "Army Laundresses: Ladies of the 'Soap Suds Row,'" *Nebraska History* 61 (Winter, 1980): 421–36; and John R. Sibbald, "Camp Followers All," *American West* 3 (Spring, 1966): 56–67, were also pertinent. Among more general accounts the following works represent the diverse literature about women: Anne Firor Scott, *The Southern Lady from Pedestal to Politics 1830–1930* (Chicago: University of Chicago Press, 1970); Barbara Welter, *Dimity Convictions: The American Woman in the Nineteenth Century* (Athens: Ohio University Press, 1976); John Mack Faragher, *Women and Men on the Overland Trail* (New Haven, Conn.: Yale University Press, 1979); and Mary P. Ryan, *The Empire of the Mother: American Writing about Domesticity, 1830–1860* (New York: Institute for Research in History and Howarth Press, 1982). Diane Johnson's brilliant "Darn That Darning," *New York Review of Books,* Apr. 12, 1984), 23–25, provides a much-needed corrective.

Secondary accounts of families are also available. Patricia Y. Stallard, *Glittering Misery: Dependents of the Indian Fighting Army* (Fort Collins and San Rafael, Colo.: Old Army Press and Presidio Press, 1978), covers the subject fairly well. Joan Ingalls, "Family Life on the Southwestern Frontier," *Military History of Texas and the Southwest* 14, no. 4, pp. 203–13, and Cora Pugmire, comp., "Unsung Heroes," *Fort Concho Report* 11 (Fall, 1979): 3–13, are also available. William H. Leckie and Shirley A. Leckie, *Unlikely Warriors: General Benjamin H. Grierson and His Family* (Norman: University of Oklahoma Press, 1984), is an intriguing account of the Grierson family and should be studied by anyone interested in the period.

The Indians of Texas have also received the attention of scholars. Primary sources of Indian-white relations include the Robert S. Neighbors Papers (Barker

Texas History Center) and Dorman Winfrey, ed. *Texas Indian Papers, 1825–1843* (Austin: Texas State Library, 1959), *Texas Indian Papers, 1844–45* (1960), and *Texas Indian Papers, 1846–1859* (1960); and Dorman Winfrey and James M. Day, eds., *Texas Indian Papers, 1860–1916* (1961). Secondary accounts include the seminal work of W. W. Newcomb, Jr., *The Indians of Texas: From Prehistoric to Modern Times* (Austin: University of Texas Press, 1961); Kenneth F. Neighbours, "Indian Exodus Out of Texas in 1859," *West Texas Historical Association Year Book* 36 (1960): 80–97; and James A. McLeod, "The Kickapoos: Migrants in Search of a Permanent Home," *Fort Concho Report* 15 (Fall, 1983). Studies of the individual tribes are also available. For army views of Indians see Thomas C. Leonard's thoughtful *Above the Battle: War-making in America from Appomattox to Versailles* (New York: Oxford University Press, 1978).

Logistics were extremely important to the daily life of every soldier and civilian on the Texas military frontiers. For general accounts Erna Risch, *Quartermaster Support of the Army: A History of the Corps, 1775–1939* (Washington, D.C.: U.S. Government Printing Office, 1962); and James A. Huston, *The Sinews of War: Army Logistics, 1775–1953* (Washington, D.C.: U.S. Government Printing Office, 1960), both in the Army Historical Series, are best. For Texas, Elvis Joe Ballew, "Supply Problems of Fort Davis, Texas, 1867–1880" (Master's thesis, Sul Ross State University, 1971), is good, as are Lowell H. Harrison, "Supplying Texas Military Posts in 1876," *Texas Military History* 4 (Spring, 1964): 23–24; and Leonora Barrett, "Transportation, Supplies, and Quarters for the West Texas Frontier under the Federal Military System, 1848–1861," *West Texas Historical Association Year Book* 5 (June, 1929): 87–99. Emmett M. Essin III, "Mules, Packs, and Packtrains," *Southwestern Historical Quarterly* 74 (July, 1970): 52–80, discusses the stubborn army mule. The much-discussed role of the camels is best described in Thomas L. Connelly, "The American Camel Experiment: A Reappraisal," *Southwestern Historical Quarterly* 69 (Apr., 1966): 442–62.

For civilian traders and controversies see the William R. Belknap Papers (Library of Congress), the James Wiley Magoffin Papers, and the John Creaton Papers (both in the Barker Texas History Center). Secondary accounts are available in Eula Haskew, "Stribling and Kirkland of Fort Griffin," *West Texas Historical Association Year Book* 32 (Oct., 1956): 55–69; and W. H. Timmons, "The Merchants and the Military, 1849–1854," *Password* 27 (Summer, 1982): 51–61. Robert W. Frazer, *Forts and Supplies: The Role of the Army in the Economy of the Southwest, 1846–1861* (Albuquerque: University of New Mexico Press, 1983), examines the situation in New Mexico.

The army's role in exploration is seen in William H. Goetzmann, *Army Exploration in the American West, 1803–1863* (1959; reprint, Lincoln: University of Nebraska Press, 1979). Primary documents, which also discuss other subjects relevant to the present study, are in S. Exec. Doc. 64, 31st Cong., 1st sess., vol. 14, ser. 562. The military's roads and telegraph lines, respectively, are discussed in Averam B. Bender, "Opening Routes across West Texas, 1848–1850," *Southwestern Historical Quarterly* 37 (Oct., 1933): 116–35, and L. Tuffly Ellis, ed., "Lieutenant

A. W. Greely's Report on the Installation of Military Telegraph Lines in Texas, 1875–1876," *Southwestern Historical Quarterly* 69 (July, 1965): 66–87. Wayne Daniel, "Fort Concho's Water Supply," *Fort Concho Report* 16 (Spring, 1984): 22–26, discusses an often overlooked aspect of daily life. Thomas J. Carleton and LaRheda Fry, "Old West Army Cookbook, 1865–1900," *El Palacio* 80 (Winter, 1974): 29–45, is interesting. Alice Kirk Grierson, *An Army Wife's Cookbook, with Household Hints and Home Remedies*, ed. Mary L. Williams (Globe, Ariz.: Southwest Parks and Monuments Association, 1972), sheds additional light on various aspects of daily life.

Extensive secondary works describe military uniforms and equipment of the nineteenth century. Among primary documents, *Ordnance Memoranda No. 29: Horse Equipments and Cavalry Accoutrements, as Prescribed by G.O. 73, A.G.O., 1885* (Pasadena, Calif.: Socio-Technical Publications, 1970) offers extensive detail. Good secondary works are those by Randy Steffen, *The Horse Soldier 1776–1943*, vol. 2, *The Frontier, the Mexican War, the Civil War, the Indian Wars, 1851–1880* (Norman: University of Oklahoma Press, 1978); Gordon Chappell, *Search for the Well-dressed Soldier 1865–1890: Developments and Innovations in United States Army Uniforms on the Western Frontier*, Museum Monograph no. 5 (Arizona Historical Society, 1972); and Sidney B. Brinckerhoff, *Boots and Shoes of the Frontier Soldier, 1865–1903*, Museum Monograph no. 7 (Arizona Historical Society). Ernest Lisle Reedstrom, *Bugles, Banners, and War Bonnets* (Caldwell, Idaho: Caxton Printers, 1977); and James E. Hicks, *U.S. Military Firearms, 1776–1956* (Alhambra, Calif.: Borden Publishing Co., 1962), are invaluable.

Military architecture is excellently covered in Willard B. Robinson, *American Forts: Architectural Form and Function* (Urbana: University of Illinois Press, published for Amon Carter Museum of Western Art, 1977); and Roy Eugene Graham, "Federal Fort Architecture in Texas during the Nineteenth Century," *Southwestern Historical Quarterly* 74 (Oct., 1970): 165–88. Archaeological surveys are found in Shirley J. Pettengill, *Report for 1975 and 1976 of Archaeological Investigations at Fort Concho* (San Angelo, Tex.: Fort Concho Museum, 1977); E. Suzanne Carter, *Fort McKavett, Menard County, Texas: Archeological and Architectural Details of the Bakery, Barracks, and Headquarters Buildings, Spring, 1973* (Austin: University of Texas Press, 1974); and Art Black, *Fort Lancaster State Historic Site, Crockett County, Texas Archeological Excavations* (Austin: Texas Parks and Wildlife Department, 1975). Ownership of the land at the forts is discussed in H. Exec. Doc. 282, 43d Cong., 1st sess., vol. 17, ser. 1615; George Ruhlen, "Quitman's Owners: A Sidelight on Frontier Reality," *Password* 5 (Apr., 1960); and Margaret Bierschwale, "Mason County, Texas, 1845–1870," *Southwestern Historical Quarterly* 52 (Apr., 1949): 379–97.

Many primary sources document general army policy. No adequate history of the military in the nineteenth century can be written without the use of these papers. The Library of Congress holds the William T. Sherman, Philip Sheridan, Edwin Stanton, Andrew Johnson, and Ulysses S. Grant papers. Microfilm copies of the Sherman, Johnson, and Grant papers are in the University of Texas. For other key leaders see the Christopher C. Augur Papers (Illinois State Historical

Society, Springfield), the Ranald S. Mackenzie Papers (U.S. Army History Research Collection, Carlisle Barracks, Pa.), and the E. O. C. Ord Papers (Bancroft Library, Berkeley, Calif.). Testimony and reports in H. Rept. 384, 43d Cong., 1st sess., ser. 1624, give a good sampling of officers' opinions about various issues. Civilian input can be found in the excellent Samuel B. Maxey Papers (Texas State Archives, Austin). Congressional debate is covered in the *Congressional Globe* (through 1873) and the *Congressional Record*. Texas newspapers such as the *Telegraph and Texas Register* (Houston) and the *Texas State Gazette* (Austin) offer interesting criticism of the army.

The National Archives holds massive collections, including Letters Sent by the Secretary of War Relating to Military Affairs, 1800–89, Record Group 107 (microcopy 6; Lamar University has copies through 1852); Letters Sent by the Office of the Adjutant General (main series), 1800–90, Record Group 94 and 407 (microcopy 565); Letters Received by the Secretary of War, Registered Series, 1801–70, Record Group 107 (microcopy 221; Lamar University has copies through 1852); Returns from U.S. Military Posts, 1800–1916, Record Group 94 and 407 (copies of the returns for Fort Bliss are in the University of Texas; copies of returns for Forts Chadbourne and Concho are in the Fort Concho Research Library). The Records of the Office of the Judge Advocate General, Court-Martial Case Files, George A. Armes are in microfilm at the Fort Concho Research Library, which also has microfilms of the Records of the U.S. Regular Army Mobile Units, Record Group 391, for the Tenth Cavalry, along with selected portions of the Records of U.S. Army Continental Commands, 1821–1920, Record Group 393. Letters Sent, Department of Texas, Record Group 393, are also worthy of mention.

The Annual Reports of the Secretary of War, 1848–90, are published in the United States Serial set. They include a rich array of reports vital to understanding army policy, and should be consulted by every serious student. Complete lists of these reports, as well as excellent secondary accounts of the Indian Wars, can be found in Robert M. Utley, *Frontiersmen in Blue: The United States Army and the Indian, 1848–1865* (1967; reprint, Lincoln: University of Nebraska Press, 1981); and Robert M. Utley, *Frontier Regulars: The United States Army and the Indian, 1866–1891* (New York: Macmillan Co., 1973), both originally published as part of Macmillan's Wars of the United States series. Other useful secondary accounts, also part of the Macmillan series, are Francis Paul Prucha, *The Sword of the Republic: The United States Army on the Frontier, 1783–1846* (1969; reprint, Bloomington: Indiana University Press, 1977); Clarence C. Clendenen, *Blood on the Border: The United States Army and the Mexican Irregulars* (New York: Macmillan Co., 1969); and Russell F. Weigley, *History of the United States Army* (1967; enl. ed., Bloomington: Indiana University Press, 1984).

For antebellum policy see George Harmon Dewey, "The United States Indian Policy in Texas, 1845–1860," *Mississippi Valley Historical Review* 17 (Dec. 1930): 377–403; and Col. Harold B. Simpson, *Cry Comanche: The 2nd U.S. Cavalry in Texas, 1855–1861* (Hillsboro, Tex.: Hill Junior College Press, 1979). For postwar policy see Robert Wooster, "The Military and United States Indian Policy, 1865–1903"

(Ph.D. diss., University of Texas, 1985). Army administration is clarified in Raphael P. Thian, comp., *Notes Illustrating the Military Geography of the United States, 1813–1880,* ed. John Carroll (1881; reprint, Austin: University of Texas Press, 1979); and Frank M. Temple, "Colonel B. H. Grierson's Administration of the District of the Pecos," *West Texas Historical Association Year Book* 38 (Oct., 1962): 85–96.

Numerous sources deal with the effects of the Civil War and Reconstruction on daily life and policy along the Texas frontiers. Secession is dealt with by Ralph A. Wooster, *The Secession Conventions of the South* (Princeton, N.J.: Princeton University Press, 1962); and Walter L. Buenger, *Secession and the Union in Texas* (Austin: University of Texas Press, 1984). William H. Bell, "Ante Bellum: The Old Army in Texas in '61," *Magazine of History* 3 (Feb., 1906): 80–86; and John T. Sprague, *The Treachery in Texas, the Secession of Texas, and the Arrest of the United States Officers and Soldiers Serving in Texas* (New York: Rebellion Record, 1862), offer Union views of the turmoil of 1861. For daily life along the frontiers during the war, the James B. Barry Papers (Barker Texas History Center) are excellent. Published accounts are in Martin Hardwick Hall, ed., "The Taylor Letters: Confederate Correspondence from Fort Bliss," *Military History of Texas and the Southwest* 15, no. 2 (1970): 53–60; and Martin Hardwick Hall, ed., "A Confederate Soldier's Letter from Fort Bliss, July 6, 1861," *Password* 25 (Spring, 1980): 17–20, 42. Union views are expressed in Oliver Willcox Norton, *Army Letters, 1861–1865* (Chicago: O. L. Deming, 1903); and the J. R. Cressinger Letters (Barker Texas History Center). For the course of the war, see the multivolume *War of the Rebellion: A Compilation of the Official Records of the Union and Confederate Armies* (Washington, D.C.: U.S. Government Printing Office). Marilynne Howsley, "Forting Up on the Texas Frontier during the Civil War," *West Texas Historical Association Year Book* 17 (Oct., 1941); 71–76, is especially illuminating.

The controversies surrounding Reconstruction had an important impact on life on the Texas military frontiers. William L. Richter has written a series of fine articles on Reconstruction in Texas. These include "Spread Eagle Eccentricities: Military-Civilian Relations in Reconstruction Texas," *Texana* 8, no. 4 (1970): 311–27; "Texas Politics and the United States Army," *Military History of Texas and the Southwest* 10, no. 3 (1972): 159–86; "'We Must Rubb [*sic*] Out and Begin Anew': The Army and the Republican Party in Texas," *Civil War History* 14 (Dec., 1973): 334–52; and "'It Is Best to Go in Strong-handed': Army Occupation of Texas, 1865–1866," *Arizona and the West* 27 (Summer, 1985): 113–42. See also Robert Walter Shook, "Federal Occupation and Administration of Texas, 1865–1870" (Ph.D. diss., North Texas State University, 1970).

A number of primary and secondary documents discuss life in the field during the Indian Wars. For the present work important primary sources include M. L. Crimmins, ed., "The Second Dragoon Indian Campaign in Texas," *West Texas Historical Association Year Book* 21 (Oct., 1945): 50–56; M. L. Crimmins, ed., "Colonel Robert E. Lee's Report on Indian Combats in Texas," *Southwestern Historical Quarterly* 39 (July, 1935): 21–32; W. Curtis Nunn, ed., "Eighty-six Hours without Water on the Texas Plains," *Southwestern Historical Quarterly* 43 (Jan., 1940):

356–64; L. F. Sheffy, ed., "Letters and Reminiscences of Gen. Theodore A. Baldwin: Scouting after Indians on the Plains of Texas," *Panhandle-Plains Historical Review* 11 (1938): 7–30; Robert C. Carriker, ed., "Thompson McFadden's Diary of an Indian Campaign, 1874," *Southwestern Historical Quarterly* 75 (Oct., 1971): 198–232; and Charles A. P. Hatfield, "Campaign of Col. R. S. Mackenzie . . . ," in Order of Indian Wars Collection (U.S. Army History Research Collection, Carlisle Barracks, Pa.). Adjutant General's Office, *Chronological List of Actions, &c., with Indians from January 15, 1837 to January, 1891* (Fort Collins, Colo.: Old Army Press, 1979), which lists every action, including commanders, troops involved, and casualties, is invaluable. Additional details are presented in John J. Finerty, *War-Path and Bivouac: The Big Horn and Yellowstone Expedition*, ed. Milo Milton Quaife (1955; reprint, Lincoln: University of Nebraska Press, 1966); and Ernest R. Archambeau, "The Battle of Lyman's Wagon Train," *Panhandle-Plains Historical Review* 36 (1963): 89–101.

Good secondary accounts of field campaigns, in addition to the volumes in the Wars of the United States series noted previously, include Douglas C. McChristian, "Grierson's Fight at Tinaja de las Palmas: An Episode in the Victorio Campaign," *Red River Valley Historical Review* 7 (Winter, 1982): 45–63; and Ronnie C. Tyler, "The Little Punitive Expedition in the Big Bend," *Southwestern Historical Quarterly* 78 (Jan., 1975): 271–91. Don Russell, "How Many Indians Were Killed? White Man versus Red Man: The Facts and the Legend," *American West* 10 (July, 1973): 42–47, 61–63, analyzes this much-debated topic.

Civilians played an important role in the daily routine at virtually every Texas military post. Their accounts provide a wealth of information on all aspects of frontier life. Unpublished sources in the Barker Texas History Center include the papers and collections of Reading W. Black, Jr., S. G. Davidson, John C. Duval, J. F. Evans, James Holmsley, Leonard Passmore, and H. B. Quimby. "Statement of Mr. R. H. Flutsch, Fort McKavett, Texas, April 6, 1956," in the Frederick Rathjen Papers, is also valuable. Published accounts include Frederick Law Olmsted, *A Journey through Texas: A Saddle-Trip on the Southwestern Frontier*, ed. James Howard (1857; reprint, Austin, Tex.: Von Boeckmann-Jones Co., 1962); M. K. Kellogg, *M. K. Kellogg's Texas Journal, 1872*, ed. Llerena Friend (Austin: University of Texas Press, 1967); "Frontier Experiences of Emmet Roberts of Nugent, Texas," *West Texas Historical Association Year Book* 3 (June, 1927): 43–58; Edgar Rye, *The Quirt and the Spur: Vanishing Shadows of the Texas Frontier* (1909; reprint, Austin: Steck-Vaughn Co., 1967); and S. Nugent Townshend, *Our Indian Summer in the Far West: An Autumn Tour of Fifteen Thousand Miles in Kansas, Texas, New Mexico, Colorado, and the Indian Territory* (London: Charles Whittingham, 1880). Editions of the *Frontier Echo* (Jacksboro) and the *Fort Griffin Echo*, on microfilm at the Barker Texas History Center, give special insights into the daily lives of civilians in these frontier communities. Randolph B. Campbell and Richard G. Lowe, *Wealth and Power in Antebellum Texas* (College Station: Texas A&M University Press, 1977), and Ralph A. Wooster, "Wealthy Texans, 1870," *Southwestern Historical Quarterly* 74 (July, 1970): 24–35, are also valuable, as are John D. Unruh, *The Plains Across:*

The Overland Emigrants and the Trans-Mississippi West (Urbana: University of Illinois Press, 1979); and N. H. Pierce and N. E. Brown, *Free State of Menard: A History of the County* (Menard, Tex.: Menard News Press, 1946).

The army's relations with the Texas Rangers were often strained. For primary accounts see Stephen B. Oates, *Rip Ford's Texas* (Austin: University of Texas Press, 1963); and James B. Gillett, *Six Years with the Texas Rangers, 1875 to 1881* (1921; reprint, Lincoln: University of Nebraska Press, 1976). Walter Prescott Webb, *The Texas Rangers: A Century of Frontier Defense*, 2d ed. (Austin: University of Texas Press, 1965), should be used carefully because of its pro-Ranger tendencies. J. R. Webb, "Henry Herron, Pioneer and Peace Officer during Fort Griffin Days," *West Texas Historical Association Year Book* 20 (Oct., 1944): 21–50, gives a related account. Henry W. Barton, "The United States Cavalry and the Texas Rangers," *Southwestern Historical Quarterly* 63 (Apr., 1960): 495–510, is interesting but argues from inference rather than direct evidence. A. E. Skinner, "Forgotten Guardians: The Activities of Company C, Frontier Forces 1870–1871," *Texana* 6 (Summer, 1968): 107–21, should also be consulted.

A few additional works also deserve mention. Joe B. Frantz, "The Significance of Frontier Forts to Texas," *Southwestern Historical Quarterly* 74 (Oct., 1970): 204–205, is brief but thoughtful. Often inaccurate in detail, T. R. Fehrenbach, *Lone Star: A History of Texas and the Texans* (New York: Macmillan Co., 1968), is nonetheless thought-provoking. Spanish military frontiers are the subjects of Max L. Moorhead, *The Presidio: Bastion of the Spanish Borderlands* (Norman: University of Oklahoma Press, 1974); and Philip Wayne Powell, "Genesis of the Frontier Presidio in North America," *Western Historical Quarterly* 13 (Apr., 1982): 125–42. Alwynn Barr, comp., "A Bibliography of Articles on the Military History of Texas," *Texas Military History* 3 (Spring, 1963): 23–32, is useful. Robert M. Utley, "Arizona Vanquished: Impressions and Reflections concerning the Quality of Life on a Military Frontier," *American West* 6 (Nov., 1969): 16–20, is another fine study worthy of special mention, as is Michael L. Tate, "The Multi-Purpose Army on the Frontier: A Call for Further Research," in Ronald Lora, ed., *The American West: Essays in Honor of W. Eugene Hollon* (Toledo, Ohio: University of Toledo Press, 1980), 171–208. Among fictional accounts of daily life at the Texas forts, the most revealing is James A. Michener, *Texas* (New York: Random House, 1985). Other fictional works are those by Richard K. McMaster, "Fort Bliss Diary, 1854–1868," *Password* 11 (Spring, 1966): 16–25; and M. L. Crimmins, "First Sergeant John W. Spangler, Company H, Second United States Cavalry," *West Texas Historical Association Year Book* 26 (Oct., 1950): 68–75.

Index